Lecture Notes in Computer Science **16421**

The series Lecture Notes in Computer Science (LNCS), including its subseries Lecture Notes in Artificial Intelligence (LNAI) and Lecture Notes in Bioinformatics (LNBI), has established itself as a medium for the publication of new developments in computer science and information technology research, teaching, and education.

LNCS enjoys close cooperation with the computer science R & D community, the series counts many renowned academics among its volume editors and paper authors, and collaborates with prestigious societies. Its mission is to serve this international community by providing an invaluable service, mainly focused on the publication of conference and workshop proceedings and postproceedings. LNCS commenced publication in 1973.

Livia Lestingi · Gwen Salaün ·
José Ignacio Requeno Jarabo
Editors

From Data to Models and Back

13th International Symposium, DataMod 2025
Toledo, Spain, November 10–11, 2025
Revised Selected Papers

Springer

Editors
Livia Lestingi
Politecnico di Milano
Milan, Italy

Gwen Salaün
Université Grenoble Alpes CONVECS, LIG,
Inria Grenoble
Montbonnot-Saint-Martin, France

José Ignacio Requeno Jarabo
Universidad Complutense de Madrid
Madrid, Spain

ISSN 0302-9743 ISSN 1611-3349 (electronic)
Lecture Notes in Computer Science
ISBN 978-3-032-25551-8 ISBN 978-3-032-25552-5 (eBook)
https://doi.org/10.1007/978-3-032-25552-5

This Springer imprint is published by the registered company Springer Nature Switzerland AG
The registered company address is: Gewerbestrasse 11, 6330 Cham, Switzerland

Preface

DataMod aims at bringing together practitioners and researchers from academia, industry and research institutions interested in the combined application of computational modelling methods with data-driven techniques from the areas of knowledge management, data mining and machine learning.

Modelling methodologies of interest include automata, agents, Petri nets, process algebras and rewriting systems. Application domains include social systems, ecology, biology, medicine, smart cities, governance, security, education, software engineering, and any other field that deals with complex systems and large amounts of data.

DataMod is an annual conference dedicated to presenting research results in any of the themes of interest for the symposium as well as application experiences, tools and promising preliminary ideas. Papers dealing with synergistic approaches that integrate modelling and knowledge management/discovery or that exploit knowledge management/discovery to develop/synthesise system models are especially welcome.

This volume comprises the papers presented at the 13th edition of the DataMod conference, held on November 10–11, 2025, in Toledo, Spain, co-located with the 23rd International Conference on Software Engineering and Formal Methods (SEFM 2025).

DataMod 2025 received 12 paper submissions, of which 7 full papers and 1 short paper were accepted. The review process was conducted by a highly international Program Committee (PC) comprising 20 experts from academia, industry, and government. Each submission underwent a rigorous double-blind review process overseen by the Program Committee Chairs, receiving three detailed review reports followed by active and thorough discussions.

In addition to the presentations of accepted papers, the conference program featured two distinguished keynotes, by Jacopo Soldani (University of Pisa, Italy) and Jose Ignacio Requeno Jarabo (Universidad Complutense Madrid, Spain).

We would like to express our gratitude to everyone who contributed to DataMod 2025. We sincerely thank the authors for submitting and presenting their work, as well as the Program Committee members and external reviewers for their dedication in providing timely, high-quality reviews and engaging in in-depth discussions. We are especially grateful to our invited speakers for delivering inspiring keynotes. Our appreciation also goes to all attendees, whose participation made the conference a success.

We deeply appreciate the support of the SEFM organizing committee members, whose help ensures the smooth execution of many practical aspects of the conference.

January 2026

Livia Lestingi
Gwen Salaün

Preface

Organization

Program Co-chairs

Livia Lestingi	Politecnico di Milano, Italy
Gwen Salaün	Université Grenoble Alpes, France

Publicity Chairs

Ouadie Khebbeb	Université Grenoble Alpes, France

Steering Committee

Oana Andrei	University of Glasgow, UK
Antonio Cerone	Nazarbayev University, Kazakhstan
Riccardo Guidotti	University of Pisa, Italy
Marijn Janssen	Delft University of Technology, The Netherlands
Stan Matwin	University of Ottawa, Canada
Paolo Milazzo	University of Pisa, Italy
Anna Monreale	University of Pisa, Italy

Program Committee

Oana Andrei	University of Glasgow, UK
Kyungmin Bae	Pohang University of Science and Technology (POSTECH), South Korea
Juliana Bowles	University of St Andrews, UK
Giovanna Broccia	ISTI-CNR, FMT Lab, Italy
Antonio Cerone	Nazarbayev University, Kazakhstan
Robert Clarisó	Universitat Oberta de Catalunya, Spain
Carla Ferreira	Universidade Nova de Lisboa, Portugal
Marc Frappier	Université de Sherbrooke, Canada
Elisa Gonzalez Boix	Vrije Universiteit Brussel, Belgium
Riccardo Guidotti	University of Pisa, Italy
Alexander Kocian	University of Pisa, Italy
Ricardo M. Czekster	Aston University, UK

José Machado	University of Minho, Portugal
Paolo Milazzo	Università di Pisa, Italy
Pedro Ribeiro	University of York, UK
Arpit Sharma	Indian Institute of Science Education and Research, India
Volker Stolz	Høgskulen på Vestlandet, Norway
Martin Tappler	TU Wien, Austria
Thais Webber	Aston University, UK
Lina Ye	CentraleSupélec, LMF, University Paris-Saclay, France

Contents

Explainable Root Cause Analysis for Microservices' Incomplete Logs

Jacopo Soldani(✉), Stefano Forti, Giovanni Cupitò, and Antonio Brogi

University of Pisa, Pisa, Italy
{jacopo.soldani,stefano.forti,antonio.brogi}@unipi.it

Abstract. Identifying the root causes of failures affecting microservice-based applications is crucial. Existing root cause analysis techniques largely focus on localising the originating faults, but typically do not provide an explicit account of how such faults propagate to produce an observed failure. The availability of propagation explanations, however, enables selecting effective mitigation strategies, e.g., introducing circuit breakers or bulkheads. In this work, we propose a declarative root cause analysis technique that reconstructs the cascading failures that may have led to an observed failure, either by inferring the root causes or by starting from known ones. The proposed technique relies solely on application logs and explicitly accounts for the fact that such logs may be incomplete, e.g., when service failures result in partial log loss. We further present a proof-of-concept implementation of the proposed technique and evaluate its effectiveness through a set of controlled experiments.

Keywords: Microservices · Cascading Failures · Root cause analysis · Explainability · Declarative Reasoning

1 Introduction

Microservices-based applications (MSAs) are widely adopted in modern software systems, with, e.g., Amazon, Netflix and Spotify already delivering their core business through MSAs [44]. This widespread adoption is largely due to the cloud-native nature of MSAs: applications are decomposed into loosely coupled services that can be deployed, scaled, and evolved independently, thereby fully leveraging the elasticity and flexibility offered by the Cloud [13].

MSAs often consist of hundreds of distinct services, each of which may be replicated through multiple running instances. The multiple instances of the services forming an MSA cooperate to handle end-user requests, possibly resulting in thousands of concurrent interactions across the system. At the same time, individual service instances may fail, e.g., by returning erroneous responses to their callers or becoming unresponsive due to crashes. If not properly handled, a failure affecting a service instance may propagate to the service instances interacting with it and subsequently spread throughout the system [1].

L. Lestingi et al. (Eds.): DataMod 2025, LNCS 16421, pp. 1–20, 2026.
https://doi.org/10.1007/978-3-032-25552-5_1

While the occurrence of service instance failures can typically be detected promptly during execution, determining their underlying causes is an offline task that is intrinsically challenging [34]. When a service instance fails, it is often unclear whether the failure originated locally or whether it resulted from interactions with another failing instance. In the latter case, additional questions arise: did the other service instance fail independently, or did it in turn fail as part of a longer cascade that spread throughout the system? Answering such questions is particularly difficult in large-scale MSAs, where thousands of interactions among service instances may be taking place in parallel [44]. Nonetheless, obtaining such answers is essential to enable effective mitigation strategies and to prevent the recurrence of the same failure cascades [34].

Existing root cause analysis (RCA) techniques can assist in identifying the service instances that are most likely to have failed first [34]. These techniques typically operate by correlating performance metrics or logged events across service instances in order to infer a set of candidate root causes, which may also be ranked according to their likelihood of having triggered the observed failure. At the same time, existing RCA techniques typically focus solely on identifying the potential root causes for an observed failure, not explaining how they propagated through the system to produce such observed failure. Providing explanations in the form of possible failure cascades – originating from a root-causing failure and affecting downstream services – would make it possible to intervene not only on the initially failing service, but also on those impacted by the cascade [34]. Such explanations would enable, e.g., introducing circuit breakers to increase service resilience [30] or setting bulkheads to confine failure propagation to specific portions of an MSA [26].

In this work, we extend an existing explainable root cause analysis technique [36], which automatically identifies both the possible root causes of a failure observed at a service instance and the failure cascades through which such root causes may have propagated to that instance. The technique can also operate in a constrained mode, where the set of potential root causes is provided as input, thereby enabling the explanation of root causes identified by existing RCA techniques. In all cases, the analysis is driven by the distributed logs produced by the running instances of the services forming an MSA. These logs are processed using declarative rules that allow us to reconstruct inter-service interactions and to determine whether a service instance failed independently or as a consequence of interacting with another failing instance. Notably, the proposed extension enables explicitly accounting for the fact that logs may be incomplete, e.g., when service failures result in partial log loss.

To assess the feasibility of the proposed RCA technique, we introduce a Proof-of-Concept (PoC) implementation, called yRCAe. We also use the PoC implementation to conduct controlled experiments based on an existing chaos engineering testbed. The experimental results show that our technique successfully identifies the possible root causes and their corresponding explanations in all the considered cases, while keeping the number of returned explanations small enough to be easily inspected by practitioners.

The paper is organised as follows. Section 2 recalls some preliminary modelling of logs from our previous work [36]. Section 3 introduces the proposed RCA technique for incomplete logs. Section 4 introduces the PoC implementation of our technique and shows its use in controlled experiments. Finally, Sects. 5 and 6 discuss related work and draw some concluding remarks, respectively.

This work extends our previous work [36] by explicitly accounting for incomplete application logs. In particular, the RCA presented in Sect. 3 is brand new, and it extends the declarative rules from [36] to enable processing incomplete logs. The PoC and experiments presented in Sect. 4 are also brand new and first presented in this work.

2 Preliminaries

2.1 The Prolog Programming Language

Our work makes use of the Prolog programming language [45] to define RCA relations relying on first-order logic. A Prolog program is a finite set of *clauses* of the form `a :- b1, ..., bn.` stating that `a` holds when `b1` $\wedge \cdots \wedge$ `bn` holds, where `n`$\geq$0 and `a`, `b1`, ..., `bn` are atomic literals. The logical or of two literals `b1` $\vee$ `b2` can be expressed as `b1 ; b2`. Clauses with empty condition are called *facts*. Prolog variables begin with upper-case letters, lists are denoted by square brackets, and negation by \+. Prolog programs can be queried, and the interpreter attempts to answer each query by applying Selective Linear Definite (SLD) resolution. The interpreter returns a computed answer substitution that instantiates the variables occurring in the query, if any. For instance, given the query:

```
?- nice(W).
```

and the following Prolog program:

```
nice(X) :- honest(X), gentle(X).
honest(alice).
honest(barbara).
gentle(barbara).
```

The interpreter returns the answer substitution {`barbara`/W}, obtained by first rewriting the query using the first clause defining `honest/1` and failing, and then applying the second clause defining `honest/1` followed by the clause defining `gentle/1`.

2.2 Knowledge Representation

We hereby lay the foundations for the declarative RCA presented in this paper, by recalling the modelling of microservices' logs in Prolog from our previous work [36]. Each log entry emitted by a service is modelled as a Prolog fact like:

```
log(SName, SInstance, Timestamp, Event, Message, Severity).
```

where `SName` and `SInstance` are the name and instance identifier of the logging service, respectively. These are followed by the log `Timestamp` and the type of the logged `Event`. The logged event type can be of either one of the following types:

- `internal`, which denotes logs related to the internal business logic of the considered service,
- `sendTo(DstService, SessionId)`, which denotes that a request was sent to an instance of `DstService` with an associated `SessionId`,[1]
- `received(SessionId)`, which denotes reception of a message by an instance of the destination service within the interaction identified by `SessionId`,
- `timeout(DstService, SessionId)`, which denotes that the interaction started towards `DstService`, identified by `SessionId`, incurred in a timeout, and
- `errorFrom(DstService, SessionId)`, which denotes that the destination service replied with an error code within the interaction identified by `SessionId`.

Finally, the Prolog fact modelling an emitted log entry includes the associated log `Message` (if any) and its `Severity` level. Severity levels are expressed according to the Syslog standard [6]:

```
severity(emerg, 0).    severity(err, 3).        severity(info, 6).
severity(alert, 1).    severity(warning, 4).    severity(debug, 7).
severity(crit, 2).     severity(notice, 5).
```

Note that Syslog severity levels can be mapped onto other existing industry standards (e.g., Log4J [40]), and compared one another via a predicate like

```
moreSevere(Sev1,Sev2) :- severity(Sev1,A), severity(Sev2,B), A<B.
```

which holds when the severity level identified by `Sev1` is more severe than the one identified by `Sev2`.

3 Declarative RCA for Incomplete Logs

The explainable RCA technique presented in [36] reconstructs failure cascades by declaratively processing service logs and by relying on the availability of interaction events (`sendTo`, `received`, `timeout`, `errorFrom`). However, the correctness of interaction reconstruction implicitly assumes that such events are consistently logged, which may not hold in real MSA deployments. Indeed, logs may be incomplete due to failures in the logging pipeline, service crashes and faults, or network partitions affecting the consistency of the logging infrastructure. To address this limitation, we extend the RCA technique presented in [36] to explicitly account for dynamic gap handling.

In this section, we summarise and illustrate a set of representative, high-level rules that we use to reconstruct a plausible cascade of failures from potentially incomplete application logs. Intuitively, the rules combine (i) existing *evidence*

[1] To easily identify messages pertaining to the same interaction, we assume that the code performing a request generates fresh session identifiers for each interaction.

(i.e., what a service has explicitly logged) with (*ii*) additional *inferred hypotheses* (i.e., events that must have occurred to make the observed interactions consistent), so as to infer missing events and build an explainable propagation chain.

While the approach described in [36] could only work by processing available logged events, the proposed extension can work both with actual `log/6` facts as well as with inferred log events. To this end, while our previous approach queried `log/6` facts directly, the extended RCA technique proposed in this paper is equipped with a wrapper predicate that can either

(a) retrieve existing logs reported within the knowledge base, or
(b) retrieve inferred logs from a list `Hs` that is being built while looking for explanations, and attempting to complete identified gaps.

Such behaviour is implemented via the two clauses in the predicate `logG/7`, uniformly abstracting over observed and inferred events, respectively:

```
% retrieves an existing log/6 fact in the knowledge base
logG(S, SI, TS, Type, Msg, Sev, _) :- log(S, SI, TS, Type, Msg, Sev, _).
% retrieves an inferred log/6 fact within the set of hypotheses Hs
logG(S, SI, TS, Type, Msg, Sev, Hs) :-
  member(log(S, SI, TS, Type, Msg, Sev), Hs).
```

3.1 Reconstructing Interactions

As in our previous work [36], the proposed RCA technique follows an interaction-based approach, trying to identify service-to-service interactions as per a request-response pattern, typical of MSAs. The modelling of logs presented above enables identifying completed interactions between instance `I` of service `SI` and instance `J` of service `SJ`, occurring between timestamps `Ts` and `Te`.

The predicate `interaction/7` infers that instance `I` of service `SI` sent a request to instance `J` of service `SJ` and that, in turn, instance `J` logged the reception of such request at time `Tr` $\in$ [`Ts`, `Te`]. Interactions are uniquely identified by their session `Id`. By means of the `logG/7` predicate, `interaction/7` operates uniformly over both observed and inferred log events.

```
interaction(Id,(SI,I),(SJ,J),HsIn,HsIn,Ts,Te) :-
    logG(SI,I,Ts,sendTo(SJ,Id),_,_,HsIn),
    logG(SJ,J,Tr,received(Id),_,_,HsIn),
    Ts =< Tr, Tr =< Te.
```

The clause above captures the baseline interaction pattern, in which both `sendTo` and `received` events are available (either observed or already inferred). In this case, `interaction/7` coincides with the original rule of yRCA [35] and enforces the temporal consistency constraint `Ts =< Tr` and `Tr =< Te`.

Besides reconstructing successful request–response exchanges, the proposed extension also detects requests that were sent but never received by the destination service as, e.g., messages got lost. Such situations are captured by the predicate nonReceivedRequest/7, which holds whenever a sendTo event is observed (or inferred), a corresponding timeout is logged, and no matching received(Id) event can be found during the interaction:

```
nonReceivedRequest(Id,(SI,I),(SJ,_),HsIn,HsOut,Ts,Te) :-
    logG(SI,I,Ts,sendTo(SJ,Id),_,_,HsIn),
    logG(SI,I,Te,timeout(SJ,Id),_,_,HsIn),
    \+ logG(SJ,_,_,received(Id),_,_,HsIn).
```

It is worth mentioning that the extensions proposed in this paper are conservative as, when no gaps are present, the explanations identified by the extended RCA technique include those identified by our original approach [36]. Instead, when interaction-related logs are incomplete, the extended RCA technique introduces additional clauses that reconstruct missing events based on the available evidence, and adds them to the Hs hypotheses list. We illustrate below a set of representative patterns implemented in the prototype for completing interactions in case of missing logs within request-response interactions.

Missing sendTo or received Logs. If the invoked service logged received(Id) at time Tr (line 2), but the corresponding sendTo event is missing (line 3), we abduce the emission event and assign it the same timestamp Tr as the reception log (line 4). This choice preserves the weakest temporal assumptions by aligning the inferred emission with the observed reception, while ensuring consistency with the enclosing interaction interval via Tr =< Te (line 5).

Notably, here and in the following, each inferred log (stored in the Hs list) is explicitly marked in its Message field to preserve explainability, making the gap-filling process traceable to the user.

```
1   interaction(Id,(SI,I),(SJ,J),Hs,[Gen|Hs],Tr,Te) :-
2       logG(SJ,J,Tr,received(Id),_,_,Hs),
3       \+ logG(SI,I,_,sendTo(SJ,Id),_,_,Hs),
4       Gen = log(SI,I,Tr,sendTo(SJ,Id),'Inferred Send Gap',info),
5       Tr =< Te.
```

Dually to the previous case, if the invoking service logged a sendTo(SJ,Id) event at time Ts (line 7), but the corresponding received(Id) event is missing (line 8), we abduce the reception event and assigns it the same timestamp Ts as the emission (line 9).

```
6   interaction(Id,(SI,I),(SJ,J),Hs,[Gen|Hs],Ts,Te) :-
7       logG(SI,I,Ts,sendTo(SJ,Id),_,_,Hs),
8       \+ logG(SJ,J,_,received(Id),_,_,Hs),
9       Gen = log(SJ,J,Ts,received(Id),'Inferred Received Gap',info),
10      Ts =< Te.
```

Missing sendTo and received Logs under timeout. If the invoking service logged a timeout(SJ,Id) event at time Te (line 12), but both the corresponding sendTo(SJ,Id) and received(Id) events are missing (lines 13–14), we reconstruct a plausible interaction start time `Ts` by estimating[2] the `TimeOut` duration (line 15) and subtracting it from `Te` (line 16). It then abduces both missing interaction events at time `Ts` (lines 17–18), thus enabling subsequent reasoning steps to traverse the interaction despite the gap.

```
11 interaction(Id,(SI,I),(SJ,J),Hs,[GenSend,GenRecv|Hs],Ts,Te) :-
12     logG(SI,I,Te,timeout(SJ,Id),_,_,Hs),
13     \+ logG(SI,I,_,sendTo(SJ,Id),_,_,Hs),
14     \+ logG(SJ,J,_,received(Id),_,_,Hs),
15     estimateTimeout(SI,Hs,Te,TimeOut),
16     Ts is Te - TimeOut,
17     GenSend = log(SI,I,Ts,sendTo(SJ,Id),'Inferred Send Gap',info),
18     GenRecv = log(SJ,J,Ts,received(Id),'Inferred Received Gap',info).
```

The clauses above illustrate how we reconstruct interactions by combining explicit evidence with inferred hypotheses, while preserving the structural and temporal constraints of the interaction model. Additional clauses in the prototype handle further gap configurations (e.g., missing send and receive logs both in presence of timeouts or cascading failures, missing timeouts in presence of send/receive logs), which we omit here for the sake of conciseness.

3.2 Explaining Failures

Once interactions have been reconstructed (possibly through hypotheses abduced in `Hs`), we determine whether an interaction completed successfully or failed, to then build explainable failure cascades. In the following, we illustrate representative rules used to (i) identify failed interactions and (ii) compose them into causal chains explaining an observed failure event.

A failed interaction is either an interaction that explicitly logged an error or a timed-out interaction, as captured by the following `failedInteraction/7` predicate that performs the inclusive disjunction of predicates `timedOutInteraction/7` and `errorInteraction/7` :

```
failedInteraction(Id,(SI,I),(SJ,J),HsIn,HsOut,Ts,Te) :-
    timedOutInteraction(Id,(SI,I),(SJ,J),HsIn,HsOut,Ts,Te);
    errorInteraction(Id,(SI,I),(SJ,J),HsIn,HsOut,Ts,Te).
```

If a reconstructed interaction towards `SJ` (line 23) is followed by the log of an `errorFrom(SJ,Id)` event by the invoking service at time `Tx` (line 24), and such event falls within the considered interaction interval (line 25), then the interaction is classified as *failed.*

[2] Predicate `estimateTimeout/4` derives the timeout duration from previously observed `sendTo-timeout` pairs for the same service, whenever available. If no such observation exists, a default value is used. This strategy allows us to reconstruct interaction start times without introducing arbitrary temporal assumptions, while remaining consistent with past executions.

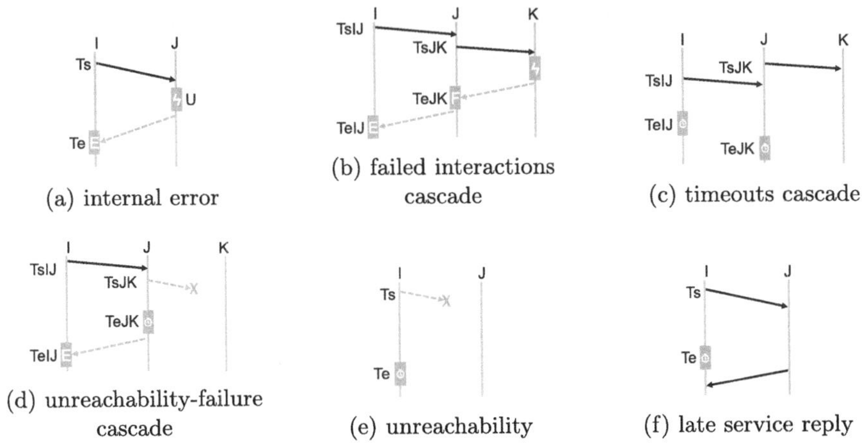

(a) internal error (b) failed interactions cascade (c) timeouts cascade

(d) unreachability-failure cascade (e) unreachability (f) late service reply

Fig. 1. Graphical sketches of six cases handled by our proposed RCA technique.

```
22 errorInteraction(Id,(SI,I),(SJ,J),HsIn,HsOut,Ts,Te) :-
23     interaction(Id,(SI,I),(SJ,J),HsIn,HsOut,Ts,Te),
24     logG(SI,I,Tx,errorFrom(SJ,Id),_,_,HsOut),
25     Ts =< Tx, Tx =< Te.
```

Similarly, if the invoking service logged a `timeout(SJ,Id)` event at time `Te` (line 28), and the corresponding interaction has been reconstructed (line 27), then the interaction is classified as *failed* due to *timeout*:

```
26 timedOutInteraction(Id,(SI,I),(SJ,J),HsIn,HsOut,Ts,Te) :-
27     interaction(Id,(SI,I),(SJ,J),HsIn,HsOut,Ts,Te),
28     logG(SI,I,Te,timeout(SJ,Id),_,_,HsOut).
```

Starting from a failure event, we recursively compose failed interactions into a causal log chain that may have caused it by means of a version of the `causedBy/5` predicate presented in our previous work [36], adapted to also consider abduced knowledge. Figure 1 sketches the main cause-effect patterns handled by the `causedBy/5` predicate, which relies on the above predicates to identify causal chains on both existing and inferred logs.

Detailedly, case (a) corresponds to a local internal error logged by the invoked service instance, which constitutes a root cause when no further failed interactions can explain it. Case (b) captures the propagation of failures across a chain of error-based interactions, where an upstream `errorFrom` event is recursively explained by a downstream failed interaction. Case (c) illustrates cascades driven by timeouts, in which a service times out while waiting for a reply from another service that is itself incurring a timeout. Case (d) represents unreachability-failure cascades, where a request is never received by the callee and the resulting timeout propagates upstream. Case (e) captures the direct unreachability of an invoked service, which crashed or never started. Finally, case (f) models late replies, where a timeout is observed despite the absence of internal errors in the callee, thus terminating the causal analysis at the caller side. All details on how these behaviours are implemented in the PoC presented in Sect. 3.3 and can be found on GitHub.[3]

3.3 PoC Implementation

To assess the feasibility of the proposed RCA technique, we developed a PoC implementation, called yRCAe, which we released open source.[4] yRCAe embeds the Prolog-based explainer that we described in Sect. 3, and it enables explaining observed failures by processing the – possibly incomplete – distributed logs produced by running MSAs.

yRCAe is essentially a command-line tool implemented in Python, which can be run by issuing the following command:

```
$ python yrcae.py KNOWLEDGE_BASE_PATH
```

where KNOWLEDGE_BASE_PATH is the path to the knowledge base embedding the distributed logs of an MSA as Prolog facts. The current PoC also assumes the knowledge base to reside in a folder also containing a file event.pl, which contains the observed failure to be explained. yRCAe then enacts the Prolog reasoning described in Sect. 3 and outputs the elapsed time and the number of identified explanations, followed by the list of such explanations. Each explanation is assigned an identifier and displays the failure cascade (i.e., the chain of events that might have possibly caused the observed failure), followed by the list of events that were inferred to fill the gaps in the available, yet incomplete, logs.

4 Evaluation

We now report on the use of yRCAe in controlled experiments (Sect. 4.1) and discuss threats to validity related to such experimental assessment (Sect. 4.2).

4.1 Controlled Experiments

This subsection presents the experimental evaluation of the proposed explainable RCA. We first introduce the research questions guiding the evaluation, then describe the experimental setup, and finally discuss the obtained results.

Research Questions. The experimental evaluation aims to assess the effectiveness and robustness of the proposed technique when applied to MSAs under realistic logging conditions, including incomplete logs. In particular, we address the following research questions:

[3] https://github.com/di-unipi-socc/yRCAe/blob/main/yRCAE-main/advanced_explainer.pl.

[4] https://github.com/di-unipi-socc/yrcae.

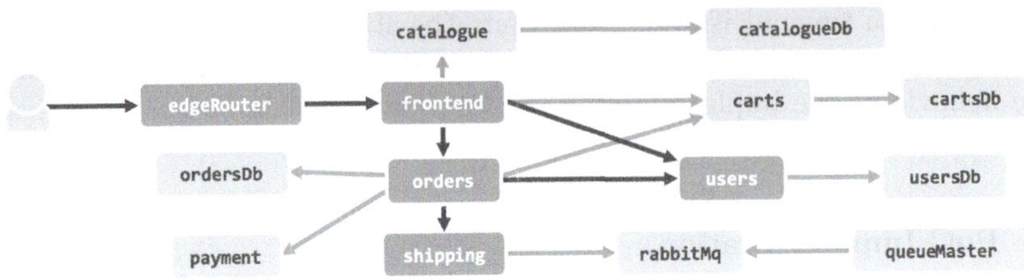

(a)

Scenario	Root Cause	Description
S1	`orders` (*failure*)	Failures injected in the `orders` service, which returns error messages. The failure then propagates to `frontend` and `edgeRouter`, in this order.
S2	`shipping` (*failure*)	Failures injected in the `shipping` service, which returns error messages. The failure then propagates to `orders`, `frontend`, and `edgeRouter`, in this order.
S3	`shipping`, `users` (*failures*)	Concurrent failures injected in the services `users` and `shipping`, which return error messages. These result in overlapping failure cascades involving `orders`, `frontend`, and `edgeRouter`, in this order.

(b)

Fig. 2. Experimental setup: (a) MSA of *Sock Echo*, with darker nodes/arcs denote the portion considered in (b) the considered scenarios.

- **RQ1**: Can the proposed RCA technique reconstruct the same failure cascades identified by the baseline RCA [36]?
- **RQ2**: Are the failure explanations inferred in the presence of incomplete logs coherent with those possibly obtained from complete executions?
- **RQ3**: What is the performance overhead introduced by the proposed RCA technique for handling incomplete logs?

Experimental Setup. The experiments are conducted using the Chaos Echo testbed [33], which we configured to mirror the MSA of Sock Shop.[5] The obtained MSA, i.e., *Sock Echo* (Fig. 2a), reproduces the interaction patterns in Sock Shop, while also supporting controlled fault injection and fine-grained manipulation of distributed logs, enabling the systematic evaluation of failure cascades. In particular, `edgeRouter` never fails autonomously. Failures are instead injected into downstream services to generate controlled failure cascades that propagate up to `edgeRouter`.

We consider three experimental scenarios of increasing complexity: (i) a single failure rooted in the `orders` service, (ii) a single failure rooted in `shipping`, and (iii) concurrent failures in `users` and `shipping`. These experimental scenarios are summarized in Fig. 2b.

[5] https://github.com/ocp-power-demos/sock-shop-demo.

For each experiment, we first execute a baseline run in which all services produce complete logs. These executions are analysed using the original RCA [36], yielding a set of baseline failure explanations that serve as ground truth. Starting from the same executions, we derive additional datasets by selectively removing log events to simulate incomplete logging scenarios, such as those caused by service crashes or logging failures. Removed events include request emission, request reception, error propagation, and timeout notifications, while the log entry corresponding to the observed failure is always preserved.[6]

Evaluation Metrics. We assess the proposed RCA technique using the following metrics:

- *Recall of Failure Explanations*: Recall measures the ability of the proposed RCA technique to recover the baseline failure explanations when logs are incomplete. Let E_b be the set of failure explanations obtained from complete logs, and E_i the set obtained from incomplete logs. Recall is defined as:

$$Recall = \frac{|E_b \cap E_i|}{|E_b|}$$

  This metric is used to answer RQ1.
- *Coherence of Inferred Explanations*: Coherence evaluates whether the additional explanations inferred due to missing log events are semantically consistent with those obtained from complete executions. An inferred explanation is considered coherent if it can be derived by the baseline RCA [36] after reintroducing the inferred missing events. Formally, let L be the incomplete knowledge base obtained by introducing gaps and let $Y_e(L)$ denote the set of pairs (y, H) produced by yRCAe, where y is an explanation and H is the set of inferred log events associated with it. The coherence of yRCAe with respect to L is defined as:

$$Coherence = \frac{|\{y \mid (y, H) \in Y_e(L) \ \wedge \ y \in Y_o(L \cup H)\}|}{|Y_e(L)|}$$

  where $Y_o(L \cup H)$ denotes the set of explanations identified by the original version of yRCA [36] over the incomplete knowledge base L augmented with the hypotheses in H. Thus, the coherence metric captures the fraction of explanations identified by yRCAe that are also derivable by yRCA once the inferred log events are incorporated into the knowledge base. A high coherence value indicates that the additional explanations found by yRCAe are consistent with the original yRCA explanation semantics, rather than being artifacts introduced by the inference process, thus answering RQ2.
- *Execution Time*: Execution time measures the total time required to compute all failure explanations for a given execution. This metric is used to evaluate RQ3 and is reported as the average execution time across runs.

[6] The logs used in our controlled experiments are publicly available online at https://github.com/di-unipi-socc/yRCAe/tree/main/yRCAE-main/EXPERIMENTS/KB.

Table 1. Results obtained with our controlled experiments on incomplete logs.

Scenario	Recall	Coherence	Average Execution Time (s)
S1	100.0%	100.0%	0.007
S2	88.5%	100.0%	0.104
S3	94.2%	100.0%	347.573

Results. As for RQ1, the results show that when logs are complete, the extended technique fully recovers the baseline failure explanations in all experimental scenarios, yielding a recall of 100%. This confirms that the proposed extension is backward compatible with the original RCA.

At the same time, when logs are incomplete, recall remains high across most scenarios. As shown in Table 1, recall ranges between 88.5% and 100% in three out of four experiments. The only notable decrease occurs in the timeout-only scenario, where the systematic removal of timing-related log events limits the amount of causal information available for reconstruction.

Even better results were achieved for RQ2, namely for the coherence on the additional explanations. Across all experimental configurations, the coherence metric is equal to 100%, as reported in Table 1. This indicates that every additional explanation inferred due to incomplete logs is semantically valid: when the inferred missing events are added back, the same explanations can be derived by the baseline RCA. The technique therefore does not introduce spurious or inconsistent failure cascades, providing a positive answer to RQ2.

Finally, handling incomplete logs introduces a moderate execution-time overhead, due to the exploration of alternative hypotheses for missing events. Nevertheless, as shown in Table 1, execution times remain bounded and bearable for the task at hand, especially if we consider that RCA is typically an offline task [49,50]. The overhead is acceptable in practice, providing a satisfactory answer to RQ3, as it still stands much lower than the time we would need to explain an observed failure by manually inspecting the thousands of events contained in the incomplete log files.

Summary. Overall, the experimental results demonstrate that the proposed explainable RCA preserves the explanatory power of the baseline approach [36] when logs are complete, remains robust in the presence of incomplete logs, infers only coherent failure explanations, and achieves practical execution times.

4.2 Threats to Validity

To conclude this section, we briefly discuss *threats to validity* following the taxonomy proposed by Wohlin et al. [46], distinguishing among construct, internal, external, and conclusion validity.

Construct Validity. Our experimental evaluation of yRCAe relies on recall, coherence, and execution time. These metrics assess correctness, semantic consistency, and computational cost, respectively. Although they do not directly measure practitioner effort nor the practical usefulness of explanations for mitigation planning, in the scope of this preliminary evaluation, we systematically compare results against baseline explanations obtained on complete logs. This ensures that the additional explanations identified by yRCAe are consistent with the original yRCA [36] reasoning model rather than artifacts of the Prolog inference mechanisms. Moreover, log gaps are systematically injected by selectively removing events and the resulting dataset is released for replicability. While such controlled settings may not fully reflect the distribution of missing logs in real MSAs, they enable reproducible assessment across various gap configurations.

Internal Validity. The experiments are conducted in a controlled environment using *Chaos Echo* [33], which enables precise fault injection and ground-truth identification. While controlled scenarios may abstract away some real-world dynamics (e.g., background noise or more complex event interleavings), they ensure repeatability and allow us to isolate the specific impact of log incompleteness on the RCA process. Additionally, timeout estimation and interaction-offset reconstruction rely on historical interaction patterns observed within the same dataset. To this end, estimation windows are bounded and progressively expanded to incrementally constrain the search space and prevent unrealistic temporal reconstructions.

External and Conclusion Validity. The evaluation is conducted on a single microservice application topology mirroring SockShop. Although the considered scenarios cover various failure cases, the results may not directly generalise to large-scale industrial systems with heterogeneous logging infrastructures. Nevertheless, the adopted request-response model is architecture-agnostic and does not rely on application-specific assumptions, which supports transferability across different microservice settings. This is a consequence of the preliminary nature of our current assessment, which we intend to strengthen in our future work by validating yRCAe on lifelike/industrial production systems.

5 Related Work

Multiple different techniques allow to analyse failures observed in running software systems. The existing techniques however target different application domains, which come with their own peculiar aspects. For instance, Travé-Massuyès [41] provides an overview on the AI-based approaches for diagnosing failures affecting controlled systems. Desai *et al.* [5] and Nandi *et al.* [24] propose two different techniques to detect anomalies in distributed software systems, with Desai *et al.* [5] also exploiting detected anomalies to drive the migration of the target applications to microservices. Gössler *et al.* [7,8] instead focuses on the analysis of the traces produced by component-based software applications, by proposing a counterfactual reasoning technique for diagnosing observed failures. With a broader scope, and starting from the notions of causes and explanations defined by Halpern and Pearl [10,11], Baier *et al.* [2] investigate on how such notions evolved into verification approaches to determine cause-effect relationships among failures observed in running software systems. Our RCA technique differs from the aforementioned works in its goal and application domain, i.e., enabling explainable RCA for failures observed in MSAs, even in the case of incomplete logs. According to existing surveys [34,38], no such technique exists yet.

A number of approaches have however been proposed to support RCA in MSAs. Among them, Guo *et al.* [9] and Zhou *et al.* [49] pursue objectives close to ours, namely the identification of the possible root causes for an observed failure and the failure cascade that may have caused such observed failure. Particularly, [9] and Zhou *et al.* [49] focus on failures observed on the frontend of an MSA, both relying on visualization techniques that enable practitioners to manually explore distributed execution traces. In contrast, our proposal is designed to uncover failure cascades that may originate from, and be observed at, any service within an MSA, while explicitly targeting a fully automated analysis process, even in the case of incomplete logs.

Other examples come from Kim *et al.* [12], Liu *et al.* [16], Liu *et al.* [17], and Mi *et al.* [23], who also propose RCA techniques that process the distributed traces of an MSA to explain a failure observed therein. Kim *et al.* [12] and Liu *et al.* [16] first reconstruct a graph modelling the service forming an MSA and their interactions. They then look for the possible root causes of an observed failure by enacting a visit of the reconstructed graph driven by the correlation among service performances. Instead, Liu *et al.* [17] and Mi *et al.* [23] directly search anomalous response time in the distributed traces, which can be correlated to – and thus can possibly have caused – an observed failure. The above discussed RCA techniques differ from ours since they require distributed tracing to be featured by an MSA, rely on complete distributed traces, and focus on returning only the possible root cause for an observed failure. We complement their results, by not only allowing to identify the possible root causes for an observed failure, but also explaining why/how a root cause propagated and caused the observed failure, even in the case of incomplete logs.

Similar observations hold for RCA techniques that rely on the monitoring specific KPIs on the services in an MSA. Concrete examples are given by the techniques proposed by Nguyen *et al.* [27,28], Shan *et al.* [32], and Wang *et al.* [42], who all infer the potential root causes for an observed failure by correlating anomalous KPI values monitored across the services in an MSA with those associated with the observed failure itself. Other examples are given by Brandón *et al.* [3], Samir and Pahl [31], Thalheim *et al.* [39], and Wu *et al.* [47,48], who also rely on the processing of monitored KPIs, but conduct the RCA over a graph representation of the MSA. While Brandón *et al.* [3], Thalheim *et al.* [39], and Wu *et al.* [47,48] derive such graphs automatically, Samir and Pahl [31] assume them to be provided as input. Other existing approaches – including those by Chen *et al.* [4], Lin *et al.* [14,15], Ma *et al.* [18–20], Mariani *et al.* [21], Meng *et al.* [22], Qiu *et al.* [29], and Wang *et al.* [43] – exploit monitored KPI data to build causality graphs, whose nodes correspond to services and whose edges capture inferred causal dependencies among their performance behaviors, which are then visited using different strategies to enact RCA. Despite their effectiveness in pinpointing the possible root causes for an observed failure, the above approaches do not explain how the identified root causes can have possibly propagated through an MSA up to causing the observed failure. We thus complement their results, by not only identifying potential root causes, but also reconstructing the complete failure cascades that explain how those causes could have propagated to produce an observed failure.

The RCA technique proposed by Aggarwal *et al.* [1] is a step closer to ours, as it does not assume the availability of distributed traces nor the monitoring of service-level KPIs, rather focusing on execution logs. Aggarwal *et al.* [1] indeed model log data as multivariate time series and apply Granger causality tests to infer a causality graph among the services in an MSA. Potential root causes of an observed failure are then identified by traversing this graph using a strategy derived from the approach of Kim *et al.* [12]. At the same time, the RCA technique proposed by Aggarwal *et al.* [1] differs from ours for the same reasons discussed above: while it is effective at locating candidate root causes for an observed failure, it does not explain how such root causes may have propagated through the MSA to produce the observed failure.

The RCA presented previous work [37] is perhaps the most closely related to that presented in this article. In that study, we pursued a similar goal, i.e., analysing the logs of an MSA to identify the failure cascades that could have led to an observed failure. At the same time, in our previous work [37], we adopted a substantially different methodological approach. We indeed assumed that application administrators would provide an explicit specification of the target MSA together with a description of the failure-aware management behaviour of the services therein. These architectural and behavioral specifications are then exploited to guide the analysis of the logs produced by the services in the target MSA to identify the possible root causes for an observed failure. Additionally, the application logs are assumed to be complete in our previous work [37]. In contrast, the RCA technique presented in this article relieves application administrators from providing any model, instead operating directly on the – possibly incomplete – logs produced by the service in the target MSA.

In summary, and to the best of our knowledge, the RCA technique presented in this article is the first to identify the potential root causes for an observed failure *and* provide an explicit explanation of why that failure occurred. In particular, ours is the first RCA technique that automatically reconstructs complete failure cascades explaining why a failure was observed in an MSA, while only relying on the – possibly incomplete – logs produced by the services in an MSA. Moreover, our technique is inherently complementary to existing RCA approaches: given a root-causing failure identified by other methods, it can be applied to *explain* how such failure may have propagated through the MSA and ultimately resulted in the observed failure.

6 Conclusions and Future Work

We have presented an explainable RCA technique for identifying cascading failures in MSA using only the logs produced by their services. Our approach reconstructs failure cascades that may have led to an observed failure, either by automatically inferring its potential root causing failures or by starting from given root causes. This enables not only localization but also an explanation of how failures propagate, complementing existing RCA techniques.

We also introduced a PoC implementation of the proposed RCA technique, and evaluated it through controlled experiments based on an existing chaos testbed. The results show that our technique identifies root causes and reconstructs their failure cascades, by also effectively handling incomplete logs. Additionally, our technique is shown to return a manageable number of explanations, keeping the inspection effort low for application administrators.

For future work, we plan to building visualization tools to present failure cascades and recommended interventions, namely the introduction of countermeasures (e.g., circuit breakers or bulkheads) to prevent a similar failure propagation to happen in the future. Additionally, we plan to validate our approach on industrial-scale applications using diverse chaos testing frameworks, e.g., Netflix's Chaos Monkey [25].

Acknowledgments. Research partly funded by the FREEDA research project (CUP: I53D23003550006), funded by the frameworks PRIN (MUR, Italy) and Next Generation EU.

References

1. Aggarwal, P., et al.: Localization of operational faults in cloud applications by mining causal dependencies in logs using golden signals. In: Hacid, H., et al. (eds.) ICSOC 2020. LNCS, vol. 12632, pp. 137–149. Springer, Cham (2021). https://doi.org/10.1007/978-3-030-76352-7_17
2. Baier, C., et al.: From verification to causality-based explications (invited talk). In: Bansal, N., Merelli, E., Worrell, J. (eds.) 48th International Colloquium on Automata, Languages, and Programming, ICALP 2021, Glasgow, Scotland (Virtual Conference), 12–16 July 2021. LIPIcs, vol. 198, pp. 1:1–1:20. Schloss Dagstuhl - Leibniz-Zentrum für Informatik (2021). https://doi.org/10.4230/LIPICS.ICALP.2021.1
3. Brandón, Á., Solé, M., Huélamo, A., Solans, D., Pérez, M.S., Muntés-Mulero, V.: Graph-based root cause analysis for service-oriented and microservice architectures. J. Syst. Softw. **159** (2020). https://doi.org/10.1016/J.JSS.2019.110432
4. Chen, P., Qi, Y., Zheng, P., Hou, D.: Causeinfer: automatic and distributed performance diagnosis with hierarchical causality graph in large distributed systems. In: Bianchi, G., Fang, Y., Shen, X. (eds.) 2014 IEEE Conference on Computer Communications, INFOCOM 2014, Toronto, Canada, 27 April–2 May 2014, pp. 1887–1895. IEEE (2014). https://doi.org/10.1109/INFOCOM.2014.6848128

5. Desai, U., Bandyopadhyay, S., Tamilselvam, S.: Graph neural network to dilute outliers for refactoring monolith application. In: Thirty-Fifth AAAI Conference on Artificial Intelligence, AAAI 2021, Thirty-Third Conference on Innovative Applications of Artificial Intelligence, IAAI 2021, The Eleventh Symposium on Educational Advances in Artificial Intelligence, EAAI 2021, Virtual Event, 2–9 February 2021, pp. 72–80. AAAI Press (2021). https://doi.org/10.1609/AAAI.V35I1.16079
6. Gerhards, R.: The Syslog Protocol. RFC 5424, IETF (2009). https://www.rfc-editor.org/info/rfc5424
7. Gößler, G., Métayer, D.L.: A general framework for blaming in component-based systems. Sci. Comput. Program. **113**, 223–235 (2015). https://doi.org/10.1016/J.SCICO.2015.06.010
8. Gössler, G., Stefani, J.: Causality analysis and fault ascription in component-based systems. Theor. Comput. Sci. **837**, 158–180 (2020). https://doi.org/10.1016/J.TCS.2020.06.010
9. Guo, X., et al.: Graph-based trace analysis for microservice architecture understanding and problem diagnosis. In: Devanbu, P., Cohen, M.B., Zimmermann, T. (eds.) ESEC/FSE '20: 28th ACM Joint European Software Engineering Conference and Symposium on the Foundations of Software Engineering, Virtual Event, USA, 8–13 November 2020, pp. 1387–1397. ACM (2020). https://doi.org/10.1145/3368089.3417066
10. Halpern, J., Pearl, J.: Causes and explanations: a structural-model approach. Part I: causes. Brit. J. Philos. Sci. **56**(4), 843–887 (2005). https://www.jstor.org/stable/3541870
11. Halpern, J., Pearl, J.: Causes and explanations: a structural-model approach. Part II: explanations. Brit. J. Philos. Sci. **56**(4), 889–911 (2005). https://www.jstor.org/stable/3541871
12. Kim, M., Sumbaly, R., Shah, S.: Root cause detection in a service-oriented architecture. In: Harchol-Balter, M., Douceur, J.R., Xu, J. (eds.) ACM SIGMETRICS/International Conference on Measurement and Modeling of Computer Systems, SIGMETRICS '13, Pittsburgh, PA, USA, 17–21 June 2013, pp. 93–104. ACM (2013). https://doi.org/10.1145/2465529.2465753
13. Kratzke, N., Quint, P.: Understanding cloud-native applications after 10 years of cloud computing - a systematic mapping study. J. Syst. Softw. **126**, 1–16 (2017). https://doi.org/10.1016/J.JSS.2017.01.001
14. Lin, J., Chen, P., Zheng, Z.: Microscope: pinpoint performance issues with causal graphs in micro-service environments. In: Pahl, C., Vukovic, M., Yin, J., Yu, Q. (eds.) ICSOC 2018. LNCS, vol. 11236, pp. 3–20. Springer, Cham (2018). https://doi.org/10.1007/978-3-030-03596-9_1
15. Lin, W., Ma, M., Pan, D., Wang, P.: Facgraph: frequent anomaly correlation graph mining for root cause diagnose in micro-service architecture. In: Li, Y., Li, F. (eds.) 37th IEEE International Performance Computing and Communications Conference, IPCCC 2018, Orlando, FL, USA, 17–19 November 2018, pp. 1–8. IEEE (2018). https://doi.org/10.1109/PCCC.2018.8711092
16. Liu, D., et al.: Microhecl: high-efficient root cause localization in large-scale microservice systems. In: Eldh, S., Falessi, D. (eds.) 43rd IEEE/ACM International Conference on Software Engineering: Software Engineering in Practice, ICSE (SEIP) 2021, Madrid, Spain, 25–28 May 2021, pp. 338–347. IEEE (2021). https://doi.org/10.1109/ICSE-SEIP52600.2021.00043
17. Liu, P., et al.: Unsupervised detection of microservice trace anomalies through service-level deep bayesian networks. In: Vieira, M., Madeira, H., Antunes, N.,

Zheng, Z. (eds.) 31st IEEE International Symposium on Software Reliability Engineering, ISSRE 2020, Coimbra, Portugal, 12–15 October 2020, pp. 48–58. IEEE (2020). https://doi.org/10.1109/ISSRE5003.2020.00014
18. Ma, M., Lin, W., Pan, D., Wang, P.: Ms-rank: multi-metric and self-adaptive root cause diagnosis for microservice applications. In: Bertino, E., Chang, C.K., Chen, P., Damiani, E., Goul, M., Oyama, K. (eds.) 2019 IEEE International Conference on Web Services, ICWS 2019, Milan, Italy, 8–13 July 2019, pp. 60–67. IEEE (2019). https://doi.org/10.1109/ICWS.2019.00022
19. Ma, M., Lin, W., Pan, D., Wang, P.: Self-adaptive root cause diagnosis for large-scale microservice architecture. IEEE Trans. Serv. Comput. **15**(3), 1399–1410 (2022). https://doi.org/10.1109/TSC.2020.2993251
20. Ma, M., Xu, J., Wang, Y., Chen, P., Zhang, Z., Wang, P.: Automap: diagnose your microservice-based web applications automatically. In: Huang, Y., King, I., Liu, T., van Steen, M. (eds.) WWW '20: The Web Conference 2020, Taipei, Taiwan, 20–24 April 2020. pp. 246–258. ACM/IW3C2 (2020). https://doi.org/10.1145/3366423.3380111
21. Mariani, L., Monni, C., Pezzè, M., Riganelli, O., Xin, R.: Localizing faults in cloud systems. In: Feldt, R., Yoo, S. (eds.) 11th IEEE International Conference on Software Testing, Verification and Validation, ICST 2018, Västerås, Sweden, 9–13 April 2018, pp. 262–273. IEEE (2018). https://doi.org/10.1109/ICST.2018.00034
22. Meng, Y., et al.: Localizing failure root causes in a microservice through causality inference. In: Wang, D., Liu, X., Melodia, T. (eds.) 28th IEEE/ACM International Symposium on Quality of Service, IWQoS 2020, Hangzhou, China, 15–17 June 2020, pp. 1–10. IEEE (2020). https://doi.org/10.1109/IWQOS49365.2020.9213058
23. Mi, H., Wang, H., Zhou, Y., Lyu, M.R., Cai, H.: Toward fine-grained, unsupervised, scalable performance diagnosis for production cloud computing systems. IEEE Trans. Parallel Distrib. Syst. **24**(6), 1245–1255 (2013). https://doi.org/10.1109/TPDS.2013.21
24. Nandi, A., Mandal, A., Atreja, S., Dasgupta, G.B., Bhattacharya, S.: Anomaly detection using program control flow graph mining from execution logs. In: Mohak Shah, B.K., Smola, A.J., Aggarwal, C.C., Shen, D., Rastogi, R. (eds.) Proceedings of the 22nd ACM SIGKDD Conference on Knowledge Discovery and Data Mining, San Francisco, CA, USA, 13–17 August 2016, pp. 215–224. ACM (2016). https://doi.org/10.1145/2939672.2939712
25. Netflix, O.S.S.: Chaos monkey. https://netflix.github.io/chaosmonkey/. Accessed 29 Apr 2026
26. Newman, S.: Building Microservices, 2 edn. O'Reilly Media, Newton (2021)
27. Nguyen, H., Shen, Z., Tan, Y., Gu, X.: Fchain: toward black-box online fault localization for cloud systems. In: Douceur, J. (ed.) IEEE 33rd International Conference on Distributed Computing Systems, ICDCS 2013, Philadelphia, Pennsylvania, USA, 8–11 July 2013, pp. 21–30. IEEE (2013). https://doi.org/10.1109/ICDCS.2013.26
28. Nguyen, H., Tan, Y., Gu, X.: Pal: propagation-aware anomaly localization for cloud hosted distributed applications. In: Bodik, P., Casas, M., Bronevetsky, G. (eds.) Managing Large-Scale Systems via the Analysis of System Logs and the Application of Machine Learning Techniques, SLAML 2011, Cascais, Portugal. ACM (2011). https://doi.org/10.1145/2038633.2038634
29. Qiu, J., Du, Q., Yin, K., Zhang, S.L., Qian, C.: A causality mining and knowledge graph based method of root cause diagnosis for performance anomaly in cloud applications. Appl. Sci. **10**(6) (2020). https://doi.org/10.3390/app10062166

30. Richardson, C.: Microservices Patterns, 1 edn. Manning Publications (2018)
31. Samir, A., Pahl, C.: DLA: detecting and localizing anomalies in containerized microservice architectures using markov models. In: Younas, M., Awan, I., Hara, T. (eds.) 7th International Conference on Future Internet of Things and Cloud, FiCloud 2019, Istanbul, Turkey, 26–28 August 2019, pp. 205–213. IEEE (2019). https://doi.org/10.1109/FICLOUD.2019.00036
32. Shan, H., et al.: ϵ-diagnosis: unsupervised and real-time diagnosis of small- window long-tail latency in large-scale microservice platforms. In: Liu, L., White, R.W., Mantrach, A., Silvestri, F., McAuley, J.J., Baeza-Yates, R., Zia, L. (eds.) The World Wide Web Conference, WWW 2019, San Francisco, CA, USA, 13–17 May 2019, pp. 3215–3222. ACM (2019). https://doi.org/10.1145/3308558.3313653
33. Soldani, J., Brogi, A.: Automated generation of configurable cloud-native chaos testbeds. In: Adler, R., et al. (eds.) EDCC 2021. CCIS, vol. 1462, pp. 101–108. Springer, Cham (2021). https://doi.org/10.1007/978-3-030-86507-8_10
34. Soldani, J., Brogi, A.: Anomaly detection and failure root cause analysis in (micro) service-based cloud applications: a survey. ACM Comput. Surv. **55**(3), 59:1–59:39 (2023). https://doi.org/10.1145/3501297
35. Soldani, J., Forti, S., Brogi, A.: Failure root cause analysis for microservices, explained. In: Eyers, D.M., Voulgaris, S. (eds.) Distributed Applications and Interoperable Systems: 22nd IFIP WG 6.1 International Conference, DAIS 2022, Held as Part of the 17th International Federated Conference on Distributed Computing Techniques, DisCoTec 2022, Lucca, Italy, 13–17 June 2022, Proceedings. Lecture Notes in Computer Science, vol. 13272, pp. 74–91. Springer, Heidelberg (2022). https://doi.org/10.1007/978-3-031-16092-9_6
36. Soldani, J., Forti, S., Roveroni, L., Brogi, A.: Explaining microservices' cascading failures from their logs. Softw. Pract. Exp. **55**(5), 809–828 (2025). https://doi.org/10.1002/SPE.3400
37. Soldani, J., Montesano, G., Brogi, A.: What went wrong? Explaining cascading failures in microservice-based applications. In: Barzen, J. (ed.) SummerSOC 2021. CCIS, vol. 1429, pp. 133–153. Springer, Cham (2021). https://doi.org/10.1007/978-3-030-87568-8_9
38. Solé, M., Muntés-Mulero, V., Rana, A.I., Estrada, G.: Survey on models and techniques for root-cause analysis. CoRR arxiv:1701.08546 (2017)
39. Thalheim, J., et al.: Sieve: actionable insights from monitored metrics in distributed systems. In: Jayaram, K.R., Gandhi, A., Kemme, B., Pietzuch, P.R. (eds.) Proceedings of the 18th ACM/IFIP/USENIX Middleware Conference, Las Vegas, NV, USA, 11–15 December 2017, pp. 14–27. ACM (2017). https://doi.org/10.1145/3135974.3135977
40. The Apache Software Foundation: Apache Log4J (2026). https://logging.apache.org/log4j/2.x/index.html
41. Travé-Massuyès, L.: Bridging control and artificial intelligence theories for diagnosis: a survey. Eng. Appl. Artif. Intell. **27**, 1–16 (2014). https://doi.org/10.1016/J.ENGAPPAI.2013.09.018
42. Wang, L., Zhao, N., Chen, J., Li, P., Zhang, W., Sui, K.: Root-cause metric location for microservice systems via log anomaly detection. In: Feng, Z., Goscinski, A., Ferrari, E., Fan, J. (eds.) 2020 IEEE International Conference on Web Services, ICWS 2020, Beijing, China, 19–23 October 2020, pp. 142–150. IEEE (2020). https://doi.org/10.1109/ICWS49710.2020.00026
43. Wang, P., et al.: Cloudranger: root cause identification for cloud native systems. In: El-Araby, E., et al. (eds.) 18th IEEE/ACM International Symposium on Cluster,

Cloud and Grid Computing, CCGRID 2018, Washington, DC, USA, 1–4 May 2018, pp. 492–502. IEEE (2018). https://doi.org/10.1109/CCGRID.2018.00076
44. Waseem, M., Liang, P., Shahin, M., Di Salle, A., Márquez, G.: Design, monitoring, and testing of microservices systems: the practitioners' perspective. J. Syst. Softw. **182**, 111061 (2021). https://doi.org/10.1016/J.JSS.2021.111061
45. Wielemaker, J., Schrijvers, T., Triska, M., Lager, T.: SWI-Prolog. Theory Pract. Logic Program. **12**(1–2), 67–96 (2012)
46. Wohlin, C., Runeson, P., Höst, M., Ohlsson, M.C., Regnell, B., Wesslén, A., et al.: Experimentation in Software Engineering, vol. 236. Springer, Heidelberg (2012)
47. Wu, L., Bogatinovski, J., Nedelkoski, S., Tordsson, J., Kao, O.: Performance diagnosis in cloud microservices using deep learning. In: Hacid, H., et al. (eds.) ICSOC 2020. LNCS, vol. 12632, pp. 85–96. Springer, Cham (2021). https://doi.org/10.1007/978-3-030-76352-7_13
48. Wu, L., Tordsson, J., Elmroth, E., Kao, O.: Microrca: root cause localization of performance issues in microservices. In: Yahia, I.G.B., Galis, A., Godor, I. (eds.) NOMS 2020 - IEEE/IFIP Network Operations and Management Symposium, Budapest, Hungary, 20–24 April 2020, pp. 1–9. IEEE (2020). https://doi.org/10.1109/NOMS47738.2020.9110353
49. Zhou, X., et al.: Fault analysis and debugging of microservice systems: industrial survey, benchmark system, and empirical study. IEEE Trans. Softw. Eng. **47**(2), 243–260 (2021). https://doi.org/10.1109/TSE.2018.2887384
50. Zolfaghari, B., Parizi, R.M., Srivastava, G., Hailemariam, Y.: Root causing, detecting, and fixing flaky tests: state of the art and future roadmap. Softw. Pract. Exp. **51**(5), 851–867 (2021). https://doi.org/10.1002/SPE.2929

Efficient Construction of Reachability Graphs for Petri Net Product Lines

Elena Gómez-Martínez(✉) and José Ignacio Requeno Jarabo

Departamento de Sistemas Informáticos y Computación, Universidad Complutense de Madrid, Calle del Prof. José García Santesmases, 9, 28040 Madrid, Spain
{mariaelena.gomez,jrequeno}@ucm.es

Abstract. This paper presents a set of algorithms for computing the reachability graph of Petri Net Product Lines (PNPLs). These algorithms address the combined challenges of concurrency and variability that arise from product-line configurations. The proposed approach integrates symbolic state representations with family-based variability handling to generate a compact, parameterised reachability graph that captures behaviour across all products without exhaustive product enumeration. The main contributions are threefold. First, we introduce a symbolic state encoding adapted to PNPL semantics. Second, we define a family-preserving successor generation procedure that applies feature constraints during exploration. Third, we propose reduction techniques to mitigate state-space explosion, including on-the-fly merging of equivalent symbolic states and selective abstraction of irrelevant state details. We prove soundness and completeness of the construction with respect to standard per-product semantics and analyse computational complexity. An implementation integrated into our modelling tool demonstrates substantial savings in memory and time compared with naive product-based exploration, while preserving diagnostic and verification capabilities. The results indicate that the method enables practical reachability analysis for realistically sized product-line models, thereby facilitating verification and design-space exploration in configurable concurrent systems.

Keywords: Petri Net Product Lines · reachability graph · symbolic analysis · family-based verification · state-space reduction

1 Introduction

Petri nets (PNs) constitute a well-established graph-based modelling formalism for concurrent systems [21,24]. Their graphical notation and firm mathematical foundations have made them a de facto choice for analysing control-flow, resource usage and behavioural properties in distributed and industrial settings.

Product-line approaches enable the compact specification of many closely related system variants by capturing variability explicitly. A Petri Net Product Line (PNPL) [12,13] combines both ideas: it encodes a family of Petri nets together with presence conditions and feature constraints, avoiding duplication

L. Lestingi et al. (Eds.): DataMod 2025, LNCS 16421, pp. 21–35, 2026.
https://doi.org/10.1007/978-3-032-25552-5_2

and enabling analyses that operate at the product-line level. Previous work has shown that structural analyses (e.g., checking net classes, structural soundness or free-choice properties) can be "lifted" to PNPLs, yielding significant efficiency gains compared to per-product analysis [13].

Despite these advantages, important gaps remain when attempting to reuse the rich set of dynamic analyses developed for traditional Petri nets in the PNPL setting. A central example is the reachability graph: a fundamental artefact for verification (e.g., model checking, liveness, deadlock detection), performance reasoning and diagnostic tasks in classical PN theory [21]. For PNPLs, however, the definition and construction of a family-preserving reachability graph are not yet standardised nor widely implemented. The interaction between variability (presence conditions, feature constraints) and state-space exploration introduces several challenges: naive per-product enumeration is infeasible for realistic product counts, symbolic encodings must preserve feature information to avoid loss of per-product semantics, and state-space explosion is exacerbated by the combinatorial interplay of control and variability [13].

These limitations hinder the applicability of PNPLs in scenarios that require behavioural analysis across variants, such as global safety checks, variant-aware verification or automated debugging of configurable concurrent systems. Bridging this gap requires: (i) a precise semantics for PNPL states that combines net marking with variability information, (ii) successor-generation algorithms that enforce feature constraints during exploration, and (iii) reduction and merging strategies that keep the family-level state space tractable while preserving soundness and completeness with respect to per-product semantics.

This paper addresses those challenges. We present a formalisation and a set of algorithms to construct a family-based reachability graph for PNPLs. Our approach defines a symbolic state representation that pairs markings with presence conditions, a family-preserving successor relation, and state-space reduction techniques to mitigate explosion. We prove soundness and completeness of the construction with respect to the standard per-product semantics, provide complexity considerations, and report an implementation integrated in the TITAN modelling environment that leverages existing tools for Petri net analysis [15]. Experimental results on benchmark PNPL models illustrate practical gains over naive product enumeration and demonstrate the utility of the reachability graph for verification and diagnosis across product families.

The rest of the paper is organised as follows. After this introduction, Sect. 2 presents the essential background for this work. Section 3 details the algorithms for successor generation and state reduction. Section 4 shows the architecture of the TITAN framework that implements our solution. Section 5 positions our contribution with respect to prior work on PNPLs and Petri net analysis. Finally, Sect. 6 summarises the conclusions and outlines future work.

2 Background

In this section, we introduce essential concepts about Petri nets (Sect. 2.1), and PNPLs (Sect. 2.2).

2.1 Petri Nets

A Petri net (PN) is a graphical and mathematical modelling tool used to describe concurrent systems [21]. Petri nets provide a natural and effective means to represent logical interactions among system components or activities, including synchronisation, sequencing, concurrency, and conflict resolution.

A PN model comprises two key elements: a net structure, which represents the static aspects of the system as a weighted, bipartite directed graph (places and transitions); and a marking, which denotes the system state by means of tokens distributed across the net structure [21]. The graphical representation of places, transitions and tokens employs circles, rectangles and dots, correspondingly.

The evolution of markings through transition firings is known as the *token game* and simulates the behaviour of the system [15]. The reachability graph (RG) of a PN is the directed graph whose vertices represent all markings reachable from the initial marking, with edges labelled by transitions corresponding to firings between markings. The RG is a central artefact to analyse dynamic properties such as reachability, boundedness, liveness, reversibility, and deadlock freedom [21]. However, RG construction suffers from state explosion for larger systems, motivating more efficient techniques such as simulation-based analysis [32] or model checking [9].

2.2 Petri Net Product Lines

Petri Net Product Lines (PNPLs) [11–13] integrate Petri nets with Software Product Line (SPL) engineering principles [5,25] to represent a collection of similar systems in a unified and compact form. A PNPL thus denotes a family of Petri nets that can be derived through distinct admissible configurations.

The adoption of a single artefact enables the concurrent analysis of all potential derivations, thereby eliminating the need for independent evaluations of each variant. Thus, this approach enables modelling and analysis of all system variants simultaneously, avoiding redundant effort for each configuration.

Definition 1 (Petri Net Product Line [12]). *A Petri Net Product Line is a tuple* $PNPL = (PN, FM, \Phi)$ *where:*

- *PN is the 150% Petri net, which includes all places, transitions, and arcs across the product family;*
- *FM is a feature model that defines the variability space; and*
- Φ *is a set of presence conditions, expressed as logical formulas, that specify under which feature combinations each element appears in a product variant.*

Elements whose presence conditions evaluate to false *are removed from the 150% net to derive the configured net for a specific variant. Variability affects only the structure of the PN; the marking, which represents the dynamic state, remains unchanged.*

As illustrated in Fig. 1, the model represents a very simple, Flexible Assembly Line capable of producing two different types of products, ItemA and ItemB. ItemA requires two tokens for its assembly, and three for ItemB. This PNPL has 3 variants: ItemA, ItemB and (ItemA $\wedge$ ItemB). This running example will be used in Sect. 3 to illustrate the construction and pruning of the feature-annotated reachability graph.

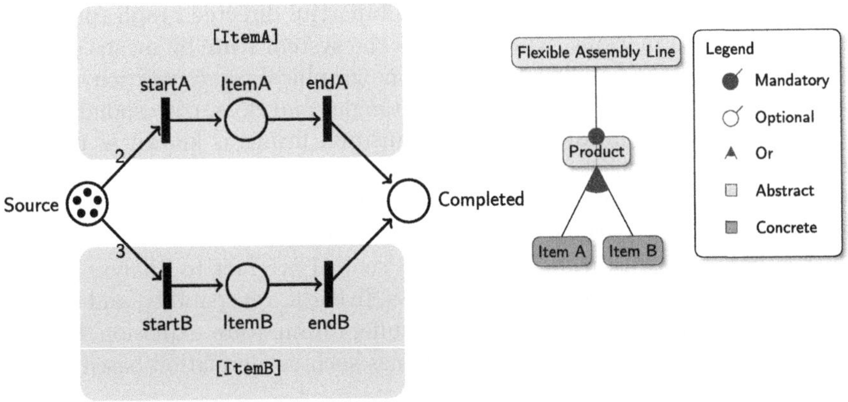

(a) 150% net annotated with PCs (b) Feature Model

Fig. 1. A PNPL representing a Simplistic Flexible Assembly Line.

Structural properties—such as marked graphs, state machines, free-choice, and extended free-choice structures—are formally analysed using lifted analysis techniques [27]. These techniques translate structural properties into first-order logical propositions that can be efficiently resolved through satisfiability (SAT) solvers [13]. Furthermore, by transforming a PNPL into a constraint programming formulation [3], P- and T-invariants can be examined at the product-line level through a lifted incidence matrix representation, as described in [11].

Prior to this work, it was not possible to construct the RG of a PNPL in order to analyse behavioural properties.

3 Construction of the Reachability Graph of a PNPL

This section outlines the formal procedure for transforming a PNPL into a reachability graph (RG) augmented with feature annotations, named the feature-annotated RG (fRG).

3.1 Feature-Annotated Reachability Graph

The Reachability Graph (RG) of a Petri Net is a state-space representation that enumerates all possible markings reachable from the initial marking through the firing of transitions. Each node in the net represents a reachable marking, while each directed edge corresponds to a transition firing that causes the system to evolve from one marking to another.

In a PNPL, variability is introduced by associating transitions, places, or arcs with presence conditions over features that govern their inclusion under specific product configurations. In order to facilitate dynamic property verification – for example, to ensure liveness or safety – across all potential products, a unified behavioural model capturing this variability must be generated.

The following formal definition introduces the concept of the feature-annotated reachability graph (fRG).

Definition 2 (Feature-Annotated Reachability Graph). *Let PNPL* $= (FM, PN, \Phi)$ *be a Petri Net Product Line, where* $PN = (P, T, F, W, M_0)$ *is the 150% Petri net with its initial marking, and* $FM = (F, C)$ *is the feature model with feature set* F *and constraints* C*. The feature-annotated reachability graph (fRG) of a PNPL is a tuple*

$$\mathit{fRG} = (V, E, f)$$

where:

- $V \subseteq \mathcal{B}(P)$ *is the set of reachable markings from* M_0*, with* $\mathcal{B}(P)$ *denoting the set of all possible markings over* P*;*
- $E \subseteq V \times T \times V$ *is the set of directed edges, where each* $(M, t, M') \in E$ *iff* $M \xrightarrow{t} M'$ *is a valid firing in the 150% net* PN*; and*
- $f : E \rightarrow 2^F$ *is a labelling function that assigns to each edge* $e = (M, t, M') \in E$ *a presence condition* $f(e) \subseteq F$ *(or its corresponding feature formula), where* F *is the set of features defined in* FM*.*

Extending the RG concept to the PNPL setting requires integrating variability information. The fRG therefore associates each transition firing with a feature expression (presence condition) that governs its activation across different product configurations. This enriched state space enables a unified analysis of behavioural properties across the entire product line.

3.2 From PNPL to Feature-Annotated RG

When constructing the fRG from a PNPL model, special care is required to ensure correct state generation, particularly in scenarios with multiple tokens and overlapping transitions. A single marking M may enable multiple transitions associated with distinct feature expressions; if these transitions fire using different tokens, the successor marking M' may implicitly combine mutually exclusive features, yielding semantically invalid states.

Conflict Detection Filter. To prevent such invalid states, we introduce a *conflict detection filter* that systematically excludes markings derived from incompatible feature combinations.

Formally, for any path $M \to M'$, if M' results from firing transitions with feature expressions $\varphi_1, \varphi_2, \ldots$ such that $\bigwedge_i \varphi_i \not\models \top$ under the feature model constraints C, then M' is pruned from the state space. The filter operates as follows:

1. **Feature Path Tracking**: Each marking $M \in V$ maintains a feature path $\Phi_M = \bigwedge_{i=1}^{k} \varphi_i$, recording the cumulative conjunction of feature expressions of all transitions fired from M_0 to reach M.
2. **Compatibility Check**: Before adding an edge $(M \xrightarrow{t} M')$ with feature expression φ_t, check that $\Phi_M \wedge \varphi_t \models \top$ under C.
3. **Pruning Rule**: Prune M' if $\Phi_{M'} = \Phi_M \wedge \varphi_t$ is unsatisfiable or violates the feature model constraints (e.g. XOR, *requires*, or *excludes* relationships). Formally:
$$M' \notin V \quad \text{if} \quad \Phi_{M'} \not\models \top \vee \Phi_{M'} \not\models C.$$
4. **Token-Level Validation**: For markings with multiple tokens in input places, ensure that the tokens enabling t originate from compatible feature branches. If some $p \in \bullet t$ contains tokens constrained by φ_p^1 and φ_p^2 with $\varphi_p^1 \wedge \varphi_p^2 = \bot$, firing t is disabled.
5. **Incremental Update**: Compute $\Phi_{M'} = \Phi_M \wedge \varphi_t$ incrementally to enable efficient SAT solving or constraint propagation.

This strategy guarantees that every state in the fRG corresponds to a valid product configuration, eliminating false positives from mixed-feature interactions while preserving completeness for valid feature combinations.

Construction Procedure. The fRG, integrating the conflict detection filter, is constructed through the following recursive procedure:

1. Initialise with the 150% net and its initial marking M_0.
2. For each enabled transition $t \in T$ in marking M, compute the successor M' according to the standard firing rule.
3. Apply the conflict detection filter by checking $\Phi_M \wedge \varphi_t \models \top$.
4. If the check succeeds, annotate the edge $(M \xrightarrow{t} M')$ with the presence condition $\chi = \Phi_M \wedge \varphi_t$ and add M' to the state space.
5. Recursively process all valid markings reachable from M_0.

Algorithm 1 implements the construction of the feature-annotated reachability graph (fRG) from a PNPL by means of a breadth-first exploration of the state space. It takes as input the set of places P, transitions T, arcs A, the initial marking M_0, the feature set $fs \subseteq FM$, and the feature model constraints C, and produces the corresponding feature-annotated reachability graph fRG together with feature paths Φ for each reachable marking.

Algorithm 1. Algorithm for generating an fRG from its PNPL (with conflict detection)

Require: P, T, A, M_0, fs ($fs \subseteq FM$), feature model constraints C
Ensure: $fRG \leftarrow$ A set of feature-annotated paths
1: $V \leftarrow \emptyset$ ▷ Set of visited markings
2: $Q \leftarrow \emptyset$ ▷ Processing queue
3: $fRG \leftarrow \emptyset$ ▷ Feature-annotated reachability graph
4: $\Phi \leftarrow \emptyset$ ▷ Map: marking $\mapsto$ feature path
5: $\Phi[M_0] \leftarrow \top$
6: $Q.add(M_0)$
7: **while** $Q \neq \emptyset$ **do**
8: $\quad M \leftarrow Q.pop()$
9: $\quad$ **for each** t_i in T **do**
10: $\quad\quad ia \leftarrow t_i.getInputArcs(A)$
11: $\quad\quad oa \leftarrow t_i.getOutputArcs(A)$
12: $\quad\quad ip \leftarrow ia.getPlaces(P)$
13: $\quad\quad op \leftarrow oa.getPlaces(P)$
14: $\quad\quad$ **if** $M[t_i.enabled(fs)]$ **then** ▷ Token + local feature enablement
15: $\quad\quad\quad M' \leftarrow M$
16: $\quad\quad\quad M'.decreaseTokens(ip, ia.getWeights())$
17: $\quad\quad\quad M'.increaseTokens(op, oa.getWeights())$
18: $\quad\quad\quad$ **if** $\forall p \in ip : M[p] \geq ia[p].weight$ **then** ▷ Firing precondition
19: $\quad\quad\quad\quad \varphi_t \leftarrow t_i.getFeatureFormula()$
20: $\quad\quad\quad\quad \Phi_{cand} \leftarrow \Phi[M] \wedge \varphi_t$
21: $\quad\quad\quad\quad$ **if** $SAT(\Phi_{cand} \wedge C)$ **then** ▷ Conflict detection filter
22: $\quad\quad\quad\quad\quad fRG.add(\text{Edge}(M \xrightarrow[\varphi_t]{} M'))$
23: $\quad\quad\quad\quad\quad$ **if** $M' \notin V$ **then**
24: $\quad\quad\quad\quad\quad\quad V.add(M')$
25: $\quad\quad\quad\quad\quad\quad \Phi[M'] \leftarrow \Phi_{cand}$
26: $\quad\quad\quad\quad\quad\quad Q.add(M')$
27: $\quad\quad\quad\quad\quad$ **end if**
28: $\quad\quad\quad\quad$ **end if**
29: $\quad\quad\quad$ **end if**
30: $\quad\quad$ **end if**
31: $\quad$ **end for**
32: **end while**
33: **return** fRG

The algorithm first initialises four data structures (lines 1–4): the set of visited markings V, the processing queue Q, the (initially empty) reachability graph fRG, and the map Φ that records, for each marking M, the cumulative feature path Φ_M. The initial feature path is set to $\Phi[M_0] = \top$ (line 5). The exploration is seeded by inserting the initial marking M_0 into the queue Q (line 6). The main loop (lines 7–32) then performs a standard breadth-first search: at each iteration, a marking M is dequeued from Q (line 8), and all transitions $t_i \in T$ are considered for firing (line 9).

For each transition t_i, the algorithm retrieves its input and output arcs (lines 10–11), and the corresponding input and output places (lines 12–13). It then checks whether t_i is enabled under the current feature configuration fs and marking M (line 14), using the predicate $M[t_i.enabled(fs)]$, which encapsulates both the usual token-enabling condition and the satisfaction of the local presence condition for t_i with respect to fs.

If t_i is enabled, a successor marking M' is computed (lines 15–17). This is done by first cloning the current marking M into M' (line 15), then decreasing the number of tokens in all input places according to the weights of the input arcs (line 16), and finally increasing the tokens in all output places according to the weights of the output arcs (line 17). The explicit firing precondition $\forall p \in ip : M[p] \geq ia[p].weight$ is then checked (line 18) to ensure that the transition is indeed fireable from M with respect to the underlying Petri net semantics.

If the firing is valid at the token level, the algorithm applies the conflict detection filter (lines 19–21). It retrieves the feature formula φ_t associated with t_i (line 19), computes the candidate feature path $\Phi_{cand} = \Phi[M] \wedge \varphi_t$ (line 20), and checks whether $\Phi_{cand} \wedge C$ is satisfiable using the feature model constraints (line 21). Only if this satisfiability check succeeds does the algorithm add a feature-annotated edge to fRG (line 22). This edge connects M to M' and is labelled with φ_t, thus realising the construction of the fRG where each transition is annotated with its presence condition. To avoid re-processing the same marking multiple times, the algorithm only enqueues M' if it has not been visited before (lines 23–26). In that case, M' is added to the visited set V (line 24), its feature path is stored as $\Phi[M'] \leftarrow \Phi_{cand}$ (line 25), and it is pushed into the queue Q for further exploration (line 26). The loop continues until Q becomes empty (line 32), meaning that all reachable feature-consistent markings have been explored.

Finally, the completed feature-annotated reachability graph fRG is returned (line 33), guaranteeing termination and completeness with respect to the reachable, feature-consistent state space of the configured PNPL.

Computational Complexity. Let $|V|$ denote the number of reachable markings and $|T|$ the number of transitions in the 150% net. Algorithm 1 performs a breadth-first exploration of the state space: each marking is dequeued from Q and processed at most once (lines 7–9), and for each processed marking M all transitions $t_i \in T$ are inspected (line 9). The inner operations for a given pair (M, t_i)—retrieving arcs and places (lines 10–13), checking enablement (line 14), computing the successor marking M' (lines 15–17), applying the firing precondition and conflict detection filter (lines 18–21), and testing membership in V (lines 23–26)—all run in constant time assuming bounded in/out degree, bounded or amortised cost for checking $\Phi_{cand} \wedge C$, and efficient data structures for sets and queues. Hence, the overall time complexity is

$$O(|V| \cdot |T|),$$

linear in the product of the number of reachable markings and transitions.

The algorithm avoids fully unfolding the PNPL for each individual feature configuration and instead constructs a symbolic RG in which variability is encoded through transition annotations. Nevertheless, if the number of reachable markings grows exponentially with the number of tokens or places, the construction may still suffer from state explosion in practice.

Illustrative Example. Figure 2 shows the reachability graph for PNPL in Fig. 1. Nodes represent the marking of the places, and edges represent the firing transitions. For instance, Source(3)ItemA(1) means that place ItemA receives one token, and Source retains three tokens when transition startA from product line [ItemA] is fired.

Nevertheless, some configurations that are naively depicted by this reachability graph are actually not feasible because of the feature constraints: e.g., reaching ItemA(1)ItemB(1) from the previous state when firing startB transition (PNPL cannot arbitrarily reach states of product [ItemB] from product [ItemA]). Hence, some of the nodes in the reachability graph must be pruned in order to restrict to valid states.

Coloured region in Fig. 2 highlights the states of the feature-annotated reachability graph that are removed by the pruning strategies because of incompatible execution paths.

4 Tool Support

We have developed TITAN (Tool for Petri net product line analysis), which supports different techniques to analyse PNPL. It can be freely accessed at [30]. The following lines describe the tool architecture in detail.

TITAN is a model-driven Eclipse plugin built in Java that leverages the Eclipse Modeling Framework (EMF) [29] for modelling and FeatureIDE [20] for defining feature models and configurations. It integrates a Sirius-based [28] graphical editor to construct 150% PNs and specify presence conditions (PCs). The extensible architecture supports additional analysis techniques and exporters via extension points. Figure 3 outlines the architecture.

TITAN provides the lifted analysis of structural properties, such as marked graph, state machine, and (extended) free-choice using Sat4j as SAT solver, as described in [13]. To analyse P- and T-invariants, TITAN transforms the PNPL into a lifted matrix equation [11]. Thus, it is expressed as a Constraint Satisfaction Problem (CSP). CSPs are solved using constraint programming techniques, concretely it relies on JaCoP, a Java library for CP solver [18]. The generation of the reachability graph and state space exploration has also been implemented. Moreover, TITAN exports PNs (both 150% net and any derivation net) to GreatSPN [1], TimeNET [31] and WoPeD [8]. It also supports the transformation of PNPL into CPN Tools [10].

TITAN currently computes reachability graphs and state spaces. Recent additions allow the use of explicit time annotations in PNPL, resulting in Timed Petri Net Product Lines (TPNPL). Time in TPNPLs aligns with the concept of time

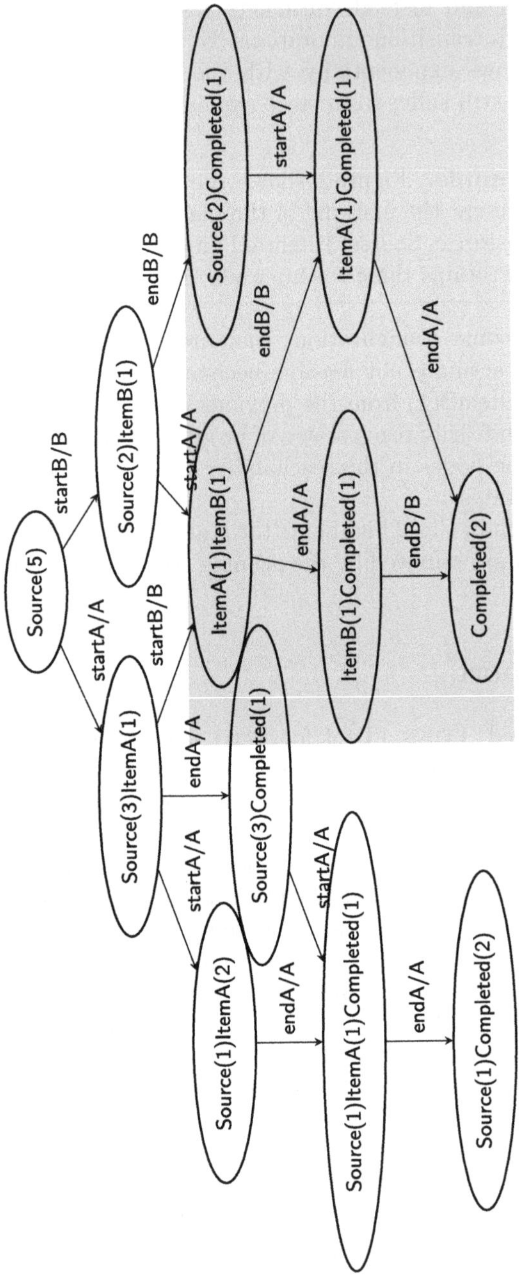

Fig. 2. Feature-annotated reachability graph for PNPL representing a Simplistic Flexible Assembly Line. (Color figure online)

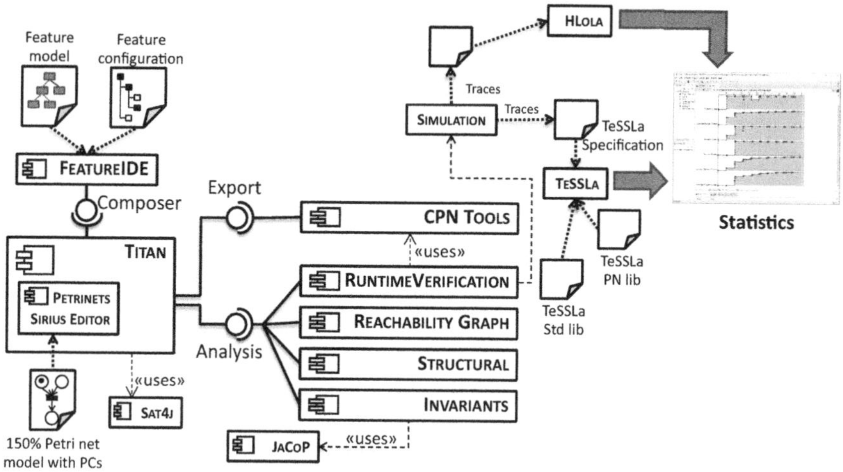

Fig. 3. Architecture overview of TITAN.

in Coloured Petri Nets [14,15], i.e., tokens carry discrete time annotations and time evolves according to a central clock. TITAN can perform runtime analysis of individual TPNPL products and compute user-specified quality metrics (e.g., performance, safety indicators) from execution events obtained by simulation traces. It relies on the TPNPL-to-CPN Tools transformation for dynamic analysis, enabling the selection of specific TPNPL products, execution of CPN Tools engines, and extraction of simulation reports. To this end, TITAN integrates two Stream Runtime Verification (SRV) frameworks (TeSSLa [6,16] and HLola [4]) for runtime analysis.

Figure 4 presents a TITAN snapshot with an example. The left panel shows the Eclipse explorer containing a FeatureIDE project with the PNPL from Fig. 1. The central panel displays the 150% net and its presence conditions, while the right panel shows the feature model. Besides the PNPL in Fig. 1, the TITAN repository includes further examples, such as vending machines, flexible manufacturing cells, and the Haukeland University Hospital case study [26].

5 Related Work

The research presented in this work builds upon a rich foundation of work in Petri net theory and software product line (SPL) engineering, with a specific focus on extending these paradigms to handle variability for dynamic analysis. This section reviews the key contributions that derive feature-annotated reachability graphs (or, similarly, Featured Transition Systems - FTS^+) from Petri Net Product Lines (PNPLs) in order to explore system dynamics via state space exploration.

The verification of Petri nets and their extensions have been a subject of extensive research. [21] laid the groundwork for Petri net theory, while [24] pro-

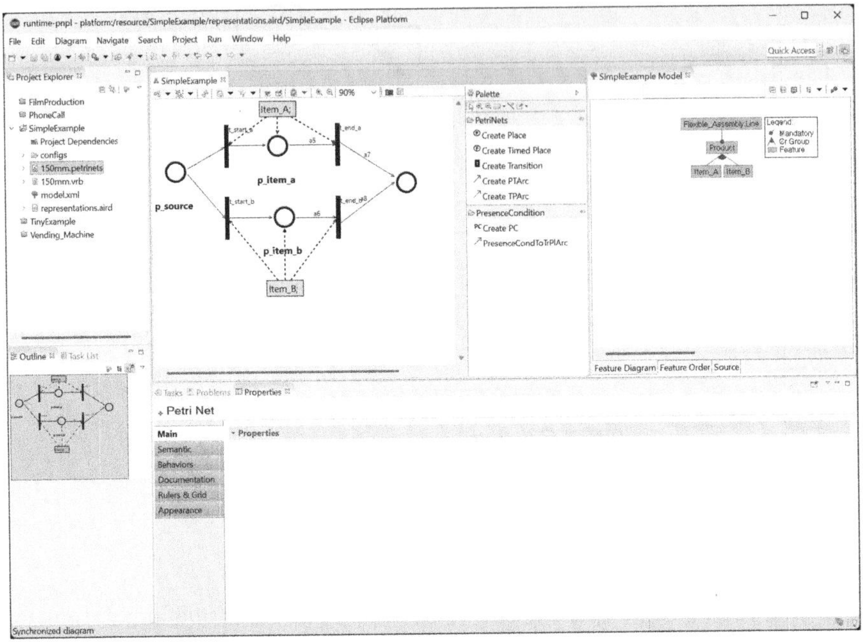

Fig. 4. PNPL modelling of Fig. 1 within the TITAN environment.

vided detailed methods for reachability analysis. Software Product Lines (SPLs) are a software engineering methodology for developing a family of related systems by leveraging a common set of features and assets. There are several mechanisms to model variability for SPL and most of them can be classified into annotation-based and composition-based techniques [2]. Here are some works have added variability to Petri nets using SPL techniques.

Feature Petri Nets (FPNs) [22] combine Petri nets with feature models by annotating net elements with propositional feature formulas, enabling feature-based enabling and disabling of behaviour. Dynamic Feature Petri Nets (DFPNs) [23] extend this framework with reconfiguration transitions (e.g. CONNECT/DISCONNECT) that modify feature states at runtime, supporting the analysis of adaptive and context-aware systems.

Petri Net Product Lines (PNPLs) are designed to model a family of Petri nets representing an SPL, where variability is captured through a Feature Model (FM) and a labelling function λ that annotates transitions with feature conditions. The focus is on statically defining all possible product configurations and their behaviours. The concept of PNPLs was pioneered by [13], who proposed a framework to model variability in concurrent systems, building on earlier work in software product lines. This approach has been extended to support slicing and configuration analysis, but verification techniques remain underdeveloped.

In [11], the authors explored feature modelling in depth, providing tools for managing configuration spaces, yet their focus was on static analysis rather than dynamic behaviour. Regarding dynamic properties analysis of PNPLs, research on that is relatively limited.

Besides reachability graph, other methods support the analysis of dynamic properties of PN: Linear Algebraic Techniques [7], Simulation-Based Analysis [19], Model Checking [17] and Transition Invariant Analysis [14]. Among all these approaches, we chose extending reachability graph with feature annotations because the RG of a Petri net offers a complete representation of the state space: it systematically generates all possible states (markings) by firing enabled transitions from the initial marking M_0. This is essential for the analysis of dynamic behaviour of PNPLs across all valid feature configurations, ensuring that properties such as reachability, deadlock, and liveness can be verified across the entire product line.

Additionally, the RG analysis methods for Petri nets, developed by pioneers like [24] and [21], include mature techniques such as state equations and coverability graphs. Although originally designed for classical Petri nets and do not extend to feature-annotated models, these methods are adapted for PNPLs through feature-extended RGs, leveraging their reliability to address variability-aware systems effectively.

6 Conclusions

This paper presents a formal framework and practical algorithms for constructing family-based reachability graphs of Petri Net Product Lines (PNPLs). Our primary contribution is a symbolic state representation that pairs net markings with presence conditions, complemented by family-preserving successor generation and conflict-aware pruning strategies that mitigate state-space explosion while preserving per-product semantics.

We prove the soundness and completeness of our construction with respect to traditional per-product analysis and analyse the main complexity trade-offs. An implementation within our PNPL modelling toolchain demonstrates significant efficiency gains over naive product enumeration, enabling scalable variant-aware verification, automated diagnostics, and design-space exploration for realistically sized product families. We provide a preliminary version of the algorithm in the Titan tool, a plug-in for the Eclipse framework.

The proposed reachability-graph construction fills a critical gap in PNPL analysis and provides a solid basis for future work, including compositional verification, hierarchical net decomposition, richer temporal logic support, and tighter integration with existing model-checking and Petri net analysis toolchains.

Acknowledgments. This work has been supported by the Spanish MINECO/FEDER projects AwESOMe (PID2021-122215NB-C31) and the Region of Madrid project DESAFíO-CM (TEC-2024/COM-235).

References

1. Amparore, E.G.: Reengineering the editor of the GreatSPN framework. In: Proceedings of PNSE@Petri Nets. CEUR Workshop Proceedings, vol. 1372, pp. 153–170. CEUR-WS.org (2015)
2. Apel, S., Batory, D.S., Kästner, C., Saake, G.: Feature-Oriented Software Product Lines - Concepts and Implementation. Springer, Cham (2013). https://doi.org/10.1007/978-3-642-37521-7
3. Brown, K.N., Miguel, I.: Chapter 21 - uncertainty and change. In: Handbook of Constraint Programming, Foundations of Artificial Intelligence, vol. 2, pp. 731 – 760. Elsevier (2006)
4. Ceresa, M., Gorostiaga, F., Sánchez, C.: Declarative stream runtime verification (hLola). In: Oliveira, B.C.S. (ed.) APLAS 2020. LNCS, vol. 12470, pp. 25–43. Springer, Cham (2020). https://doi.org/10.1007/978-3-030-64437-6_2
5. Clements, P., Northrop, L.: Software Product Lines: Practices and Patterns. Addison-Wesley Longman Publishing Co., Inc, Boston, MA, USA (2002)
6. Convent, L., Hungerecker, S., Leucker, M., Scheffel, T., Schmitz, M., Thoma, D.: TeSSLa: temporal stream-based specification language. In: Massoni, T., Mousavi, M.R. (eds.) SBMF 2018. LNCS, vol. 11254, pp. 144–162. Springer, Cham (2018). https://doi.org/10.1007/978-3-030-03044-5_10
7. Desel, J.: Basic linear algebraic techniques for place/transition nets. In: Reisig, W., Rozenberg, G. (eds.) ACPN 1996. LNCS, vol. 1491, pp. 257–308. Springer, Heidelberg (1998). https://doi.org/10.1007/3-540-65306-6_18
8. Freytag, T., Sänger, M.: WoPeD - an educational tool for workflow nets. In: Limonad, L., Weber, B. (eds.) Procs. of the BPM Demo Sessions 2014 Co-located with the 12th International Conference on Business Process Management (BPM 2014), Eindhoven, The Netherlands, September 10, 2014. CEUR Workshop Proceedings, vol. 1295, p. 31. CEUR-WS.org (2014). https://ceur-ws.org/Vol-1295/paper3.pdf
9. Girault, C., Valk, R.: Petri Nets for Systems Engineering: A Guide to Modeling, Verification, and Applications. Springer, Cham (2013)
10. Gómez-Martínez, E., Guerra, E., de Lara, J.: Analysing product lines of concurrent systems with coloured petri nets. In: The 34th Intl. Conf. on Software Engineering and Knowledge Engineering, SEKE 2022, pp. 118–123. KSI Research Inc. (2022). https://doi.org/10.18293/SEKE2022-015
11. Gómez-Martínez, E., Guerra, E., de Lara, J., Garmendia, A.: Lifted structural invariant analysis of Petri net product lines. J. Log. Algebraic Methods Program. **130**, 100824 (2023). https://doi.org/10.1016/J.JLAMP.2022.100824
12. Gómez-Martínez, E., de Lara, J., Guerra, E.: Towards extensible structural analysis of petri net product lines. In: PNSE@Petri Nets/ACSD. CEUR Workshop Proceedings, vol. 2424, pp. 37–46. CEUR-WS.org (2019)
13. Gómez-Martínez, E., de Lara, J., Guerra, E.: Extensible structural analysis of petri net product lines. Trans. Petri Nets Other Model. Concurr. **15**, 27–49 (2021). https://doi.org/10.1007/978-3-662-63079-2_2
14. Jensen, K.: Coloured Petri nets: A high level language for system design and analysis. In: International Conference on Application and Theory of Petri Nets, pp. 342–416. Springer, Cham (1989)
15. Jensen, K., Kristensen, L.M., Wells, L.: Coloured petri nets and CPN tools for modelling and validation of concurrent systems. Int. J. Softw. Tools Technol. Transf. **9**(3–4), 213–254 (2007). see also https://cpntools.org/

16. Kallwies, H., Leucker, M., Schmitz, M., Schulz, A., Thoma, D., Weiss, A.: TeSSLa - An ecosystem for runtime verification. In: Dang, T., Stolz, V. (eds.) Runtime Verification (RV 2022). LNCS, vol. 13498, pp. 314–324. Springer, Cham (2022). https://doi.org/10.1007/978-3-031-17196-3_20
17. Khomenko, V.: Model checking based on prefixes of Petri net unfoldings. Ph.D. thesis, Newcastle University (2003)
18. Kuchcinski, K., Szymanek, R.: JaCoP - Java constraint programming solver. In: CP Solvers: Modeling, Applications, Integration, and Standardization (2013)
19. Lu, Z., Liu, J., Dong, L., Liang, X.: Maintenance process simulation based maintainability evaluation by using stochastic colored petri net. Appl. Sci. **9**(16) (2019). https://doi.org/10.3390/app9163262, https://www.mdpi.com/2076-3417/9/16/3262
20. Meinicke, J., Thüm, T., Schröter, R., Benduhn, F., Leich, T., Saake, G.: Mastering Software Variability with FeatureIDE. Springer, Cham (2017)
21. Murata, T.: Petri nets: properties, analysis and applications. Proc. IEEE **77**(4), 541–580 (1989)
22. Muschevici, R., Clarke, D., Proença, J.: Feature petri nets. In: Botterweck, G., Jarzabek, S., Kishi, T., Lee, J., Livengood, S. (eds.) Software Product Lines - 14th International Conference, SPLC 2010, Jeju Island, South Korea, September 13-17, 2010. Workshop Proceedings (Volume 2 : Workshops, Industrial Track, Doctoral Symposium, Demonstrations and Tools), pp. 99–106. Lancaster University (2010). http://splc2010.postech.ac.kr/SPLC2010_second_volume.pdf
23. Muschevici, R., Proença, J., Clarke, D.: Feature nets: behavioural modelling of software product lines. Softw. Syst. Model. **15**(4), 1181–1206 (2016). https://doi.org/10.1007/S10270-015-0475-Z
24. Petri, C.A.: Kommunikation mit Automaten. Ph.D. thesis, Universität Hamburg, Germany (1962)
25. Pohl, K., Böckle, G., van der Linden, F.J.: Software Product Line Engineering. Foundations, Principles and Techniques. Springer, Cham (2005). https://doi.org/10.1007/3-540-28901-1
26. Requeno, J.I., Gómez-Martínez, E., Kallwies, H., Haustein, M., Leucker, M., Stolz, V., Stünkel, P.: Runtime verification of timed petri nets. In: Köhler-Bussmeier, M., Moldt, D., Rölke, H. (eds.) Procs. of the Int. Workshop on Petri Nets and Software Engineering 2024 co-located with the 45th Int. Conf. on Application and Theory of Petri Nets and Concurrency (PETRI NETS 2024). CEUR Workshop Proceedings, vol. 3730, pp. 122–131. CEUR-WS.org (2024). https://ceur-ws.org/Vol-3730/paper07.pdf
27. Salay, R., Famelis, M., Rubin, J., Sandro, A.D., Chechik, M.: Lifting model transformations to product lines. In: Jalote, P., Briand, L.C., van der Hoek, A. (eds.) 36th International Conference on Software Engineering, ICSE 2014, pp. 117–128. ACM (2014). https://doi.org/10.1145/2568225.2568267
28. Sirius: https://www.eclipse.org/sirius/
29. Steinberg, D., Budinsky, F., Paternostro, M., Merks, E.: EMF: Eclipse Modeling Framework 2.0. Addison-Wesley Professional, 2nd edn. (2009)
30. TITAN - Tool for PetrI net producT line ANalysis. https://doi.org/10.5281/zenodo.13993436
31. Zimmermann, A.: Modelling and performance evaluation with TimeNET 4.4. In: QEST. LNCS, vol. 10503, pp. 300–303. Springer, Cham (2017)
32. Zurawski, R., Zhou, M.: Petri nets and industrial applications: a tutorial. IEEE Trans. Industr. Electron. **41**(6), 567–583 (1994)

Probabilistic Algorithm with Dynamic Load Balancing for GPU-Accelerated Tumor Growth Simulations

Manuel I. Capel(✉) and Luis Rodríguez Domingo

ETSIIT, Software Engineering Department, Universidad de Granada, 18071 Granada, Spain
{manuelcapel,luisrd}@ugr.es
https://lsi2.ugr.es/mcapel

Abstract. Efficiently simulating tumor growth using cellular automata (CA) requires high computational power. This paper presents a probabilistic CA model with a GPU–accelerated dynamic load balancing strategy implemented using CUDA, which enhances execution efficiency and scalability. The proposed approach integrates a probabilistic formulation of tumor cell transitions with adaptive GPU scheduling to avoid costly synchronization and improve parallel efficiency. Experimental results demonstrate execution time reductions of up to 54% on a 1024×1024 grid of CUDA thread blocks, while maintaining accuracy, thereby showcasing the effectiveness of our load balancing mechanism. This work bridges the gap between biologically realistic modeling and scalable GPU execution, contributing to the design of efficient computational oncology simulations.

Keywords: Cellular Automata · Tumor Growth Model · CUDA · Parallelization · Dynamic Load Balancing

1 Introduction

Tumor growth simulation plays a crucial role in biomedical research and clinical decision-making, providing computational insight into cancer progression and treatment response. By modeling tumor growth dynamics using high-performance computing (HPC), researchers can predict tumor behavior under certain conditions, optimize medication delivery strategies, and evaluate treatment efficacy before conducting clinical trials [1].

Advances in high-performance computing (HPC) and GPU acceleration have enabled increasingly complex tumor models, making it possible to simulate large-scale, biologically realistic models that were previously computationally infeasible [19]. However, despite their biological expressiveness, cellular automata(CA)-based models remain computationally expensive. Accurate simulation of tumor growth is essential for advancing precision oncology and improving patient outcomes [2].

L. Lestingi et al. (Eds.): DataMod 2025, LNCS 16421, pp. 36–53, 2026.
https://doi.org/10.1007/978-3-032-25552-5_3

Despite extraordinary advances in computational modeling, tumor growth simulations still face significant challenges in terms of efficiency and scalability. Traditional mathematical approaches, based on CA [17] or reaction-diffusion differential equations, demand substantial computational power, particularly when aiming for realistic biological fidelity. Scalability issues stem from the complex interactions between tumor cells, the microenvironment, and treatment responses, which require models with high spatial and temporal resolution [13]. Furthermore, adapting these models to modern heterogeneous architectures, such as GPU clusters or distributed HPC systems, remains difficult due to inefficient load balancing, memory bottlenecks, and parallelization constraints [16]. Overcoming these challenges is essential to achieve real–time simulations that support clinical decision–making and personalized treatment design.

Parallel computing has demonstrated its effectiveness across many domains involving the simulation of complex processes, and recent advances in distributed HPC and GPU architectures have further extended this potential. Several studies have improved the efficiency of CA implementations for tumor growth modeling [5,9]. Nonetheless, existing parallelization strategies often encounter scalability limitations due to synchronization overheads and inefficient workload distribution among processing units. In [8] and [11], the degree of parallelism had to be restricted to prevent race conditions between processes. Previous dynamic balancing approaches, such as [21], improve performance but still rely on synchronization mechanisms that limit scalability.

Other current approaches have explored computational dynamic load balancing in specific subproblem domains. For example, [10] propose techniques for efficiently executing a CA in parallel in a two-dimensional domain divided into rectangular regions, while [18] adapt load balancing to a processor grid aligned with the geometry of the problem.

In this paper, we introduce a probabilistic CA model with a GPU-accelerated dynamic load balancing mechanism that avoids costly synchronization. By updating cells independently across CUDA threads, our approach enhances scalability while preserving model accuracy. CUDA (Compute Unified Device Architecture) is a parallel computing platform developed by NVIDIA that enables general-purpose computation on GPUs. Unlike the approach in [21], which processes each tumor cell independently but requires synchronization for shared-data update, we revisit and extend the probabilistic model in [17] to ensure that each grid cell's state is updated independently in the next iteration. This guarantees that each thread processes its own cell without requiring global synchronization or extensive atomic operations, thereby eliminating contention overhead and enabling efficient large–scale simulations.

2 Related Work

Tumor growth has been widely modeled using cellular automata (CA) due to their ability to capture complex biological behavior through simple local interaction rules [17]. In CA-based models, each cell evolves according to neighborhood-dependent transition rules, enabling the simulation of tumor expansion, invasion, and microenvironment interactions. Unlike continuous approaches such as reaction–diffusion models [7] or systems of differential equations [15,23], CA explicitly represent individual cell dynamics and stochastic effects, making them particularly suitable for multiscale tumor modeling. Comprehensive surveys, such as [12], highlight the relevance of CA models for studying cell-cycle regulation and therapeutic response.

As model complexity increases, computational efficiency becomes a limiting factor. Parallelization techniques have therefore played a central role in enabling large-scale CA simulations. GPU-based implementations have demonstrated substantial performance improvements over CPU-based approaches. For instance, Cagigas-Muñiz et al. [3] optimized stencil-based CA simulations on CUDA architectures, reporting significant acceleration compared to sequential baselines. Similarly, Du et al. [6] introduced a GPU-powered 3D hybrid simulator capable of handling tens of millions of cells, achieving speedups of approximately 150× over parallel CPU implementations. These studies illustrate the transformative impact of GPU acceleration in computational oncology.

Load balancing remains a critical challenge in parallel CA simulations. Dynamic load balancing (DLB) strategies aim to distribute workload evenly across processing units, especially in spatially heterogeneous domains where tumor density evolves dynamically. Giordano et al. [10] proposed analytical workload redistribution methods for distributed-memory architectures, while Salguero et al. [21] developed a parallel CA tumor growth model incorporating dynamic balancing to reduce execution time. Although these approaches improve resource utilization, synchronization overhead and communication costs often limit scalability, particularly when frequent workload redistribution is required.

Despite significant progress in computational optimization, fewer works explicitly connect modeling semantics with architectural design. Most GPU-based CA studies prioritize raw throughput, often relying on deterministic update rules or simplified transition schemes to reduce synchronization costs. In contrast, probabilistic CA formulations introduce additional computational complexity but enhance biological expressiveness. Bridging the gap between probabilistic modeling and scalable GPU execution therefore remains an open methodological challenge.

Our work contributes to this line of research by integrating a probabilistic CA formulation with a GPU-oriented dynamic load balancing strategy designed to minimize synchronization overhead while preserving biological realism. By explicitly aligning modeling decisions with GPU execution constraints, the proposed approach advances both computational efficiency and methodological coherence in large-scale tumor growth simulations.

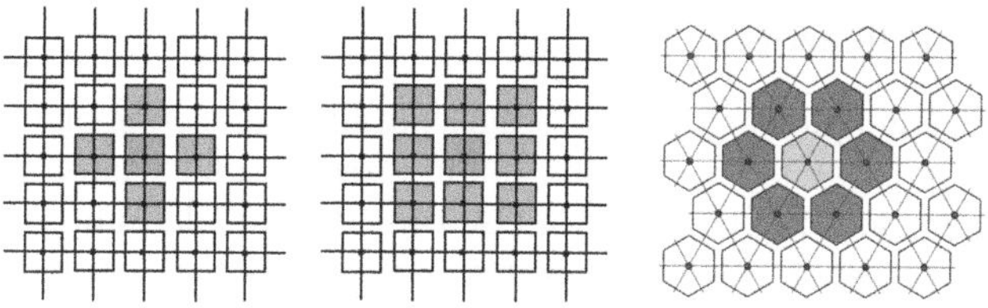

Fig. 1. Comparison of common neighborhood configurations in two-dimensional cellular automata.

3 Methodology

3.1 Tumor Growth Simulation Model

The CA model focuses on simulating tumor growth through local rules that govern the behavior of each cell according to its immediate environment. The model can be described through three fundamental components: spatial representation, behavioral rules, and underlying model assumptions.

Regarding spatial representation, the system is defined on a discrete two-dimensional grid in which each position represents either a tumor cell or a surrounding tissue element (see Fig. 1). The type of neighborhood used for interaction—such as the Moore neighborhood with $\mathbf{b} = 8$ neighbors or the von Neumann neighborhood with $\mathbf{b} = 4$ neighbors—determines how each cell is influenced by its local environment. The system evolves in discrete time steps, meaning that all state changes occur synchronously at regular intervals.

Concerning behavioral rules, each cell follows a set of probabilistic mechanisms that regulate three principal parameters. The proliferation capacity (ρ_{max}) defines how frequently a cell is allowed to divide. The migration capacity (μ) determines the likelihood that a cell will move within the surrounding tissue. The spontaneous death capacity (α) specifies the probability that a cell will die without external intervention. These parameters vary depending on the cell type, particularly distinguishing tumor stem cells from tumor daughter cells.

The model further assumes that tumor growth is driven by two main cell populations. Tumor stem cells are considered immortal, characterized by unlimited proliferation ($\rho = \infty$) and zero spontaneous death probability ($\alpha = 0$), and they are capable of generating both self-renewing copies and tumor daughter cells. In contrast, tumor daughter cells have limited proliferation capacity ($\rho = \rho_{max}$) and a non-zero probability of spontaneous death ($\alpha > 0$). A key aspect of the model is competition for space. When no neighboring positions are available, a cell enters a quiescent state, becoming inactive until environmental conditions allow further activity.

Overall, this model provides a structured framework for studying tumor growth dynamics and can be efficiently optimized for high-performance computing environments through parallelization strategies implemented on GPU hardware.

3.2 GPU Parallelization Strategy

The CUDA-based implementation leverages parallel processing on Graphics Processing Units (GPUs) to accelerate tumor growth simulations. The strategy addresses three main aspects: the CUDA threading model and grid structure, memory optimization, and synchronization with race condition handling.

The computational domain is partitioned into a grid of thread blocks, where each thread is responsible for updating a single cell of the cellular automaton. Each block processes a subregion of the global grid, with threads mapped directly to individual cells. Shared memory is used within each block to temporarily store intermediate cell state updates, thereby reducing expensive accesses to global memory. The number of threads per block is carefully tuned to balance computational workload and ensure efficient memory access patterns, maximizing Streaming Multiprocessor (SM) occupancy.

From a memory optimization perspective, the implementation exploits several CUDA-specific mechanisms. Shared memory is employed to cache frequently accessed cell states locally within thread blocks, significantly reducing latency compared to global memory accesses. Global memory coalescing is enforced to align memory access patterns with warp execution, ensuring that contiguous threads access contiguous memory locations. In addition, constant memory is used to store static model parameters, minimizing redundant memory fetches and further improving bandwidth efficiency.

To guarantee correctness while maintaining performance, appropriate synchronization mechanisms are incorporated to prevent race conditions. CUDA's `_syncthreads()` primitive is used to synchronize threads within a block, ensuring consistent intermediate updates before proceeding to subsequent computation stages. Atomic operations are applied when multiple threads attempt to modify shared memory locations, thereby preserving data integrity. At a broader level, grid-level synchronization strategies are implemented to ensure coherent state updates across blocks during successive simulation steps.

The complete CUDA implementation is publicly available in our repository [4], ensuring full reproducibility. The description above summarizes the core computational strategy for clarity.

Overall, these design choices ensure data consistency across threads while maximizing parallel efficiency. The use of synchronization primitives and atomic operations effectively eliminates race conditions and preserves the integrity of cell updates. Profiling results indicate that synchronization and atomic operations account for approximately 5% of total execution time, confirming that contention overhead remains limited. As a result, the CUDA-based cellular automaton implementation achieves substantial computational acceleration, enabling large-scale tumor growth simulations to be performed within feasible time frames.

4 Computational Model and Algorithmic Approach

The tumor growth simulation follows a structured computational approach based on CA. The CUDA-based implementation leverages parallelization to efficiently model the stochastic evolution of tumor cells.

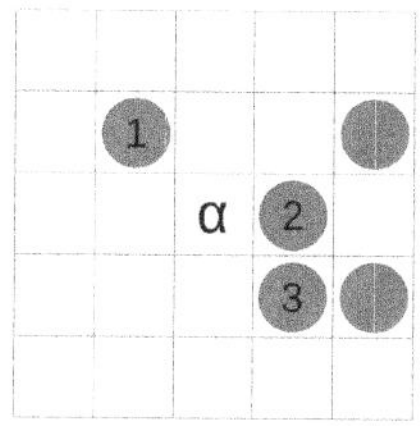

Fig. 2. Indexing of the neighbors of cell α in the Moore neighborhood.

4.1 Computational Model

The CUDA implementation follows a parallelized probabilistic approach designed to ensure efficient and consistent state updates across the two-dimensional grid. Each CUDA thread is assigned to process a single node of the grid, enabling fully parallel execution of cell state transitions. This thread-to-cell mapping ensures that the automaton evolves concurrently across the entire computational domain.

To prevent race conditions during updates, the implementation employs a double buffering strategy. Two grid states are maintained simultaneously: one stores the current configuration of the system, while the second holds the updated states computed for the next iteration. At the end of each simulation step, the buffers are swapped, ensuring that all threads operate on a consistent and immutable snapshot of the previous state.

Cancerous transformation probabilities are computed locally using the Moore neighborhood, allowing each cell's evolution to depend exclusively on its immediate surroundings. This localized computation model preserves the intrinsic spatial nature of the cellular automaton while maintaining parallel scalability. To further enhance memory efficiency, random memory accesses are minimized by enforcing an ordered neighbor processing scheme. Each neighbor is indexed systematically, beginning from the upper-left position and proceeding clockwise (Fig. 2). Neighboring cells containing cancerous states contribute directly to the probability of the α cell transitioning to a cancerous state in the subsequent iteration.

Overall, this computational model combines probabilistic local interactions with GPU-oriented memory and execution optimizations, ensuring both correctness and high parallel efficiency.

4.2 Definition of the α-Cell Transition Probabilities

This section considers two possible scenarios for computing the probability that the cell α contains a cancer cell in the next iteration. In the first case, α is initially non-cancerous and may transition to a cancerous state due to probabilistic influence from neighboring tumor cells. In the second case, α already contains a cancer cell and may either persist in its current state or be affected by additional contributions from neighboring cancerous cells, according to the defined transition probabilities.

Definitions and Notation. Let α be a cell in a grid that may or may not contain a cancer cell. We define the following terms:

- $N(\alpha)$: the neighborhood of α (typically a Moore neighborhood, consisting of up to 8 adjacent cells in 2D).
- v: the number of neighboring cells of α that contain cancer cells.
- $V = \{a_1, a_2, \ldots, a_v\}$: the set of these cancerous neighboring cells.
- K_a: the probability that a neighboring cell $a \in V$ generates a cancer cell in α, defined as:

$$K_a = \frac{p_{mi} + p_{re}}{l_a}, \tag{1}$$

  where l_a is the number of nodes in $N(\alpha)$ that do not yet contain cancer cells.
- p_{re}: the probability that a cancer cell in α persists if it is already present.
- p_{mi}: the probability that a cancer cell migrates into α from a neighboring cell.

Case 1: Probability of Cancer Cell Generation in α. To compute the probability that at least one of the neighbors of α will generates a cancer cell in α, given that α does not initially contain one, we consider all possible permutations σ of the set V. For a neighbor a_0 occupying position n in the ordering σ, the probability that it is the first to generate a cancer cell in α is:

$$P(a_0, n) = \frac{1}{v!} K_{a_0} (n-1)!(v-n)! \sum_{j=1}^{\binom{n-1}{v-1}} \prod_{i=1}^{n-1} (1 - K_{\sigma(i)}). \tag{2}$$

Probability of the first neighbour generating a cancer cell in α.

Summing over all possible positions n where a_0 can generate the cell in α, we obtain the total probability:

$$P_\alpha = \sum_{a \in V} \sum_{n=1}^{v} P(a, n). \tag{3}$$

Final probability of cancerous transition in α.

This equation expresses the probability that a cancer cell arises in α due to the influence of its cancerous neighbors.

Case 2: Probability of Cancer Cell Persistence in α. If α already contains a cancer cell, the probability that it will persist in the next iteration or receive a new cancer cell is:

$$P_\alpha = p_{\alpha_{re}} + (1 - p_{\alpha_{re}}) \sum_{a \in V} \sum_{n=1}^{v} P_\alpha(a, n). \tag{4}$$

Probability of α remaining cancerous or receiving a new cancer cell.

Here, $P_\alpha(a, n)$ represents the probability that the neighbor a generates a cancer cell in α at position n:

$$\begin{aligned} P_\alpha(a_0, n) &= \frac{(1 - p_{\alpha_{re}})}{(v+1)!} K_{a_0} (n-1)!(v-n+1)! \\ &\times \sum_{j=1}^{\binom{n-1}{v-1}} \prod_{i=\sigma(\alpha)-1}^{n-1} (1 - K_{\sigma(i)}). \end{aligned} \tag{5}$$

Here, K_{a_0} represents the probability of migration and reproduction from neighbour a_0. All possible cases where α is accessed after a_0 in the ordering are summed.

Finally, summing over all probabilities from each neighbor, we obtain the total probability formula:

$$P = \sum_{a \in V} \sum_{n=1}^{v} P_\alpha(a, n). \tag{6}$$

Final probability of cancerous transition in α.

This equation accounts for all possible contributions from neighbors, considering the order in which they are evaluated, ensuring the correct dynamics for persistence and generation of new cancer cells in α.

4.3 Algorithmic Framework and Complexity Analysis

The tumor growth simulation begins with the initialization of a two-dimensional grid representing both initial tumor cells and surrounding healthy tissue. Once initialized, the system evolves through probabilistic state update rules applied at each discrete time step. A tumor cell may proliferate with probability P_{re} provided that neighboring space is available, migrate with probability P_{mi}, or undergo programmed cell death (apoptosis) with probability P_d. These transitions are evaluated locally for each cell, preserving the spatial interaction principles of the cellular automaton.

Parallel execution is achieved through CUDA kernels, allowing all cells in the grid to be updated concurrently. Proper synchronization mechanisms are

Algorithm 1. Transition Function for Tumor Growth Simulation with CUDA

```
currentCell ← threadIdx + blockIdx * blockDim
if currentCell is cancerous then
    if currentCell.nNeighbours > 0 then
        if currentCell.nNeighbours == 8 then
            nextCell ← currentCell
        else
            P ← calcProbabilities()
            r ← Random(0, 1)
            if r < P then
                nextCell ← neighbourCell
            else
                nextCell ← currentCell
            end if
        end if
    else
        nextCell ← currentCell
    end if
else
    if currentCell.nNeighbours > 0 then
        P ← calcProbabilities()
        r ← Random(0, 1)
        if r < P then
            nextCell ← neighbourCell
        else
            nextCell ← currentCell
        end if
    else
        nextCell ← currentCell
    end if
end if
```

employed to maintain data consistency across threads, ensuring that state transitions are computed from a coherent snapshot of the previous iteration. The simulation proceeds iteratively until a steady-state growth regime or predefined convergence condition is reached. This CUDA-based design significantly enhances computational efficiency, enabling large-scale tumor growth simulations to be performed with high performance and numerical stability.

The implementation relies on three specialized CUDA kernels that structure the computational workflow. The neighborhood update kernel scans the Moore neighborhood of each cell to determine the number of cancerous neighbors contributing to local transition probabilities. The transition function kernel evaluates these probabilities and determines the next state of each cell according to the defined stochastic rules. A dedicated cancer stem cell persistence kernel ensures that stem cells maintain their immortal characteristics throughout the simulation, preserving the biological assumptions of the model. The function **calcProbabilities()** described in Algorithm 1 computes the probability that each neighboring tumor cell generates a cancer cell in α, storing these values in a vector. The specific neighboring cell responsible for inducing the transition is then selected according to the computed probability distribution. The recursive probability combination functions for both cancerous and non-cancerous cells follow the Poleszczuk model and are available in the public code repository.

From a computational perspective, the probability calculation procedure involves nested loops, recursive calls, and combinatorial operations that influence overall complexity. In the theoretical worst case, the recursive formulation leads to a complexity of $\mathcal{O}(v!)$, where v denotes the number of relevant neighboring cells. However, in practice, GPU parallelization distributes these computations across threads, reducing the effective per-thread computational cost to $\mathcal{O}(v)$. This parallel reduction in complexity makes large-scale simulations computationally feasible while preserving the probabilistic accuracy of the underlying biological model.

4.4 Experimental Setup

Simulations were performed on an NVIDIA GeForce GTX 1650 with Max-Q design, using CUDA. We tested grid sizes of 512×512 and 1024×1024 nodes used for 25-day and 50-day simulations, respectively. A single stem cell was placed at the center of the grid as the initial condition, with each simulation step representing one hour, resulting in 600 steps for 25-day simulations and 1200 steps for 50-day simulations. The performance evaluation focused on three key metrics: *execution time*, measuring the computational time required for each iteration; *speedup*, assessing the performance improvement of the GPU implementation over a sequential execution; and *load balancing efficiency*, analyzing the workload distribution across CUDA thread blocks. The sequential implementation serves as the baseline for measuring speedup. While qualitative comparisons with [21] are included, our aim is not to replicate their setup but to evaluate the proposed probabilistic model's scalability and efficiency under comparable conditions. Although execution times are slightly higher than those reported in [21], the proposed strategy provides improved scalability and more uniform GPU utilization, highlighting its potential for larger-scale simulations.

Model Parameters and Calibration. Table 1 summarizes the main probabilistic parameters used in the tumor growth simulation. The proliferation rate ($\rho_{\max}$), migration probability (μ), and spontaneous death rate (α) define the biological behavior of tumor stem and daughter cells, while p_{mi} and p_{re} correspond to the migration and persistence probabilities used in the stochastic transition rules (Eqs. 1–6). Parameter values were drawn from previous studies on high-performance CA tumor models [17] and adjusted empirically to reproduce realistic growth dynamics and spatial expansion patterns consistent with [10,18]. These values balance computational feasibility with biological plausibility and were verified through stability tests of the growth curve over multiple simulation runs.

Table 1. Representative parameter values used in the probabilistic CA tumor growth model.

Parameter	Symbol	Range	Value	Description
Proliferation capacity	$\rho_{\max}$	3–6 div.	5	Max. divisions per daughter cell
Migration probability	μ	0.05–0.15	0.10	Probability of migration
Spontaneous death rate	α	0.01–0.10	0.05	Probability of apoptosis
Cell migration factor	p_{mi}	0.05–0.20	0.12	Probability of cancer cell inflow
Persistence factor	p_{re}	0.70–0.95	0.85	Probability of persistence in α

Parameter Selection and Calibration. The probabilistic parameters of the model were selected using a two-stage calibration process based on the reference biological model of Poleszczuk and Enderling, as well as the experimental validation performed in the underlying study.

First, the parameters governing cell dynamics –namely, proliferation capacity (ρ_{max}), migration probability (μ), spontaneous death rate (α), migration factor (ρ_{mi}) and persistence factor (ρ_{re}) –were initialised within the biologically plausible ranges reported in previous CA tumour growth models. These ranges were chosen to reflect typical avascular tumour behaviour and spatial expansion patterns.

Secondly, the parameter values were empirically calibrated through repeated simulation runs to ensure that the resulting tumour growth dynamics satisfied the following criteria: (i) monotonic expansion without numerical instability; (ii) spatially compact tumour morphology with a dense core; and (iii) growth curves consistent with classical tumour growth models (logistic and Gompertz), and (iv) stability of results across multiple stochastic realisations.

Model reliability was assessed by fitting the simulated growth curves to analytical growth functions, and by evaluating the goodness of fit using standard error metrics. The selected parameter configuration corresponds to the median setting that produced stable growth behaviour and minimal fitting error across repeated experiments. The detailed experimental procedure and growth-curve validation are reported in the underlying implementation study [20].

This calibration procedure ensures that the chosen parameters strike a balance between biological plausibility, numerical stability and computational feasibility, as demonstrated by the experimental analysis of the underlying implementation.

5 Experimental Results

Since tumor growth simulations require a high resolution, we have chosen a 1024×1024 grid to represent the tumor tissue. This grid size limits the tumor to 1,048,576 cells, which are initially empty (non-cancerous tissue) at the beginning of the simulation and can be progressively occupied by tumor cells.

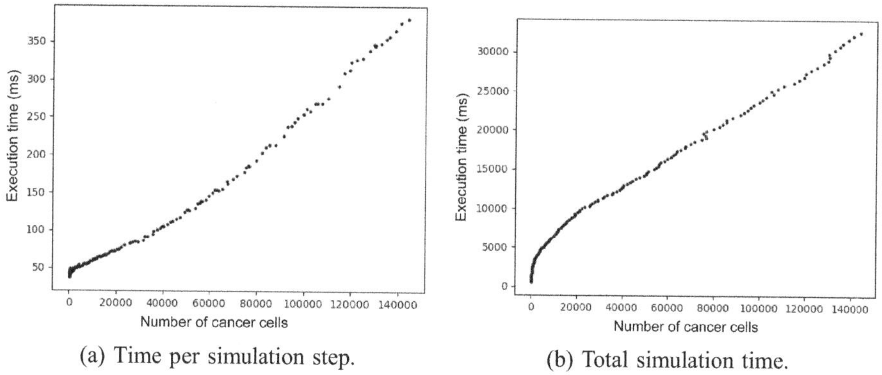

Fig. 3. Comparison between the number of cancer cells and simulation time.

5.1 Performance Comparison

The performance of the proposed tumor growth simulation was evaluated using various execution parameters and CUDA grid configurations. The total execution time and the number of processed cells per time unit were measured with a 1024×1024 grid over 150 simulation days. A comparison with previous work [21] highlights three key points: (a) the proposed algorithm processes a similar number of cells as in [21], demonstrating that the tumor growth model remains consistent. (b) Unlike [21], which used 4000 steps, this work uses 3600 steps to match the 150-day simulation time window, where each day consists of 24 steps, $150\,\text{days} \times 24\,\text{steps/day} = 3600$ steps. (c) Although the best execution times of the proposed approach are slightly worse that those in [21], the grid cell distribution strategy enhances scalability, which was not achieved in the previous work. This work primarily evaluates computational performance.

CUDA Grid Size and Speedup Analysis. The speedup achieved when varying the CUDA grid size is detailed in Table 2. The results show a significant speedup compared to single-thread execution.

Speedup increases with grid size, reaching 218.647× for a 1024×1024 configuration. The simulation achieves 8.79M processed cells/s in only 17.187s.

Execution Time Curve Analysis. The relationship between number of tumor cells and execution time per step is crucial. Execution time grows approximately linearly with tumor size, with minor deviations due to increased neighborhood interactions (Fig. 3a).

Similarly, Fig. 3b shows that total execution time initially increases rapidly as the tumor grows, but eventually, growth stabilizes and follows an approximately linear trend. This confirms that the probabilistic model remains efficient even for larger simulations.

Table 2. Performance of the simulations carried out with the probabilistic model, varying the size of the CUDA grid.

CUDA Grid	Size	Processed	Processed/s	Seconds	Speedup
1×64	164,401	191,918,090	40,234.41	4769.998	1
2×64	136,588	146,984,801	78,683.08	1868.061	1.956
4×64	153,697	173,264,862	84,914.98	2040.451	2.111
8×64	146,279	169,838,837	147,932.54	1148.083	3,677
16×64	146,784	160,235,895	250,391.66	639.941	6.223
16×16	147,533	176,305,011	136,524.60	1291.379	3.393
32×64	137,424	154,349,732	498,481.24	309.64	12.389
32×32	158,803	180,625,230	262,416.52	688.315	6.522
64×64	141,702	161,861,208	908,587.38	178.146	22.582
128×128	119,016	123,115,379	2,344,429.65	52.514	58.269
256×256	139,710	147,640,588	4,906,306.92	30.092	121.943
512×512	129,254	142,093,466	5,581,705.07	25.457	138.729
1024×1024	134,349	151,196,626	8,797,150.52	17.187	218.647

Comparative Discussion with GPU CA Models. To contextualize the performance results in Table 2, we compared our probabilistic GPU-based cellular automaton with other recent GPU implementations for CA-driven tumor or biological simulations.

Cagigas-Muñiz *et al.* [3] reported a speed-up of approximately 150× over CPU implementations for large-scale CA stencils optimized with CUDA, while Du *et al.* [6] achieved a 150-fold acceleration in their 3D hybrid simulator (*Gell*), which handles tens of millions of cells through simplified deterministic update rules. Our implementation reaches a maximum speed-up of about 219× relative to a sequential baseline for a 1024^2 grid (approximately one million cells).

Table 3. Kernel execution times and execution times examined using Nvprof.

Kernel/Operation	Time (%)	Total	Calls	Avg	Min	**Max**
transitionFunction()	80.76%	169.448 s	3600	47.069 ms	5.3988 ms	175.90 ms
updateNeighbors()	18.41%	38.6204 s	3600	10.728 ms	10.392 ms	11.412 ms
`CUDA memcpy DtoH`	0.77%	1.61256 s	31	52.018 ms	51.493 ms	53.980 ms
setup_kernel()	0.03%	65.804 ms	1	65.804 ms	65.804 ms	65.804 ms
`CUDA memcpy HtoD`	0.02%	51.896 ms	1	51.896 ms	51.896 ms	51.896 ms
stemCellTest(Cel)	0.01%	18.802 ms	3600	5.2220 µs	2.3040µs	7.3920 µs

Although the absolute throughput of our simulator is roughly 40–50% of the per-cell update rate reported in [6] for comparable grid sizes, our model incorporates probabilistic transition rules and dynamic load balancing, which increase computational complexity but yield greater biological realism and scalability. Therefore, the obtained performance is consistent with the state-of-the-art GPU CA models, demonstrating that probabilistic formulations can approach the efficiency of deterministic GPU frameworks while providing a more expressive modeling capability for tumor growth dynamics.

Profiling (Table 3) shows transitionFunction() dominates runtime ($\approx$ 81%). GPU occupancy of the function decreases to $\approx$ 36% in later iterations, due to uneven workload distribution.

5.2 Sensitivity Analysis

A local sensitivity analysis was conducted around the calibrated parameter values to evaluate the robustness of the model and its suitability for heterogeneous biological scenarios. Sensitivity analysis is widely used in computational biology to assess model robustness and parameter identifiability under uncertainty [14]. The adopted procedure follows standard practices in local sensitivity analysis for complex computational models [22]. Each key parameter was varied independently while the others were kept fixed. (a) migration probability μ: ±20%; (b) The spontaneous death rate (α): ±20%; and (c) the persistence factor (ρ_{re}): ±10%. For each configuration, 10 simulation runs were performed. Two indicators were measured: (1) the final tumour size after 50 simulated days, and (2) the average execution time per simulation step (Table 4).

Table 4. Local sensitivity analysis

Parameter variation	Change in final tumor size	Change in execution time
μ −20%	−8.7%	+0.6%
μ +20%	+9.3%	+0.8%
α −20%	+11.5%	+0.4%
α +20%	−10.2%	+0.5%
ρ_{re} −10%	−14.8%	+1.1%
ρ_{re} +10%	+16.2%	+1.3%

As expected for avascular growth dynamics, results indicate that biological outcomes are moderately sensitive to persistence and death parameters, while computational performance varies by less than 1.5% in all cases.

This confirms that: (a) model behaviour is robust to moderate parameter uncertainty; (b) GPU performance is largely independent of biological parameter tuning; and (c) the proposed implementation can be adapted to different biological scenarios without a significant computational impact.

The sensitivity trends are consistent with the growth-curve stability analysis reported in the underlying experimental study.

The sensitivity methodology follows standard practices in computational biology and uncertainty analysis. These trends are consistent with the stability analysis of tumor growth dynamics reported in the experimental study [20].

5.3 Scalability Analysis

When designing a parallel GPU implementation for tumor growth simulations, the grid partitioning strategy strongly affects SM occupancy, memory behavior, and load balancing.

We evaluated two partitioning schemes: (a) division into 16 full rows or columns, and (b) division into 64 smaller regions. A hybrid strategy combining both approaches was then designed to improve overall efficiency.

In the 16-row/column scheme, workload imbalance occurs because tumor growth is concentrated near the center, leaving some SMs underutilized. This configuration also shows reduced cache efficiency and uneven execution times, since the processing cost depends on the tumor density assigned to each block.

	Average	Min	Max	Sum
SM Active Cycles	435.886.667,94	428.384.647	443.847.847	6.974.186.687
SMSP Active Cycles	428.369.846,02	399.514.675	444.196.286	27.415.670.145
L1 Active Cycles	435.886.667,94	428.384.647	443.847.847	6.974.186.687
L2 Active Cycles	410.789.433,50	410.592.168	410.975.932	3.286.315.468
DRAM Active Cycles	621.931.620	620.156.424	623.757.140	2.487.726.480

Fig. 4. Load distribution on the different SMs of the GPU for the distribution of the cell grid in 64 regions.

The 64-region scheme, Fig. 4, improves load balance by distributing active cells more evenly across SMs. However, this approach increases scheduling overhead and may degrade memory locality due to more scattered access patterns.

The proposed hybrid strategy combines the memory locality of the row-based scheme with the load balancing of the region-based approach. This design ensures a more uniform workload distribution while preserving contiguous memory accesses.

Table 5. Comparison of Workload Distribution Strategies

Factor	Comparison of Workload Distribution Strategies		
	16 Rows/Columns	64 Regions	Hybrid Grid (Expected)
SM Utilization	× Poor	✓ Good	✓ Best
L1/L2 Cache	× Lower efficiency	✓ Better caching	✓ Optimal cache utilization
DRAM Usage	× Lower, but inefficient	✓ Higher but contemption	✓ Balanced throughput

Profiling results confirm that the hybrid strategy achieves near-uniform SM utilization. As shown in Fig. 4, all SMs operate within a narrow execution range (approximately 428–443 million cycles), whereas the row-based configuration exhibits significant imbalance (not shown). In addition, improved spatial locality increases L1/L2 cache effectiveness and reduces global memory traffic, resulting in lower memory latency and better overall performance (Table 5).

6 Discussion

The proposed probabilistic model combined with hybrid load balancing improves GPU utilization and scalability, enabling efficient large-scale tumor growth simulations. Compared to row-, column-, or region-based partitioning, the hybrid strategy achieves more uniform GPU occupancy, illustrating how modeling semantics directly influence both biological realism and computational feasibility. Profiling indicates that execution time is primarily concentrated in the transition and neighborhood-update kernels, suggesting future optimizations through kernel fusion and improved memory access patterns. Overall, the approach aligns modeling methodology with scalable GPU execution, contributing to computational oncology within a feasible and fully available framework.

The probabilistic formulation increases biological expressiveness by explicitly modeling stochastic proliferation, migration, and persistence. This realism introduces additional computational overhead relative to deterministic CA, as transition probabilities must be evaluated for every cell at each iteration. The transition kernel accounts for approximately 80% of total runtime, reflecting this cost. Nevertheless, GPU parallelism sustains high throughput and scalability, demonstrating that biologically meaningful stochastic dynamics can be supported at scale. Proper architectural mapping allows enhanced realism without sacrificing performance. Correctness is ensured through intra-block synchronization using `_syncthreads()` and limited atomic operations for shared updates. These mechanisms account for roughly 5% of total runtime and remain stable across grid sizes and tumor densities, indicating that synchronization is not a scalability bottleneck. By restricting coordination to localized operations and avoiding global communication, the design minimizes contention while preserving numerical integrity. Alternative lock-free approaches would require restructuring transition semantics and increasing global memory traffic. The chosen strategy therefore balances efficiency, scalability, and implementation simplicity.

7 Conclusion and Future Work

This paper presents a probabilistic algorithm with dynamic load balancing for GPU-accelerated tumor growth simulations, achieving significant improvements in execution time, scalability, and load balancing efficiency compared to static approaches. The proposed hybrid workload distribution ensures balanced GPU utilization and enhanced computational performance. Future work will focus on extending the probabilistic model toward biologically validated simulations and incorporating adaptive balancing in multi-GPU and distributed environments to further improve scalability and applicability to complex biomedical scenarios. The C++/CUDA implementation of the tumor growth simulation code is available at [4].

References

1. Anderson, A., Chaplain, M.: Continuous and discrete mathematical models of tumor-induced angiogenesis. Bull. Math. Biol. **60**(5), 857–900 (1998)
2. Dlamini, Z., Francies, F.Z., Hull, R., Marima, R.: Artificial intelligence and machine learning in cancer research: current applications and future perspectives. Comput. Struct. Biotechnol. J. **18**, 2300–2311 (2020). https://doi.org/10.1016/j.csbj.2020.08.019
3. Cagigas-Muñiz, D., del Rio, F.D., Sevillano-Ramos, J.L., Guisado-Lizar, J.L.: Efficient simulation execution of cellular automata on GPU. Simul. Model. Pract. Theory **118**, 102519 (2022). https://doi.org/10.1016/j.simpat.2022.102519
4. Capel, M.I., Rodríguez Domingo, L.: Load balancing strategies for parallel tumor growth simulations (2025). https://github.com/mcapeltu/Load-Balancing-Strategies-for-Parallel-Tumor-Growth-Simulations. Accessed 13 Oct 2025
5. Cicirelli, F., Forestiero, A., Giordano, A., Mastroianni, C.: Parallelization of space-aware applications: modeling and performance analysis. J. Netw. Comput. Appl. **122**, 115–127 (2018)
6. Du, J., Zhou, Y., Jin, L., Sheng, K.: Gell: a GPU-powered 3d hybrid simulator for large-scale multicellular system. PLoS ONE , 18 (2023)
7. Gatenby, R., Gawlinski, E.: A reaction-diffusion model of cancer invasion. Can. Res. **56**, 5745–5753 (1996)
8. Gerakakis, I., Gavriilidis, P., Dourvas, N.I., Georgoudas, I.G., Trunfio, G.A., Sirakoulis, G.C.: Accelerating fuzzy cellular automata for modeling crowd dynamics. J. Comput. Sci. **32**, 125–140 (2019)
9. Giordano, A., Amelia, F., Gigliotti, S., Rongo, R., Spataro, W.: Load balancing of the parallel execution of two dimensional partitioned cellular automata. In: Proceedings of the 30th Euromicro International Conference on Parallel, Distributed and Network-based Processing (PDP), pp. 205–210. (2022)
10. Giordano, A., Rango, A.D., Rongo, R., D'Ambrosio, D., Spataro, W.: Dynamic load balancing in parallel execution of cellular automata. IEEE Trans. Parallel Distrib. Syst. **32**(2), 470–484 (2021)
11. Grama, A.Y., Gupta, A., Kumar, V.: Isoefficiency: measuring the scalability of parallel algorithms and architectures. IEEE Parallel Distrib. Technol. Syst. Appl. **1**(3), 12–21 (1993)
12. Ma, Ch., Gurkan-Cavusoglu, E.: A comprehensive review of computational cell cycle models in guiding cancer treatment strategies. npj Systems Biology and Applications. **10**(71), 1–28 (2024). https://doi.org/10.1038/s41540-024-00397-7
13. Rockne, R.C., Hawkins-Daarud, A., Swanson, K.R., et al.: The 2019 Mathematical Oncology Roadmap. Phys. Biol. **16**(4), 041005 (2019). https://doi.org/10.1088/1478-3975/ab1a09
14. Marino, S., Hogue, I.B., Ray, C.J., Kirschner, D.E.: A methodology for performing global uncertainty and sensitivity analysis in systems biology. J. Theor. Biol. **254**(1), 178–196 (2008). https://doi.org/10.1016/j.jtbi.2008.04.011
15. Padder, A., Shah, T.R., Afroz, A., et al.: A mathematical model to study the role of dystrophin protein in tumor micro-environment. Sci. Rep. **14**, 1–15 (2024)

16. Metzcar, J., Wang, Y., Heiland, R., Macklin, P.: A review of cell-based computational modeling in cancer biology. JCO Clin. Cancer Inform. **3**, 1–13 (2019). https://doi.org/10.1200/CCI.18.00069
17. Poleszczuk, J., Enderling, H.: A high-performance cellular automaton model of tumor growth with dynamically growing domains, (2013)
18. Rango, A.D., Giordano, A., Mendicino, G., Rongo, R., Spataro, W.: Tailoring load balancing of cellular automata parallel execution to the case of a two-dimensional partitioned domain. J. Supercomput. **79**, 9273–9287 (2023)
19. Du, J., Zhou, Y., Jin, L., Sheng, K.: Gell: A GPU-powered 3D hybrid simulator for large-scale multicellular system. PLOS ONE **18**(7), e0288721 (2023). https://doi.org/10.1371/journal.pone.0288721
20. Domingo, Rodríguez, L.: Dynamic Load Balancing Strategy for Tumor Growth Simulations on GPU Hardware, Granada, Spain (2024). Bachelor thesis
21. Salguero, A.G., Capel, M.I., Tomeu, A.J.: Parallel cellular automaton tumor growth model. In: Practical Applications of Computational Biology and Bioinformatics, 12th International Conference, PACBB 2018. Advances in Intelligent Systems and Computing, **803**, 175–182 (2018). https://doi.org/10.1007/978-3-319-98702-6_21
22. Saltelli, A.: Global Sensitivity Analysis: The Primer, Wiley, Chichester, UK (2008). https://doi.org/10.1002/9780470725184
23. Yin, A., Moes, D., van Hasselt, J., et al.: A review of mathematical models for tumor dynamics and treatment resistance evolution of solid tumors. Pharmacometrics Syst. Pharmacol. **8**(9), 720–737 (2019)

Reachability Specification Adaptation for Continuous Dynamical Systems

Zhi Zhang[1(✉)], Dalal Alrajeh[1], Yue Gu[2], Roberto Metere[3], Michele Sevegnani[2], Kangfeng Ye[3], and Poonam Yadav[3]

[1] Imperial College London, London, UK
zhi.zhang90@outlook.com
[2] University of Glasgow, Glasgow, UK
[3] University of York, York, UK

Abstract. Continuous dynamical systems are fundamental in modelling a wide range of real-world phenomena, from cyber-physical systems to industrial automation. Such systems operate in dynamic environments where unanticipated situations can arise. Requirements specified at design time may become partially unachievable when the system is deployed. We propose a novel method for reachability specification degradation tailored to continuous dynamical systems. Our approach involves sampling points within the initial state space region, estimating reachability regions over time using the Lipschitz constant, and augmenting the original specification through disjunction operations. We implement our method to support how a system can adapt to requirements in real time.

Keywords: Continuous dynamical systems · Reachability · Specification degradation

1 Introduction

Continuous dynamical systems are fundamental in modelling a wide range of real-world phenomena, from cyber-physical systems [15,20] and communication systems [13,16,26] to biological processes [9] and industrial automation [21]. These systems operate in environments that are often dynamic, uncertain, or partially known, making it essential for the system requirements (specified at design time) to continually adapt as the environment changes or new information about the environment becomes available. For example, consider a workload management system for next-generation communication base stations [26]. The system must balance resource allocation across processing units and communication channels, despite fluctuating network demands and traffic patterns. Such requirement could be expressed as a safety property that states "a base station workload must never exceed 1 terabits per second (Tbps)" or formally in signal temporal logic as: $\mathbf{G}_{[a,b]}(\mathrm{WL}_{bs} \leq 1\mathrm{Tbps})$, where $\mathbf{G}$ is *always*, a, b represent time values, and WL_{bs} is the base station workload. However, in a major event,

L. Lestingi et al. (Eds.): DataMod 2025, LNCS 16421, pp. 54–66, 2026.
https://doi.org/10.1007/978-3-032-25552-5_4

the number of users connected to a station may increase dramatically, causing this requirement to be (temporarily) violated. When modelling a continuous dynamical system, this violation may manifest as a subset of trajectories from an initial state-space region (e.g., a high number of connected users) that never reach desirable states (e.g., a workload below 1 Tbps). One possible repair to the predefined requirement might be "a base station workload must never exceed 1 Tbps, or if it does, then it must reduce it to below 1 Tbps within 5 min".

Several approaches have been proposed to enable adaptation of specifications (a.k.a. specification degradation) expressed in a temporal logic formalism in the face of environmental changes, such as [3,6,8,10,27]. However, these are limited in that they either (i) only handle discrete systems and thus require discretisation of the state space, causing a lack of precision in the requirements specification, or (ii) do not provide means for detecting violations of the specification for continuous dynamical systems from an initial region to trigger the adaptation.

In this paper, we propose a novel method for safety requirements' degradation in continuous dynamical systems. Our approach to safety requirements expressed in non-nested Signal Temporal Logic (STL) [19] and considers their satisfaction checking as a reachability analysis problem [2,11,14]. Given an initial condition (representing a state-space region, which is the blue region of Fig. 1) for the system and a safety requirement, the approach uses the system's Lipschitz constant to estimate the reachability regions (yellow region of Fig. 1) for the system starting from the sampling points in the initial state-space region. Since the considered STL specifications are non-nested, their satisfaction can be checked independently for each atomic temporal subformula, which simplifies the degradation process. The estimated region is then used to extract a weakening of the original specification, ensuring that the adapted specification is satisfied by all trajectories starting from this initial state-space region.

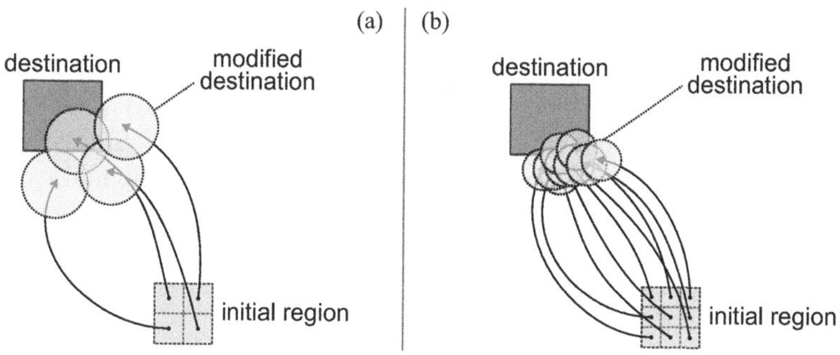

Fig. 1. The specification repair is based on the Lipschitz constant with (a) a 2×2 partition, and (b) a 3×3 partition. The yellow regions denote the reachable regions. (Color figure online)

2 Related Work

The closest work to ours focuses on the degradation of specifications in STL when deviations in the environment's expected behaviour are detected [6,7]. The primary challenge for these approaches lies in verifying whether the predefined specification has been violated, as it often requires checking an infinite number of trajectories. For instance, the work of [6] cannot detect specification violations when the time interval of the specification is long, and the action set is large, since this requires checking numerous trajectories generated by various combinations of actions within the specified time frame. To overcome this problem, Ghosh et al. [10] employed mixed-integer linear programming (MILP) to verify the violation of STL specifications and facilitated specification adaptation by reformulating the repair process as a model predictive control problem, for a dynamical system originating from an initial point. However, MILPs can only be used to check the violation of the specification for certain simple scenarios, since they often face infeasibility issues, such as running for extended periods without producing a solution. This is caused by large problem sizes, tight or complex constraints, or ill-conditioned problems [5].

The work of [3] presents an automated approach to the degradation of specifications expressed in a subclass of Linear Temporal Logic, for which tractable synthesis methods exist, in response to the detection of violations of environmental assumptions. Their approach considers violations of safety assumptions about the environment as a trigger for the adaptation process. As in this work, their research focuses on computing weaknesses of the original specification. Different from ours, they focus on discrete systems. In [1], a meta-learning framework is proposed to support the adaptation of learners during specification degradation tasks. They propose using a reinforcement learning agent to configure a learner that identifies the optimal degradation at runtime. However, these approaches cannot be applied to continuous dynamical systems, nor can they handle specifications without loss of accuracy.

At the same time, alternative set representations have been explored in reachability analysis, which could also be applied in the context of specification repair for continuous systems. For example, polygonal (polyhedral) sets have been used to represent the behaviour of anisotropic systems [12]. Similarly, Taylor model-based representations, which combine high-order polynomial expansions with rigorous remainder bounds, have been employed to construct flowpipes for nonlinear systems [4,18]. While our framework is currently formulated using Lipschitz based approximations, it could in principle be extended to incorporate these alternative representations.

Our work can be viewed as complementary to approaches to synthesising correct-by-construction control strategies for dynamical systems, as [17,22]. These assume specifications are correct initially. Our approach complements these approaches by accounting for requirements that are too strong and cannot always be achieved, requiring their degradation.

3 Preliminary

3.1 Dynamical System

A continuous dynamical system (CDS) describes the evolution of a system's state over time, and an external dynamical environment can influence its dynamics. This system may need to satisfy certain specifications, such as safety or reachability.

Definition 1 (Continuous Dynamical System). *Given $\mathcal{S} \subseteq \mathbb{R}^n$ as the bounded state space for a system, and $\mathcal{E} \subseteq \mathbb{R}^m$ as the bounded state space for the dynamical environment, we define a* continuous dynamical system *as the tuple $\Sigma_s := (\mathcal{S}, \mathcal{E}, f)$, where $f : \mathcal{S} \times \mathcal{E} -> \mathcal{S}$ is a measurable function characterising the state evolution of Σ_s. Assume that this dynamical system starts from the initial state space region $B_0 \subset \mathcal{S}$. That is, given $x(t) \in \mathcal{S}$ and $e(t) \in \mathcal{E}$ at some time t, its dynamical system is defined as*

$$\dot{x}(t) = f\left(x(t), e(t)\right), \ t \in \mathbb{R}^+, \tag{1}$$

where the dynamics of state $e(t)$ is governed by

$$\dot{e}(t) = \Theta(e(t)), \tag{2}$$

and $\Theta : \mathcal{E} \to \mathcal{E}$ is a measurable function.

If the function $e : \mathbb{R}_{\geq 0} \to \mathbb{R}^m$ is a constant vector function, the CDS runs in an environment with a constant rate of variation. The static environment is the special case, in which $e(t)$ is always the zero vector for any $t \in \mathbb{R}^+$.

By selecting a sufficiently small time step h_t and an initial time t_0, Eq. (1) can be approximated by the Euler method, as follows,

$$x(k+1) = x(k) + h_t f(x(k), e(k)), \tag{3}$$

where $k = \frac{t-t_0}{h_t}$. For any time $t^* \in \mathbb{R}^+$, the time interval $[t_0, t^*]$ can be represented as $[0, k^*]$, where $k^* = \frac{t^*-t_0}{h_t}$, $k^* \in \mathbb{Z}^+$. Its initial condition $x(0)$ denotes x_0 and x_k denotes $x(k)$. In the following discussion, we only consider this form for the CDS. Thus, the evolution of the system described in Eq. (1) is characterised by the trajectories of its states and measurements.

In this paper, we assume that the models of Eq. (1) and (2) are all known and autonomous dynamical systems. In the following sections, we will study the specification adaptation, such as the properties of safety and reachability.

3.2 Signal Temporal Logic

Signal Temporal Logic (STL) was originally developed as an extension of Metric Interval Temporal Logic (MITL), designed to analyse and reason about the behaviour of real-valued, dense-time signals [19]. Thus, STL can be used to specify the time-varying behaviour of a system based on the real value signal. In this paper, we focus on the STL with non-nested temporal operators fragment, which includes all the key temporal operators of STL except for their nesting.

STL is consisted of predicates h which is $\texttt{true}$ if and only if a function $h : \mathbb{R}^n \to \mathbb{R}$ is such that $h(x) \geq 0$. The syntax for an STL formula ϕ is defined as

$$\phi := \texttt{true} \mid h(x) \geq 0 \mid \neg\phi \mid \phi_1 \wedge \phi_2 \mid \mathbf{F}_{[a,b]}\phi \mid \mathbf{G}_{[a,b]}\phi \mid \phi_1 \mathbf{U}_{[a,b]}\phi_2,$$

where ϕ_1, ϕ_2 are STL formulas and a, $b \in \mathbb{R}_{\geq 0}$ with $a \leq b$. $\mathbf{U}$ is the until operator, and $\phi_1 \mathbf{U}_{[a,b]}\phi_2$ means ϕ_1 must hold until ϕ_2 becomes true within a time interval $[a, b]$. The temporal operator $\mathbf{F}$ and $\mathbf{G}$ are *eventually* and *always* operator. Let $\vDash$ denote the satisfaction relation between a time-state pair (x, t) and an STL formula ϕ, i.e., $(x, t) \vDash \phi$ which means ϕ holds true in the signal x at the time moment t, where the function $x : \mathbb{R}_{\geq 0} \to \mathbb{R}^n$.

Definition 2. *For a signal x the satisfaction of a formula ϕ as described in [19], as follows*

$$
\begin{aligned}
&(x,t) \vDash h \iff h(x(t)) \geq 0\\
&(x,t) \vDash \neg h \iff \neg((x,t) \vDash h)\\
&(x,t) \vDash \phi_1 \wedge \phi_2 \iff (x,t) \vDash \phi_1 \wedge (x,t) \vDash \phi_2\\
&(x,t) \vDash \phi_1 \mathbf{U}_{[a,b]}\phi_2 \iff \exists t_1 \in [t+a, t+b] \cdot (x,t_1) \vDash \phi_2 \wedge \forall t_2 \in [t, t_1] \cdot (x,t_2) \vDash \phi_1\\
&(x,t) \vDash \mathbf{F}_{[a,b]}\phi \iff \exists t_1 \in [t+a, t+b] \cdot (x,t_1) \vDash \phi\\
&(x,t) \vDash \mathbf{G}_{[a,b]}\phi \iff \forall t_1 \in [t+a, t+b] \cdot (x,t_1) \vDash \phi
\end{aligned}
$$

4 Problem Statement

We are interested in checking the trajectory of a system whose behaviour is prescribed by Eq. (1), starting from the initial region B_0, against a reachability property specified as an STL formula.

Definition 3. ***(Regional Satisfaction)*** *Given a specification ϕ and its time interval $[0, t^*]$, the system described in Eq. (1) can satisfy this specification ϕ, when starting from initial region B_0, i.e., for all $x(k)$ generated from Eq. (3), the set $\mathcal{X}_\phi := \{x_0 \in B_0 | \exists k \in \{0, \ldots, k^*\}, x_k \vDash \phi\}$ is equal to B_0. We say this system has a* Regional Satisfaction *w.r.t. ϕ, when starting from the initial region B_0.*

Definition 4 (Partially Regional Satisfaction). *Given a specification ϕ and its time interval $[0, t^*]$, the system described in Eq. (1) can partially satisfy this specification ϕ, when starting from the given region B_0, i.e., the set $\mathcal{X}_\phi \subset B_0$. We say this system has a* partially regional satisfaction *w.r.t. ϕ, when starting from the given region B_0.*

Definition 5 (Strong Regional Unsatisfaction). *Given a specification ϕ, the system described in Eq. (1) cannot satisfy this specification ϕ, when starting from the given region B_0, i.e., for all $x(0) \in B_0$, the set $\mathcal{X}_\phi$ is empty. We say this system has a* strong regional unsatisfaction *with respect to ϕ, when starting from the given region $B_0 \subset S$.*

Remark 1. It is easy to obtain that: if the system described in Eq. (1) fails to achieve regional satisfaction with respect to ϕ, then its trajectories from the initial region B_0 either satisfy ϕ only partially or are strongly unsatisfactory.

Definition 6 (Specification Repair). *Given a specification ϕ, the system described in Eq. (1) whose initial region is B_0 has strong regional unsatisfactory w.r.t. ϕ. Then, a new generated specification ϕ^* is such that for Eq. (3) the set $\mathcal{X}_{\phi^*} := \{x_0 \in B_0 | \exists k \in \{0, \ldots, k^*\}, x_k \models \phi^*\}$ is equal to B_0. We say this specification ϕ^* is the specification repair of ϕ for this system described in Eq. (1) whose initial region is B_0.*

Problem. Let the system described in Eq. (1), whose initial region is B_0, not have regional satisfaction with respect to an STL formula ϕ. Based on the dynamics of this system and the parameters of STL, generate a new specification ϕ^* such that this system, whose initial region is B_0, can have regional satisfaction w.r.t. the new specification ϕ^*.

In this problem, we face two key challenges:

C1 Determining when a system described in Eq. (1) whose initial region is B_0, does not have regional satisfaction w.r.t. specification ϕ?
C2 Determining an adaptation to the specification that ensures regional satisfaction w.r.t. specification ϕ?

For C1, since the initial region B_0 for the system described in Eq. (1) is a dense and uncountable set, it is impossible to check the trajectory of this system starting from every point in B_0. Additionally, it is difficult to degrade the specification based on the limited information (C2). The following section will try to address these challenges.

5 Methodology

We propose here a method to verify whether a system described in Eq. (1) whose initial region is B_0 has regional satisfaction w.r.t. specification ϕ, and to degrade when it does not.

For Eq. (1), the satisfaction of the specification can be verified by evaluating the function h values corresponding to the system's state variables. Typically, for systems with a continuous state space, evaluating the function h can be reduced to a reachability analysis. This involves determining whether the state variables can enter some specified value ranges while meeting the given temporal requirements. In this section, we adopt the Lipschitz constant $\mathcal{L}$ of the vector field of Eq. (1) to verify the specification.

For the dynamical system described in Eq. (1), it has a Lipschitz constant $\mathcal{L}$, such that for any x and x^* in $\mathcal{S}$, $\|f(x_k) - f(x_k^*)\| \leq \mathcal{L}\|x_k - x_k^*\|$. The Lipschitz constant $\mathcal{L}$ can be used to quantify the distance between two trajectories of Eq. (1), each starting from a different initial point. According to Eq. (3),

$$\begin{aligned}\|x_{k+1} - x^*_{k+1}\| &\leq h_t\|f(x_k) - f(x^*_k)\| + \|x_k - x^*_k\| \\ &\leq (\mathcal{L}h_t + 1)\|x_k - x^*_k\| \leq (\mathcal{L}h_t + 1)^{k+1}\|x_0 - x^*_0\|.\end{aligned} \tag{4}$$

This property is useful for quickly estimating the reachable region of Eq. (1) by sampling a limited number of trajectories from a small set of initial points, as shown in Algorithm 1. In detail, we can partition the initial region into many cells, as shown in Step 1, and then sample the central point of each cell as the initial point, as indicated by the blue region in Fig. 1. For each initial point, the system described in Eq. (1) generates the associated trajectory. According to the specification ϕ, we find the point in each trajectory, as shown in Step 5, satisfying that the value of the function h at this point is the closest to the value region of the same function in the specification ϕ. Alongside, the relevant maximum time moment is recorded. Using the maximum distance between any point in a cell and its centre in Step 2, the inequality described in Eq. (4) is applied to estimate the reachable region, which calculation can be represented as the Step 9, as illustrated by the yellow circle in Fig. 1. By comparing the overlap between the specification region and the estimated region, it is possible to quickly determine whether a system starting from the initial region B_0 has regional satisfaction (i.e., C1 can be solved). Through Step 7 in Algorithm. 1, the new specification is generated, ensuring that trajectories from B_0 pass through the estimated region while meeting the time constraints of specification ϕ, which C2 is addressed.

Remark 2. In this paper, we restrict our analysis to the known-model setting. Nonetheless, the framework naturally extends to the unknown-model case, where an upper bound on the LC can be estimated directly from data using methods based on extreme value theory [24,25]. This upper bound may result in an estimated region that is excessively large.

6 Case Study

We present two case studies to demonstrate the capability of our proposed method in estimating the reachability region based on the given specification and initial region, and subsequently degrading the specification. Our first case analyses a workload management system for next-generation communication base stations with dynamic loads. Our second case examines the dynamics of a nonlinear car-like model in response to environmental changes. Both use the Lipschitz constant to weaken specifications and ensure compliance. The computations are performed on a laptop with an Apple M1 Pro CPU and 32 GB RAM, running MATLAB R2024a. The source code can be found at https://github.com/zcode-pa/SRofCDS.

Algorithm 1 Automated Weakening Specification of Continuous Dynamical System

Require: Initial region B_0, STL specification ϕ, time interval $I := [t_{\text{start}}, t_{\text{end}}]$, partition parameter (n, m), time step h_t, LC $\mathcal{L}$
Partition B_0 into $n \times m$ cells, ensuring each cell $B_0^i, i \in \{1, \dots, n \times m\}$ has equal width and height
Quantify $r := \max_{x \in B_0^i} \|x - x_c^i\|$, where x_c^i is central point of B_0^i
for $i = 1 : n \times m$ **do**
  Simulate the trajectory starting from x_c^i
  Locate the trajectory point $x_c^{i,*}$ whose distance to specification ϕ is minimised and record the moment
end for
Take the maximum moment t^*
Calculate $(\mathcal{L}h_t + 1)^{k^*}$, where $k^* = \frac{t^* - t_{\text{start}}}{h_t}$
At each point $x_c^{i,*}, i = 1, \dots, n \times m$, generate a circle of radius $r(\mathcal{L}h_t + 1)^{k^*}$; denote this circle by $\mathcal{B}_i$
Generate the new region $\mathcal{B}$ as the union of all circles $\mathcal{B}_i$, $i = 1, \dots, n \times m$, where $\mathcal{B} := \bigcup_{i=1}^{n \times m} \mathcal{B}_i$.
Compare with the region of specification ϕ, denoted this region by $\mathcal{B}_\phi$
Replace $\mathcal{B}_\phi$ with the new region $\mathcal{B}$

Example 1 (Workload management system).
Consider a workload management system for next-generation Base Stations (BSs) [26]. Assume each BS in active mode has the same load dynamics. The dynamics of each BS in active mode of the wireless network are

$$\dot{l}_i = f(l_i) + \sum_{j=1, j \neq i}^{N} a_{ij} g(l_i, l_j), \tag{5}$$

where N is the number of BSs, $l_i := \frac{\sum_{u=1}^{U_i(t)} \hat{B}_{u,i}}{B_i(t)}$ is the load of BS station i at time t and continuous-time variable, $B_i(t)$ is the number of physical resource blocks (PRBs) of BS i can assign to users at time t, $\hat{B}_{u,i} := Q_u / w(P_{u,i}, N_0)$ is the minimum number of PRBs that should be assigned to user u, Q_u is the minimum data rate that needs to be provided, $w(P_{u,i}, N_0)$ is the rate function, $P_{u,i}$ is the power that user u receives from BS i and N_0 is the noise power. f_i is the load dynamics in BS i, and $g(\cdot, \cdot)$ is the offloading dynamics. The stable state is $l_i = 1$.

Here, we consider the model with two BSs: $\dot{l}_1 = (1 - l_1^2) + (l_1 - l_2), \dot{l}_2 = (1 - l_2^2) + (l_2 - l_1)$. The original specification can be the requirement $\mathbf{F}_{[t_0, t_c]}(1 - \epsilon \leq l_1 \leq 1 + \epsilon \wedge 1 - \epsilon \leq l_2 \leq 1 + \epsilon)$, where t_0 is the moment when many users are connecting to the network. This specification dictates that the system must converge to the stable state's neighbourhood within the time interval $[t_0, t_c]$, ensuring eventual stabilisation..

As shown in the phase portrait of system (5) in Fig. 2 (a) and (b), the estimated reachability regions do not have any overlaps with the destination region of $\mathbf{F}_{[0,0.4]}\left(\wedge_{i=1}^{2} 0.9 \leq l_i \leq 1.1\right)$, i.e., the trajectories of system (5) starting from initial region $B_0 = [1.8, 2] \times [1.8, 2]$ cannot satisfy this specification. Thus, the destination region specified in the original specification needs to be combined with the estimated reachability region using a disjunction, depicted as circles in Fig. 2(a) and (b), where the radii are 0.1054 and 0.0703, respectively. This ensures that the trajectory from every point within the initial region B_0 satisfies the updated specification. For another initial region $B_0^* = [1.05, 1.25] \times [1.8, 2]$, the similar results can be found in Fig. 2(e) and (f). In addition, the estimated reachability region based on the specification with large time interval $\mathbf{F}_{[0,1]}\left(\wedge_{i=1}^{2} 0.9 \leq l_i \leq 1.1\right)$ can be found in Fig. 2(c) and (d). Besides that, in Fig. 3, under finer partitions of the initial region, the area of the estimated region becomes smaller and smaller.

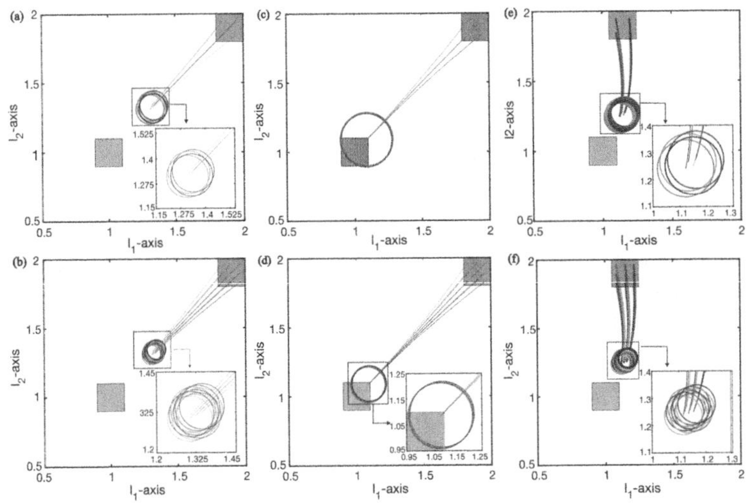

Fig. 2. Reachability regions estimated from different initial regions under different partitions: 2×2 (a), (c), (e), and 3×3 (b), (d), (f), where the purple regions represent the initial regions, the red regions denote the destination regions, and the circles represent the estimated regions. (Color figure online)

Example 2 (Non-linear car model).
Consider the non-linear car-like model as presented in [23]:

$$\begin{aligned} &\dot{x} = v\cos\theta,\ \ \dot{y} = v\sin\theta, \\ &\dot{\theta} = v\kappa,\ \ \dot{v} = u_v,\ \ \dot{\kappa} = u_\kappa, \end{aligned} \tag{6}$$

where $(x, y, \theta, v, \kappa)^T \in \mathbb{R}^5$ is state vector, consisting of its planar position (x, y) [m], its orientation θ [rad], speed v [m/s], and curvature κ $\left[\mathrm{m}^{-1}\right]$. The control

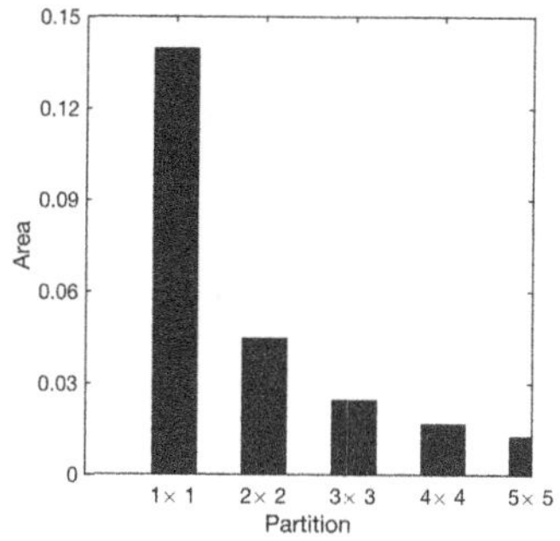

Fig. 3. The area of the estimated reach regions under varying partitions of the initial region.

input $u = (u_v, u_\kappa)^T$ is two-dimensional and consists of the derivatives of speed and curvature, respectively. In our simulation, we let the control input $u = (0, 0)^T$, i.e., v and κ are constant, respectively. The initial value of the speed and curvature decides the derivative of orientation.

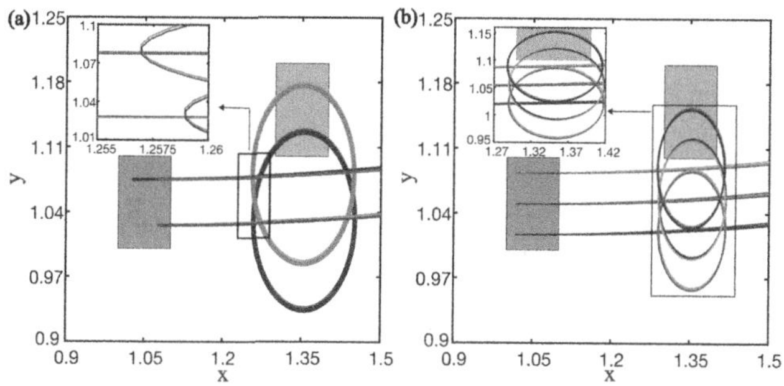

Fig. 4. Reachability regions estimated from the initial condition with different partitions: (a) 2×2 and (b) 3×3.

In addition, if the external environment, such as wind conditions, varies, the model is presented as follows:

$$\begin{aligned} &\dot{x} = v\cos\theta + w_x,\ \dot{y} = v\sin\theta + w_y, \\ &\dot{\theta} = v\kappa + w_\theta, \dot{v} = u_v,\ \dot{\kappa} = u_\kappa, \end{aligned} \tag{7}$$

where variable $w_x : \mathbb{R}^+ \to \mathbb{R}$, $w_y : \mathbb{R}^+ \to \mathbb{R}$, and $w_\theta : \mathbb{R}^+ \to \mathbb{R}$. The evolution of w_x, w_y, and w_θ is governed by system (2). In this example, we only consider the constant wind, $w_x = 0.3$, $w_y = 0.1$, and $w_\theta = 0.1$.

The estimated reachability regions shown in Fig. 4 and 5 are for specifications:

$$\mathbf{F}_{[0,1]}(1.3 \le x \le 1.4 \wedge 1.1 \le y \le 1.2)$$
$$\mathbf{F}_{[0,0.4]}(1.3 \le x \le 1.4 \wedge 1.1 \le y \le 1.2)$$

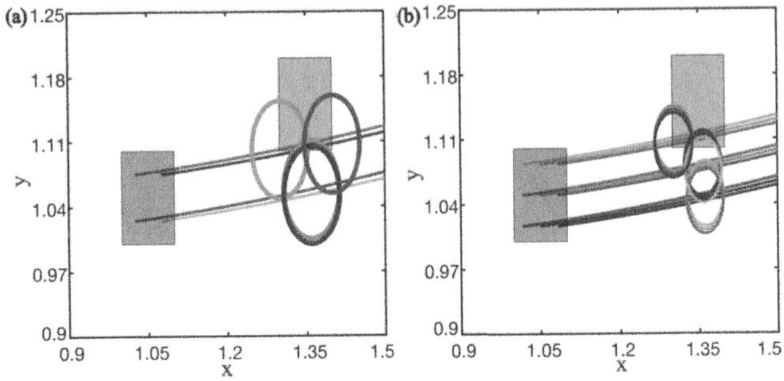

Fig. 5. Reachability regions estimated from the initial condition under wind condition, with different partitions: (a) 2×2 and (b) 3×3.

These two specifications indicate that the non-linear car eventually reaches the region defined by $1.3 \leq x \leq 1.4$ and $1.1 \leq y \leq 1.2$ within time intervals $[0, 1]$ and $[0, 0.4]$, respectively. They all demonstrate that the estimated regions (i.e., circles) obtained with finer partitions are smaller and more precise compared to those from coarser partitions. By applying a disjunction operation to the estimated regions, the newly modified specification can be satisfied by all trajectories starting from the relevant initial region.

Remark 3. The two examples demonstrate how reachability estimation using Lipschitz constants can be applied to achieve specification degradation. This approach ensures that system trajectories, starting from an initial state-space region, can satisfy the newly modified specifications, even in the face of environmental changes.

7 Conclusion and Future Works

We proposed a novel method for gracefully degrading reachability specifications of continuous dynamical systems operating in the dynamical environment, which has not been studied before. The proposed approach enables systems to adapt their requirements dynamically by sampling points within the initial state space, estimating reachability regions using the system's Lipschitz constant, and employing a disjunction operation to augment the original specification. Validation of a workload management system for next-generation base stations, along with a non-linear car-like model, demonstrates the effectiveness and practicality of the method. In the future, we aim to develop a formal framework that integrates online reachability analysis with specification transformation, enabling provably correct and minimally conservative requirement adaptations in real time. We also plan to extend this framework to control continuous dynamical systems with dense feasible control inputs and to handle more complex specifications, including reach-avoid tasks and specifications featuring nested temporal operators.

Acknowledgment. The EPSRC supports this work through the Communications Hub for Empowering Distributed Cloud Computing Applications and Research (CHEDDAR) under grants EP/X040518/1 and EP/Y037421/1.

References

1. Alrajeh, D., Benjamin, P., Uchitel, S.: Adaptation 2: adapting specification learners in assured adaptive systems. In: 2021 36th IEEE/ACM International Conference on Automated Software Engineering (ASE), pp. 1347–1352. IEEE (2021)
2. Alur, R., et al.: The algorithmic analysis of hybrid systems. Theor. Comput. Sci. **138**(1), 3–34 (1995)
3. Buckworth, T., Alrajeh, D., Kramer, J., Uchitel, S.: Adapting specifications for reactive controllers. In: 2023 IEEE/ACM 18th Symposium on Software Engineering for Adaptive and Self-Managing Systems (SEAMS), pp. 1–12. IEEE (2023)
4. Chen, X., Abraham, E., Sankaranarayanan, S.: Taylor model flowpipe construction for non-linear hybrid systems. In: 2012 IEEE 33rd Real-Time Systems Symposium, pp. 183–192. IEEE (2012)
5. Chinneck, J.W.: Feasibility and Infeasibility in Optimization: Algorithms and Computational Methods, vol. 118. Springer, Heidelberg (2007). https://doi.org/10.1007/978-0-387-74932-7_6
6. Chu, S., Koe, J., Garlan, D., Kang, E.: Integrating graceful degradation and recovery through requirement-driven adaptation. In: Proceedings of the 19th International Symposium on Software Engineering for Adaptive and Self-Managing Systems, pp. 122–132 (2024)
7. Chu, S., et al.: Runtime resolution of feature interactions through adaptive requirement weakening. In: 2023 IEEE/ACM 18th Symposium on Software Engineering for Adaptive and Self-Managing Systems (SEAMS), pp. 115–125. IEEE (2023)
8. D'Ippolito, N., Braberman, V., Kramer, J., Magee, J., Sykes, D., Uchitel, S.: Hope for the best, prepare for the worst: multi-tier control for adaptive systems. In: Proceedings of the 36th International Conference on Software Engineering, pp. 688–699 (2014)
9. DiStefano III, J.: Dynamic Systems Biology Modeling and Simulation. Academic Press (2015)
10. Ghosh, S., et al.: Diagnosis and repair for synthesis from signal temporal logic specifications. In: Proceedings of the 19th International Conference on Hybrid Systems: Computation and Control, pp. 31–40 (2016)
11. Giorgetti, N., Pappas, G.J., Bemporad, A.: Bounded model checking of hybrid dynamical systems. In: Proceedings of the 44th IEEE Conference on Decision and Control, pp. 672–677. IEEE (2005)
12. Greenstreet, M.R., Mitchell, I.: Reachability analysis using polygonal projections. In: Vaandrager, F.W., van Schuppen, J.H. (eds.) HSCC 1999. LNCS, vol. 1569, pp. 103–116. Springer, Heidelberg (1999). https://doi.org/10.1007/3-540-48983-5_12
13. Grindrod, P., Higham, D.J.: A dynamical systems view of network centrality. Proc. Roy. Soc. A: Math. Phys. Eng. Sci. **470**(2165), 20130835 (2014)
14. Henzinger, T.A., Kopke, P.W., Puri, A., Varaiya, P.: What's decidable about hybrid automata? In: Proceedings of the Twenty-Seventh Annual ACM Symposium on Theory of Computing, pp. 373–382 (1995)

15. Ijspeert, A.J., Nakanishi, J., Schaal, S.: Movement imitation with nonlinear dynamical systems in humanoid robots. In: Proceedings 2002 IEEE International Conference on Robotics and Automation (Cat. No. 02CH37292), vol. 2, pp. 1398–1403. IEEE (2002)
16. Jacobsson, K.: Dynamic modeling of Internet congestion control. Ph.D. thesis, KTH (2008)
17. Jagtap, P., Soudjani, S., Zamani, M.: Formal synthesis of stochastic systems via control barrier certificates. IEEE Trans. Autom. Control **66**(7), 3097–3110 (2020)
18. Makino, K., Berz, M.: Taylor models and other validated functional inclusion methods. Int. J. Pure Appl. Math. **6**, 239–316 (2003)
19. Maler, O., Nickovic, D.: Monitoring temporal properties of continuous signals. In: Lakhnech, Y., Yovine, S. (eds.) FORMATS/FTRTFT -2004. LNCS, vol. 3253, pp. 152–166. Springer, Heidelberg (2004). https://doi.org/10.1007/978-3-540-30206-3_12
20. Qu, Z.: Cooperative Control of Dynamical Systems: Applications to Autonomous Vehicles. Springer, Heidelberg (2009) https://doi.org/10.1007/978-1-84882-325-9
21. Rigatos, G.G.: Modelling and control for intelligent industrial systems. In: Adaptive Algorithms in Robotics and Industrial Engineering (2011)
22. Tabuada, P.: Verification and Control of Hybrid Systems: A Symbolic Approach. Springer, Heidelberg (2009). https://doi.org/10.1007/978-1-4419-0224-5
23. Webb, D., Berg, J., Kinodynamic, R.: Optimal motion planning for systems with linear differential constraints. arXiv preprint arXiv: 1205.5088 (2012)
24. Weng, T.W., et al.: Evaluating the robustness of neural networks: an extreme value theory approach. In: International Conference on Learning Representations (2018). https://openreview.net/forum?id=BkUHlMZ0b
25. Wood, G.R., Zhang, B.: Estimation of the Lipschitz constant of a function. J. Global Optim. **8**(1), 91–103 (1996)
26. Zou, M., Guo, W.: Cascade network stability of synchronized traffic load balancing with heterogeneous energy efficiency policies. In: GLOBECOM 2024 - 2024 IEEE Global Communications Conference, pp. 1083–1088 (2024). https://doi.org/10.1109/GLOBECOM52923.2024.10901638
27. Zudaire, S.A., Nahabedian, L., Uchitel, S.: Assured mission adaptation of UAVs. ACM Trans. Auton. Adapt. Syst. (TAAS) **16**(3–4), 1–27 (2022)

Ruleless Digital Twins

Ivan Spajić(✉) and Volker Stolz

Western Norway University of Applied Sciences, Bergen, Norway
{ispa,vsto}@hvl.no

Abstract. We introduce a transparent digital twin (DT) decision-making approach without the use of explicit decision rules or rule-based models. Our approach utilizes ontological inference and simulation models to explore possible decisions before applying them to the twinning target. As proof of concept, we provide an implementation of the proposed framework purely based on widely-known technologies and standards, and subsequently demonstrate the feasibility of our approach. We discuss benefits and drawbacks, and recognize that a *ruleless* approach to DT decision-making ultimately rests on an effective method of choosing from a multitude of possibilities. Lastly, we consider potential future work and exploration in the context of more effective automation and simulation model usage.

Keywords: digital twins · IoT · ontologies · inference · simulation · FMUs · MAPE-K

1 Introduction

Digital twins (DTs) are a domain overlapping with various other ICT fields, such as the Internet of Things (IoT), modeling, simulation, runtime verification, and many others [16]. At their core, DTs consist of a digital system traditionally acting as a model for a physical one, often regarded as the physical twin (PT), particularly in contexts of cyber-physical systems (CPSs). This notion has, however, become more generalized whereby DTs are no longer used exclusively for modeling PTs. Instead, they have developed to reflect what are now more broadly referred to as twinning targets (TTs) [18].

According to Larsen *et al.* [16], DTs add value to their PTs[1] without unduly compromising their operations. To meet this goal, a DT includes a level of connectivity that allows data to be received from and transmited to its TT [15]. In CPSs, this is typically manifested in the context of a sensor-actuator network (SAN). In such scenarios, data is gathered by sensors on the PT side and sent to a smart node capable of processing it on the DT side. Thereafter, based on some logic or rules, certain actions are taken and commands are transmitted back to the actuators on the PT side. The same process generalizes beyond CPSs and

[1] Although they use the term "PT", it should be noted that Larsen *et al.* do not limit themselves to DTs modeling physical objects.

L. Lestingi et al. (Eds.): DataMod 2025, LNCS 16421, pp. 67–84, 2026.
https://doi.org/10.1007/978-3-032-25552-5_5

SANs, although instead of data only being transmitted between a DT and its physical devices, such as sensors and actuators, it may also be transmitted in a pure cyber context. In such cases, DTs may also be used for optimizing or reconfiguring processes [16], networking, or software [9] in general.

To facilitate their data processing and decision-making, various kinds of models are essential for DTs [16,18]. Apart from architectural [13] and data models [5], they often also depend on simulations [3] used for creating hypothetical scenarios whose results are subsequently utilized in making actuation or reconfiguration decisions for the TT. Moreover, DTs may use ontological knowledge graphs for conceptual modeling, which allows for semantic data validation and additional reasoning techniques [4,19]. Furthermore, for increased accuracy, numerous IoT and DT decision-making processes utilize rule-based models [20,23,31], many of which typically follow an `IF-THEN` pattern.

Perhaps somewhat obviously, a DT will always require models containing information about its TT's structure and behavior. In addition, given numerous examples of DTs making use of ontologies, simulations, and behavioral rule models, as well as an abundance of model-driven techniques in the literature [18], there is a naturally-arising question concerning the possibility of using ontological reasoning with simulations to power decision-making processes without behavioral rule models. Thus, our paper explores this question as follows: in Sect. 2, we present a more specific context from related works in the literature as well as our own contributions. In Sect. 3, we outline our idea on a conceptual level, and in 4, we describe its implementation and proof of concept. In Sect. 5, we discuss drawbacks and other potential approaches, and in Sect. 6, we introduce ideas for future work. Lastly, we conclude in Sect. 7.

2 Background

As outlined in Larsen *et al.* [16], models are vital to DTs. Furthermore, as highlighted by Lehner *et al.* [18], model-driven engineering (MDE) techniques additionally yield various benefits within the general field of DTs. For instance, models can be used in model-to-model transformations, where source and target models adhere to different hosting platforms. Moreover, one may also apply model-to-model transformations to more generative purposes, such as executable code generation. Regardless of the specific goal, it is evident that MDE techniques carry a shared aspect of increased automation. For this reason, we study the extent of this automation in the context of ontological inference, simulations, and rule-based models throughout the exploration of our own problem statement and related work.

2.1 Related Work

Gabor *et al.* [7] partition the different levels of control exerted by a DT into several tiers. Our work directly addresses their second tier for "immediate reaction", where actions are triggered by system state observations, and enables the third tier of "planned reaction", where reward functions steer planning.

Talasila *et al.* [25] introduce the "DT-as-a-Service" with valuable insights about composing new DTs. While they identify simulation ("`WHAT-IF`" analysis) as a key requirement, they do not explore decision planning in detail.

Kamburjan *et al.* [12] reflect their *program state* into a knowledge base to use the expressivity of ontologies. We take the opposite approach and initially realize several of the necessary components entirely in the knowledge base.

Compagnucci *et al.* [4] utilize the Semantic Sensor Network (SSN) ontology [29] for semantic data validation and class mapping to input models used for DT code generation. They make use of finite-state machines as rule-based models for defining the internal logic of their generated DTs. Although they acknowledge the potential of using ontological inference from SSN, Compagnucci *et al.* ultimately do not use this type of reasoning for any kind of automated rule or rule-based model generation.

Korth *et al.* [14] demonstrate DTs in the context of decision support systems (DSSs) based on digital models and simulations comprising an event-driven architecture. Crucially, our approach shares their list of five criteria for good decisions and planning: (*i*) current state knowledge, (*ii*) future situation (hypothetical) knowledge, (*iii*) functions identifying disruptions, (*iv*) functions generating (feasible) decisions, and (*v*) functions evaluating these decisions. Although their DTs demonstrate a level of decision support by investigating hypothetical scenarios through simulations, they leave full decision-making to the users.

Michael *et al.* [20] present a model-driven software architecture for DT generation. For a DT to accurately plan and make its decisions, they propose the use of case-based reasoning models in the form of `{IF pattern THEN actions EXPECT result}`. They provide examples of parameterized commands containing conditions for the DT. With this, the DT attempts to find a matching system condition case from an available repository of case-based models supplied by domain experts. If the case is applicable to the observed system conditions, its solution is applied. Otherwise, the DT's reasoner chooses a similar case and adjusts it. When the adjusted case mitigates the situation, it is added to the repository of cases. Additionally, Michael *et al.* focus on the aspect of explainability whereby a system should transparently explain its decision-making processes. To achieve this, they use a feedback loop framework similar to MAPE-K [24]. Although they rely on explicit rule models, they leave the rule adjustment details of their example cases outside of the scope of their work.

While they do not strictly focus on DTs, some of the more related work comes from Päßler *et al.* [23], who present a formal model of an architecture for controlling an IoT-based smart home solution. They define decision-making models and, through simulation experiments, show improved performance of the system's ability to satisfy its requirements with respect to regulating air temperature and quality. They utilize all MAPE-K phases to perform different tasks, such as the *Analyze* phase for checking current system configuration satisfiability and the *Plan* phase for potentially choosing system reconfigurations. An interesting point to note is that for the *Knowledge* portion of the MAPE-K, Päßler *et al.* rely on a formal, ontological meta-model that describes elements such as *objectives* and *functions.* In Sub-sect. 4.1, we will demonstrate how our ontological contributions (interestingly) represent similar concepts.

2.2 Contributions

Having highlighted some of the relevant literature with respect to the use of rules in DT and IoT decision-making processes, we will now outline the primary and secondary contributions of this paper.

Primary Contribution: We demonstrate the feasibility of *ruleless* DTs through ontological reasoning and simulations for powering autonomous decision-making processes. By removing the need for manually crafting and maintaining hand-written rule models, we also show increased automation and reduced complexity, albeit at the expense of greater computational cost.

Secondary Contributions: We present lightweight additions to the SSN ontology to facilitate the primary contribution and further demonstrate how this ontology already contains most of the required concepts. Additionally, we present this idea in the context of only using widely-known and well-accepted technologies and standards. Lastly, as part of an available artifact[2], we provide a generic control loop solution that conforms to our proposed ontology and is complete with examples and interfaces intended for additional user-provided implementations. This solution demonstrates autonomous DT decision-making by evaluating system condition constraints, finding available mitigations, simulating hypothetical scenarios, and, as a result, picking optimal actions.

3 Approach

Figure 1 visualizes an architectural perspective of all of the components of our proposed system. Our approach begins with using an ontology to infer additional model data from what was originally provided by the stakeholder. Since a DT requires models that describe the structure and behavior of its TT anyway, the idea is to let stakeholders create these in the form of knowledge graphs that conform to the ontology as instance models. The ontology thus requires concepts that allow stakeholders to describe sensors and actuators, in case of physical TT components, and soft sensors [11] and configurable software parameters, in case of cyber ones. In both cases, stakeholders would also need to describe their properties of interest, which can be observed and/or actuated on. For this, we ultimately envision stakeholders using a form of automated model export in conjunction with tools such as Protégé [21].

[2] The ontology, inference rules, example instance models, simulation model, and the feedback loop solution are all available at https://doi.org/10.5281/zenodo.18741472.

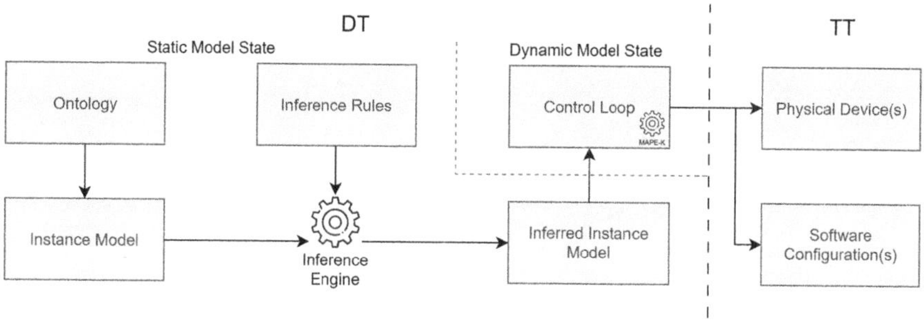

Fig. 1. An overview of the proposed system's components. Here, the inference rules and the control loop rely on the ontology.

The ontology should allow the instance models to contain desirable conditions for the DT to maintain, e.g., `{18 <= roomTemperature < 25}`. In addition, to express the power of DTs adding value to their TTs [16], they should also specify optimizations (e.g., minimizing energy consumption), since, for example, given a desired condition as `{roomTemperature > 18}`, the system could simply keep the heater on the warmest setting for as long as possible to satisfy it.

Most importantly, as part of the semantic descriptions of the actuators and reconfigurable parameters, it is also necessary for the ontology to provide different types of effects these elements can have on their respective properties. By knowing *how* an action changes a property, we can subsequently infer all relevant actions the DT can take to potentially restore its desirable conditions. For example, if a stakeholder is interested in observing a room temperature property and defines a heater as an actuator that (generally) increases its value, then, should the temperature drop below desired levels, it becomes inferrable that actuating the heater might mitigate the problem.

Further following Fig. 1, the instance model is run through an inference engine to produce an inferred (expanded) one. In addition to the initial TT component descriptions, their respective properties, and the desired conditions, the inferred model will now also contain elements representing all possible optimization actions as well as actions for mitigating any unsatisfied conditions.

Next, this initial inferred model is supplied into the control loop component during its initialization. The control loop is responsible for controlling physical devices and software configurations on the TT side, and effectively acts as the DT's processing center. Since DTs need to handle both data input and output in a feedback fashion, we propose for the control loop to follow the MAPE-K [24] architecture. This allows us to organize different DT processing phases into the corresponding phases of the MAPE-K. We envision the loop to function as detailed in Fig. 2: first, the *Monitor* phase handles value observations for the specified properties. With the observed property values, the *Analyze* phase evaluates which, if any, desired conditions are unsatisfied and selects a set of all possible mitigation and optimization actions from the knowledge base (initial inferred model). From this set of actions, the *Plan* phase constructs and

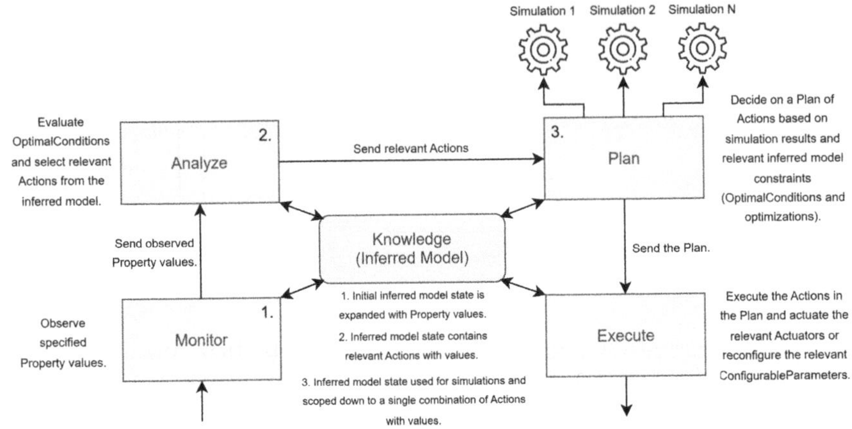

Fig. 2. A visualization of the parts comprising the control loop component based on the MAPE-K [24] architecture.

executes all possible simulation configurations, which may be split into several intervals. This approach allows a simulation configuration to change component states throughout various stages of its execution. A fitness function identifies the optimal simulation's combination of actions which the *Execute* phase enacts.

Throughout the different stages in this process, the framework uses the stakeholder-provided instance model to expand or filter its data. Initially, the static instance model is dynamically expanded with the set of inferred actions and then reduced by evaluating conditions and selecting possible mitigations. The model is dynamically expanded again with all possible simulation configurations before being reduced to a single combination of concrete actions.

In summary, our overall approach of *ruleless* DT decision-making can be represented analogously with a tree of possibilities, as visualized in Fig. 3. In this tree, each path to a leaf node represents a sequence of possible combinations of actions the DT can choose to attempt to restore a condition and/or to optimize for certain properties, whereby the DT's ultimate goal is to prune the tree of possibilities down to a single option. Initially, with actions inferred from the instance model, the number of possible decisions grows. By analyzing which, if any, desired conditions are unsatisfied, the DT selects the subset of actions that positively affect the model. From these, the DT constructs simulation combinations, and the number of possible decisions grows again. Finally, a simulation fitness function prunes the tree, ultimately yielding the DT's final decision.

3.1 Technologies and Standards

Firstly, we require an ontology that can semantically represent IoT-relevant concepts such as hosting systems, physical devices, software or soft sensors, and observable properties. For this, we recognize the Semantic Sensor Network (SSN) and Smart Applications REFerence (SAREF) [6] ontologies as some of the more

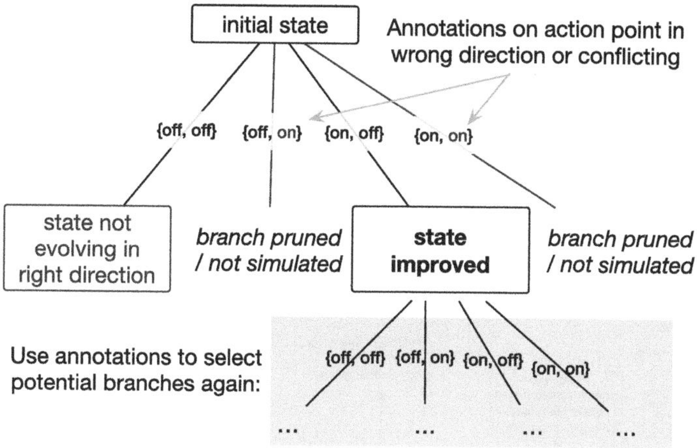

Fig. 3. The tree of possible decisions the DT can take based on the number of inferred actions and possible simulation configurations.

established and widely-used candidates [4,8,22]. Of the two, we evaluate SSN to be more representative of what is needed for our approach, based on the lower number of missing required concepts. Although SAREF Core provides numerous extension ontologies that could provide some of those concepts, it already contains 33 classes, 64 object properties, and 8 data properties. Conversely, while SSN is itself an extension of the Sensor, Observation, Sample, and Actuator (SOSA) [29] ontology, it only contains 23 classes, 36 object properties, and 2 data properties, making it the more light-weight option.

Among inference engines, we opted to use Apache Jena [26] as it is one of the most widely-known open-source technologies in the field with a long history and wide-ranging standard feature support. Apart from allowing for different levels of inference, Jena's API also provides model-checking features for additional verification against inferred models breaking ontological constraints.

We selected the Functional Mock-up Interface (FMI) [27] standard to power our simulations due to its wide-spread industry support and increasing usage in the field of DTs [1,10]. Our approach relies on the use of Functional Mock-up Units (FMUs) as self-contained, executable simulation models for creating relevant hypothetical scenarios. Moreover, apart from wide-spread adoption, FMUs are fairly lightweight components and thus exhibit a high degree of execution performance.

Lastly, to interact with RDF/OWL knowledge graphs and execute FMUs, we utilize the dotNetRDF [30] and Femyou [2] .NET libraries, respectively.

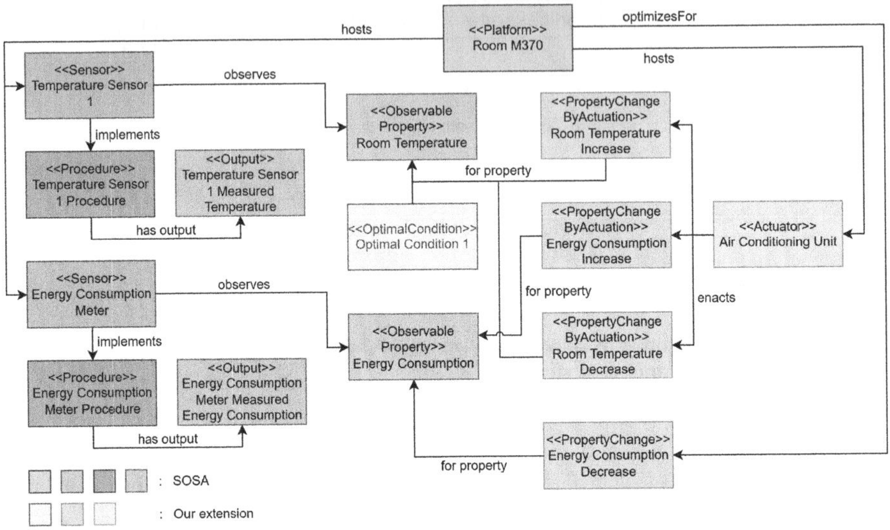

Fig. 4. Some of example 1's components annotated with their classes. Note that *sosa:ObservableProperty* is a subclass of *ssn:Property*.

4 Implementation

We designed two examples for our proof of concept: example 1 (shown partially in Fig. 4) describes a room containing sensors measuring temperature, humidity, and energy consumption, as well as actuators for affecting each property. As such, it is representative of a TT containing physical components as part of a CPS. Example 2 (in the digital artifact) describes a soft sensor using an online lossy compression algorithm with configurable parameters for adjusting the input data size and the degree of lossiness, and is therefore representative of a TT containing cyber elements. Throughout this paper, we mostly use example 1 as a case for demonstrating the different stages of our implementation.

4.1 Ontology

As outlined in Sect. 3, although we make thorough use of SSN, this ontology still lacks concepts crucial to our approach. Hence, we introduce a lightweight extension by adding classes required to complete stakeholder-provided instance models as well as the resulting inferred ones.

```
// OptimalCondition
'for property' exactly 1 Property
hasValueConstraint exactly 1 rdfs:Literal
reachedInMaximumSeconds max 1 xsd:int
```

Listing 4.1.1. *:OptimalCondition* class definition triples in Manchester syntax.

An important missing concept is that of desired conditions on targeted property values. Here, we introduce the *:OptimalCondition* class whose definition triples are shown in Listing 4.1.1. An *:OptimalCondition* requires three things: (*i*) an *ssn:Property*, (*ii*) constraints on its value, and (*iii*) an upper limit on the time taken to restore it, should the value of the respective *ssn:Property* fall out of bounds.

Moreover, to facilitate cyber TTs, we add a *:ConfigurableParameter* class as a subclass of *ssn:Property* and *ssn:Input*. *:ConfigurableParameters* represent adjustable soft sensor inputs used to affect their algorithms and subsequent *ssn:Outputs*. In terms of example 2, both the size of input data and the degree of lossiness *ssn:Properties* would be *:ConfigurableParameters*.

```
// PropertyChangeByReconfiguration is a subclass of PropertyChange
'for property' exactly 1 Property
affectsPropertyWith exactly 1 Effect
alteredBy exactly 1 Effect
enactedBy min 1 ConfigurableParameter
```

Listing 4.1.2. *:PropertyChangeByReconfiguration* definition triples in Manchester syntax.

Two more classes we add are those of *:Effect* and *:PropertyChange*. The *:Effect* class in our prototype contains just two individuals, *:ValueIncrease* and *:ValueDecrease*, representing the type of change done to an *ssn:Property*. The purpose of the *:PropertyChange* class is to act as a wrapper facilitating the mapping between *ssn:Properties* and the *:Effects* applied to them. Furthermore, to support both physical and cyber TT elements, the *:PropertyChange* class has two subclasses, namely *:PropertyChangeByActuation* and *:PropertyChange-ByReconfiguration*, the latter of which is shown in Listing 4.1.2. These classes contain references to *sosa:Actuators* and *:ConfigurableParameters*, respectively, and thus facilitate the construction of inferred models later in the process. As shown in Fig. 4, example 1 contains four *:PropertyChangeByActuation* individuals (without *Effect* references) relating to temperature and energy consumption changes.

```
:optimizesFor rdf:type owl:ObjectProperty ;
              rdfs:domain <http://www.w3.org/ns/sosa/Platform> ;
              rdfs:range :PropertyChange ;
```

Listing 4.1.3. *:optimizesFor* definition triples in OWL.

Somewhat related to the *:OptimalCondition* class, but without the hard value constraints, is the concept of targeted system optimizations. As shown in Listing 4.1.3, this was introduced as the *:optimizesFor* object property, with *ssn:Platform* as its domain and *:PropertyChange* as its range. In example 1, a system optimization for lower energy consumption is defined through the relation *:RoomM370 :optimizesFor :EnergyConsumptionDecrease*. Overall, this concept enables stakeholders to specify their optimizations while also facilitating simulation result filtering, as discussed further in Subsect. 4.3.

```
// ActuationAction is a subclass of Action
hasActuator exactly 1 Actuator
setsActuatorToState exactly 1 rdfs:Literal
```

Listing 4.1.4. *:ActuationAction* definition triples in Manchester syntax.

Moreover, we added the *:Action* class, which defines an action the DT can take as part of its eventual decision. Individuals belonging to this class are not directly supplied by the stakeholder but are instead inferred from the definitions of *:OptimalConditions*, optimizations, and *:PropertyChanges*. Much like *:PropertyChange*, the *:Action* class has two subclasses, namely *:ActuationAction* and *:ReconfigurationAction*. Whereas the former reconfigures *physical* components, the latter is for *cyber* components. As shown in Listing 4.1.4, each *:ActuationAction* contains a reference to a *sosa:Actuator* and a literal representing its state. Similarly, a *:ReconfigurationAction* contains a reference to a *:ConfigurableParameter* and a literal representing the value to configure it to.

Lastly, it should be noted that, as an adjustable input variable, a *:ConfigurableParameter* (as e.g., a float, double, etc.) can have a virtually infinite number of values. Furthermore, there may be specific limitations on its value ranges or distributions. Similarly, a *sosa:Actuator*, such as *:AirConditioningUnit* in example 1, may have a wide range of programmable states that would be unsuitable to represent as explicit instance model components. Thus, we include the *:ActionValueGenerator* class as a subclass of *ssn:Procedure* to represent a method (e.g., FMU execution, REST API call, or other) for deriving possible *sosa:Actuator* states and *:ConfigurableParameter* values, respectively.

4.2 Ontological Inference

There are two main objectives in using ontological inference rules in our system. First, inference rules are used to verify the structural invariants of the model, an example of which is shown in Listing 4.2.1. Second, they are used for deriving additional information from what is initially provided by the stakeholder. To simplify both verification and additional triple creation, some inference rules leave intermediate marker comments for subsequent rules to match on.

```
[rule4e:     (?restriction1 rdf:comment ?property)
             (?restriction1 rdf:comment "verification mark")
             (?restriction1 xsd:minExclusive ?value1)
             (?restriction2 rdf:comment ?property)
             (?restriction2 rdf:comment "verification mark")
             (?restriction2 xsd:maxExclusive ?value2)
             notEqual(?property, "verification mark")
             ge(?value1, ?value2)
             -> ... print("Conflicting conditions detected!") ... ]
```

Listing 4.2.1. An example verification rule checking for conflicting *OptimalCondition* constraints based on markings applied by a previous rule.

Since the DT ultimately has to pick a set of *Actions* that restore *OptimalConditions* and/or optimize for a *Property*, it is important that these *Actions* not be contradicting. Most potential user-related constraint problems would typically be prevented by using their tools' built-in reasoners. For a single individual, they would immediately highlight problematic cases, such as simultaneously defining a constraint value to be <18 and >25. However, if stakeholders define multiple *OptimalCondition* individuals pertaining to the same *Property*, they will also be able to freely define them with mutually contradicting constraints such that the reasoner cannot highlight the issue. Without constraint verification rules, the DT could encounter scenarios where it was forced to simultaneously simulate *Actions* with *Actuators* that apply conflicting *Effects* on the same *Property*, ultimately preventing it from arriving to a meaningful decision.

```
[rule3a:    (?thing rdf:comment ?propertyChange)
            (?propertyChange meta:enactedBy ?actuator)
            (?actuator rdf:type sosa:Actuator)
            uriConcat(?actuator, meta:ActuationAction, ?actionName)
            ->  (?actionName rdf:type meta:ActuationAction)
                (?actionName meta:hasActuator ?actuator) ]
```

Listing 4.2.2. An example rule for inferring *ActuationActions.*

To derive additional triples, the inference rules rely on instance models containing crucial information, such as the *PropertyChanges* caused by various TT components. As shown in Listing 4.2.2, the inference rules match on this information and expand an instance model with the *Actions* the DT can take. Each *Action* will therefore either contain an *Actuator* or a *ConfigurableParameter* capable of causing the kind of *PropertyChange* required for restoring a specific *OptimalCondition* constraint or optimizing for a *Property.*

The rules do not, however, simply infer *Actions* as a result of any *PropertyChanges* present. In terms of the tree of possible DT decisions (see Fig. 3), branches are potentially immediately pruned away during the creation of an inferred model. This is done by initially focusing on the specified *OptimalConditions'* value constraints. Given a particular type of constraint, such as an upper or lower bound, only the corresponding, mitigating *PropertyChanges* are selected and thus only a subset of all possible *Actions* is inferred.

Since example 1 contains *OptimalConditions* with upper and lower bounds for *RoomTemperature*, both the *Actuators* causing *PropertyChanges* with *ValueIncrease* and those causing *PropertyChanges* with *ValueDecrease* become relevant. Because the *AirConditioningUnit* component is responsible for both types of relevant *PropertyChanges*, an *ActuationAction* is inferred with it as its *Actuator.* Moreover, due to a specified optimization on *RoomHumidity* in the full instance model, an additional *ActuationAction* with the *Dehumidifier* is inferred. Note that, due to reasons discussed in Sect. 4.1, these inferred *ActuationActions* have no concrete *Actuator* states specified and thus serve as placeholders until the execution of their respective *ActionValueGenerators* (discussed further in Sect. 4.3).

4.3 Control Loop

In line with the MAPE-K [24] architecture, the control loop component features four main phases assisted by the inferred model as its knowledge base. Each phase interacts with the inferred model's knowledge graph through the use of SPARQL [28] queries. The control loop features interfaces for stakeholder-provided *Sensor* and *Actuator* implementations used for *Property* observations and *Action* executions, respectively. These implementations handle the DT's data input and output during the *Monitor* and *Execute* phases of the loop. The following sub-subsections outline the phases in greater detail.

Monitor Phase. The *Monitor* phase invokes stakeholder-provided *Sensor* implementations and observes all relevant *Property* values to store them in a dedicated *Property* cache, thereby effectively augmenting the inferred model.

Analyze Phase. As discussed in Sect. 3 and shown in Fig. 2, the overall aim of the *Analyze* phase is to further reduce the set of *Actions* used for simulating hypothetical scenarios, thereby further pruning the tree of possible decisions. To achieve this, the phase begins by querying the knowledge base (inferred model) for all *OptimalConditions* and evaluating their constraints against the respective *Property* values observed earlier.

```
SELECT ?optimalCondition ?property ?reachedInMaximumSeconds WHERE {
  ?optimalCondition rdf:type meta:OptimalCondition .
  ?optimalCondition ssn:forProperty ?property .
  ?optimalCondition meta:reachedInMaximumSeconds ?reachedInMaximumSeconds . }
```

Listing 4.3.1. The SPARQL query used for selecting all *OptimalConditions* and most of their elements. The constraints are selected with more complex, subsequent queries.

After selecting all *OptimalConditions* (Listing 4.3.1), each one's constraints are evaluated against the values of their respective *Properties*. This evaluation determines whether an *OptimalCondition* is unsatisfied and thus whether an *Action* should be taken to restore it. During evaluation, each constraint is broken down into its constituent atomic constraints (e.g., upper and lower bounds) whose operators are used to determine the *Effect* and thus the *PropertyChange* required from potential mitigation *Actions*. With this, a subset of *Actions* is selected from those in the knowledge base, as shown in Listing 4.3.2.

```
SELECT ?actuationAction ?actuatorState ?actuator ?property WHERE {
    ?actuationAction rdf:type meta:ActuationAction.
    ?actuationAction meta:hasActuatorState ?actuatorState .
    ?actuatorState meta:enacts ?propertyChange .
    ?actuator meta:hasActuatorState ?actuatorState .
    ?actuator rdf:type sosa:Actuator .
    ?propertyChange ssn:forProperty ?property .
    ?property owl:sameAs @property .
    ?propertyChange meta:affectsPropertyWith @filter . }
```

Listing 4.3.2. The SPARQL query used for selecting all mitigating *ActuationActions* with a `filter` parameter representing the *Effect*.

As outlined in Subsect. 4.2, the knowledge base initially only contains placeholder *Actions* without specified *Actuator* states or *ConfigurableParameter* values. To obtain concrete *Actions* with specific states and values, stakeholder-provided *ActionValueGenerators* are executed for every *Action's Actuator* or *ConfigurableParameter*. Assuming example 1's *OptimalConditions* are unsatisfied, the relevant mitigation *Action* is the one containing *AirConditioningUnit*. Executing *AirConditioningUnit's ActionValueGenerator* thus produces all possible states for the *Actuator* and subsequently yields a concrete *ActuationAction* for each one. This process is also used for optimization *Actions*.

Plan Phase. The overall purpose of the *Plan* phase is to explore via simulation, within the scope of the provided mitigation and optimization *Actions*, all hypothetical scenarios possible and subsequently pick the optimal one to execute. This process can be divided into several steps: (*i*) generate all allowed combinations of provided *Actions*, (*ii*) generate all possible configurations of simulation intervals with *Action* combinations, (*iii*) execute all simulation configurations and obtain their results, and (*iv*) select the optimal configuration.

Upon receiving potential mitigation and optimization *Actions*, all of their allowed combinations are generated such that no *Actions* in a given set share *Actuators* or *ConfigurableParameters*. Next, we generate simulation configurations, each of which represents a unique simulation scenario setup. Because different *Actuator* states might affect *Property* values differently, we divide our simulations into timed intervals to join with different *ActuationAction* combinations. This allows *Actuators* to potentially restore *OptimalConditions* through a variety of states in a given simulation. We deliberately choose not to include *ReconfigurationActions* as part of the timed simulation intervals since changes in cyber TTs depending on *ConfigurableParameters* do not necessarily occur as time-dependent processes. Updated *ConfigurableParameter* values may produce results instantly, or they may take longer than the *OptimalConditions* allow, due to, e.g., cyber implementation details. Thus, combinations of *ReconfigurationActions* are appended to simulation configurations as post-simulation *Actions*. With this, a unique configuration is generated for every combination of *ActuationActions* in every interval and with every combination of post-simulation *ReconfigurationActions*. In example 1, for 4 *AirConditioningUnit* states, 2 *Dehumidifier* states, and a simulation granularity (depth of tree) of 4, a total of 4096 unique simulation configurations are generated.

We retrieve the simulation model (FMU) URI from the knowledge base. Although our example uses a stakeholder-provided URI, it could alternatively be derived through a query. This model represents the hosting *Platform* and thus needs to comprise its *Actuators* as input parameters, as well as all of its system *Properties* as both input and output parameters. With these FMUs, all simulation configurations are executed based on values in the *Property* cache (current state of the model), whereby for each simulation interval, *Actuator* states and *Properties* are supplied, the simulation time is advanced to the duration of the interval, and the resulting *Property* values are recorded for the next step.[3]

The Fitness Function. Finding the optimum effectively relies on a fitness function that successively filters simulation configurations out based on their resulting *Property* values. Our current implementation of this function contains several steps. Firstly, the function prioritizes simulation configurations that result in the most *OptimalConditions* satisfied. In case of more than one configuration sharing the highest number, the function checks their values of the *Properties* to optimize for. In this step, each *Property* the system wishes to optimize for has its

---

[3] The simulation of *ReconfigurationActions* is not currently implemented but may easily be performed through, e.g., API calls.

value compared with the same *Property* from every other remaining simulation configuration. In case that *Property* is optimized for with *ValueIncrease*, simulation configurations with the highest value for that *Property* have their scores incremented. Similarly, if a *Property* is optimized for with *ValueDecrease*, configurations with the lowest value for that *Property* have their scores incremented instead. Scores are compared between all remaining simulation configurations, and those with the highest total are chosen. Finally, if there are still multiple configurations remaining, the function arbitrarily chooses from the collection. Note that our fitness function currently does not address totally avoiding prohibited TT states or the exclusion of *Actions* that might lead to them, both of which are intended as future work.

Execute Phase. Having identified the optimal simulation configuration, the *Execute* phase performs all *ActuationActions* by invoking the corresponding *Actuator* implementations, e.g. through API calls, and *ReconfigurationActions* by updating the *ConfigurableParameters* in the *Property* cache. These are then used for the next *Monitor* phase's soft sensor value observations.

5 Discussion

One of the biggest strengths of this approach is its flexibility to adapt to frequently-changing TT components and conditions. Because the system repeatedly queries its knowledge base, it is also resilient against changing stakeholder requirements. Unlike with a rule-based system, our approach allows stakeholders to change their *OptimalCondition* specifications and have the resulting DT decisions automatically adapt in response. Moreover, in a rule-based system, the stakeholder must provide a whole new rule (`IF-THEN`) for each new condition (the `IF`) and desired decision (the `THEN`), whereas *OptimalConditions* (the `IF`) allow inference and simulations in our approach to yield the decision (the `THEN`) automatically. Furthermore, because our approach utilizes simulations, it also effectively looks ahead into any potential future before making its decision.

Conversely, because it relies on FMUs for simulations, our approach requires that they be provided by the stakeholder beforehand. Adopting our method thus effectively creates a trade-off between the development time spent on rule-based models versus FMUs, although this is arguably mitigated due to the aforementioned simulation benefits. Moreover, because FMUs may contain default or starting values for their input parameters, it is possible to utilize them without exact parameter matching, thus adding to their flexibility at the cost of simulation accuracy. In addition, because we explore all potential scenarios within the scope of the previously inferred *Actions* and all of their possible states and values, our approach makes use of heuristics to combat combinatorial blowup, which we anticipate to be especially problematic for low-powered or embedded IoT processing devices. This blowup can be reduced further through more information about the types of possible *Effects* in the ontology. Our changes to the SSN ontology only introduced two (qualitative) individuals, namely *ValueIncrease* and *ValueDecrease*, for simplicity. Specifying more detailed *Effect* types would increase instance model complexity, but would simultaneously help in pruning down the tree of possibilities during the DT's *Plan* phase.

In comparison to Päßler *et al.* [23], our method exhibits some key differences between our respective simulations and decision-making functions. Our method utilizes FMUs while Päßler *et al.* encode their simulation models entirely in Maude. Furthermore, they apply domain knowledge to assign quantitative *quality attribute* values with respect to objective fulfilment in their decision-making process, which subsequently allows them to select the maximum out of an available pool of scores and thus to choose the most appropriate model of premade decision-making rules. Since our approach is intended for more general applications, our own default decision-pruning function aims to be domain-independent, and, as a result, does not consider quantitatively scoring with respect to *OptimalCondition* restoration, although this does leave plenty of opportunity for user-provided logic with scoring to be used instead. Regardless, one of the most prominent differences between our works is in our solution's *rulelessness*. Whereas Päßler *et al.* rely on the aforementioned premade rule models, our approach ultimately enables DTs to make decisions without them.

In general, however, if a ruleless DT is to successfully decide on a combination of *Actions* to execute, it must still explore its tree of possibilities. Without streamlining, the DT is forced to consider all possible combinations of all *Actions*, both necessary and unnecessary, occurring within every possible simulation interval, all of which realistically equates to an expensively simulated trial-and-error approach. For this reason, to ensure the drawbacks of combinatorial explosions do not outweigh the benefits of flexibility, removing rules from DTs ultimately comes down to employing a reasonably effective decision-pruning process.

6 Future Work

Currently, our framework is purely reactive such that actions are triggered only by unmet *OptimalConditions*. It is straightforward to use the same simulation process for all possible *Actions* or a subset thereof, to preemptively avoid violating *OptimalConditions* in the *simulated state*, i.e., after the next simulation interval. As an example, a *Property* whose value is within its *OptimalCondition* requires no *Actions*. However, given an FMU showing that taking no *Actions* results in the *Property*'s value falling outside *OptimalConditions*, the same process would demonstrate that *Actions* should instead be taken proactively.

Our focus is on harnessing the power of simulation, and we plan to evaluate against real TTs in the future. We will thus also investigate the feasibility of implementing our planning solution on Talasila *et al.*'s [25] "DT-as-a-Service" platform that comprehensively addresses model management, including FMUs.

In addition to providing the instance model (which is easily automated for a given TT) with manual annotations for *OptimalConditions* and *PropertyChanges*, the quality of the simulations still hinges on the availability and fidelity of the respective FMUs. We plan to explore lightweight methods for implementing stakeholder preferences in the fitness function without extensive programming effort; e.g., SPARQL queries over simulated configurations could provide the required flexibility in writing custom functions, though they might still be far from user-friendly.

During construction of the initial DT, instead of annotating *PropertyChanges* in the knowledge base, we could leverage FMUs to derive them. The FMUs must already contain information essential for describing *how Properties* are affected, so *PropertyChanges* might be automatically inferable from simple FMU test executions. This may also allow for more accurate *PropertyChanges*, not only describing *Effects*, but also *Property* value ranges they hold for, subsequently representing that, e.g., running an *Actuator* in different states causes different kinds of *Effects*. Additionally, historical data about specific *Action* combinations taken for specific TT conditions could comprise cases to power a framework akin to that of Michael *et al.* [20]. This could thus alleviate combinatorial blowups by matching on previously encountered TT conditions that already reference the optimal set of *Actions* to take.

Other potential future work includes exploring the feasibility of matching DTs with FMUs, based on ontological *Property* descriptions. The semantic data in the instance model, such as minimum/maximum values and SI units, could be used in conjunction with FMI model descriptions to facilitate FMU and/or parameter matching. With a given *matching threshold*, it may be possible to automatically offer ontologically compatible FMUs and alleviate stakeholder burden. Furthermore, with the introduction of solutions such as UniFMU [17], it may prove feasible to utilize model-driven code generation techniques to produce the required FMUs from additional information in the knowledge base. For example, identifying or deriving an FMU from the body of engineering knowledge for a room of a given size with components of given specifications sounds attainable. Moreover, we envision vendors potentially providing FMUs for their systems.

7 Conclusion

In this paper, we explore and demonstrate the feasibility of *ruleless* DTs. By utilizing widely-accepted technologies and standards (the SSN ontology, SPARQL queries, and FMUs), we present an implementation comprising ontologies, inference rules, simulations, and the MAPE-K architecture that enables the removal of explicit rule-based models from DT decision-making processes. We provide two instance models (available in the artifact) as examples and use one of them to demonstrate the different stages of the approach. The resulting combinatorial explosion of combinations needs heuristics that select promising simulations to remain manageable. Furthermore, we discuss the pros and cons of both the approach and the technologies used. Lastly, we discuss future work, among which are implementation improvements as well as explorations into the semantic matching of simulation models.

Acknowledgment. This work was supported by Bergens Rederiforening and the Norwegian Research Council project CroFlow: Enabling Highly Automated Cross-Organisational Workflow Planning (grant no. 326249).

References

1. Abrazeh, S., et al.: Virtual hardware-in-the-loop FMU co-simulation based digital twins for heating, ventilation, and air-conditioning (HVAC) systems. IEEE Trans. Emerg. Top. Comput. Intell. (2023). https://doi.org/10.1109/TETCI.2022.3168507
2. Azeau, O.: Femyou (2020). https://github.com/Oaz/Femyou
3. Cimino, C., Leva, A., Ferretti, G.: Ensuring consistency in scalable-detail models for DT-based control. In: 17th IFAC Symposium on Information Control Problems in Manufacturing (INCOM 2021) (2021). https://doi.org/10.1016/j.ifacol.2021.08.158
4. Compagnucci, I., Snoeck, M., Asensio, E.S.: Supporting digital twins systems integrating the MERODE approach. In: 2023 ACM/IEEE International Conference on Model Driven Engineering Languages and Systems Companion (MODELS-C) (2023). https://doi.org/10.1109/MODELS-C59198.2023.00079
5. Dalibor, M., et al.: Generating customized low-code development platforms for digital twins. J. Comput. Lang. (2022). https://doi.org/10.1016/j.cola.2022.101117
6. European Telecommunications Standards Institute: SAREF: the Smart Applications REFerence ontology (2024). https://saref.etsi.org/core/v4.1.1/
7. Gabor, T., Belzner, L., Kiermeier, M., Beck, M.T., Neitz, A.: A simulation-based architecture for smart cyber-physical systems. In: 2016 IEEE International Conference on Autonomic Computing (ICAC), pp. 374–379 (2016). https://doi.org/10.1109/ICAC.2016.29
8. Guittoum, A., Aïssaoui, F., Bolle, S., Boyer, F., Palma, N.D.: Inferring threatening IoT dependencies using semantic digital twins toward collaborative IoT device management. In: SAC 2023: Proceedings of the 38th ACM/SIGAPP Symposium on Applied Computing (2023). https://doi.org/10.1145/3555776.3578573
9. Huang, X., Hu, S., Yang, H., Wang, X., Pei, Y., Shen, X.: Digital twin-based network management for better QoE in multicast short video streaming. IEEE Trans. Wirel. Commun. (2024). https://doi.org/10.1109/TWC.2024.3438159
10. Hugues, J., Hristosov, A., Hudak, J.J., Yankel, J.: TwinOps – DevOps meets model-based engineering and digital twins for the engineering of CPS. In: MODELS 2020: Proceedings of 23rd ACM/IEEE International Conference on Model Driven Engineering Languages and Systems: Companion Proceedings (2020). https://doi.org/10.1145/3417990.3421446
11. Jiang, Y., Yin, S., Dong, J., Kaynak, O.: A review on soft sensors for monitoring, control, and optimization of industrial processes. IEEE Sens. J. (2021). https://doi.org/10.1109/JSEN.2020.3033153
12. Kamburjan, E., Klungre, V.N., Schlatte, R., Johnsen, E.B., Giese, M.: Programming and debugging with semantically lifted states. In: Verborgh, R., et al. (eds.) The Semantic Web - 18th International Conference, ESWC 2021. Lecture Notes in Computer Science, vol. 12731, pp. 126–142. Springer (2021). https://doi.org/10.1007/978-3-030-77385-4_8
13. Kirchhof, J.C., Malcher, L., Rumpe, B.: Understanding and improving model-driven IoT systems through accompanying digital twins. In: Proceedings of 20th ACM SIGPLAN International Conference on Generative Programming: Concepts and Experiences (2021). https://doi.org/10.1145/3486609.3487210
14. Korth, B., Schwede, C., Zajac, M.: Simulation-ready digital twin for realtime management of logistics systems. In: 2018 IEEE International Conference on Big Data (Big Data), pp. 4194–4201. IEEE, Seattle, WA, USA (2018). https://doi.org/10.1109/BigData.2018.8622160

15. Kritzinger, W., Karner, M., Traar, G., Henjes, J., Sihn, W.: Digital twin in manufacturing: a categorical literature review and classification. IFAC-PapersOnLine (2018). https://doi.org/10.1016/j.ifacol.2018.08.474
16. Larsen, P.G., Fitzgerald, J., Gomes, C.: Engineering Digital Twins for Cyber-Physical Systems, chap. 1. Springer (2024). https://doi.org/10.1007/978-3-031-66719-0_1
17. Legaard, C.M., Tola, D., Schranz, T., Macedo, H., Larsen, P.G.: A universal mechanism for implementing functional mock-up units. In: Proceedings of 11th International Conference on Simulation and Modeling Methodologies, Technologies and Applications - SIMULTECH, vol. 1, pp. 121–129 (2021). https://doi.org/10.5220/0010577601210129
18. Lehner, D., et al.: Model-driven engineering for digital twins: a systematic mapping study. Softw. Syst. Model. (2025). https://doi.org/10.1007/s10270-025-01264-7
19. Lin, Y.J., Tu, Y.M.: A scalable IoT-driven smart agriculture system: ontology-based inference and automation for hydroponic farming. Sens. Mater. (2025). https://doi.org/10.18494/SAM5410
20. Michael, J., Schwammberger, M., Wortmann, A.: Explaining cyberphysical system behavior with digital twins. IEEE Softw. (2023). https://doi.org/10.1109/MS.2023.3319580
21. Musen, M.A.: the Protégé Team: The Protégé Project: A Look Back and a Look Forward. AI Matters (2015). https://doi.org/10.1145/2757001.2757003
22. Ouedraogo, E.B., et al.: Digital twin data management: a comprehensive review. IEEE Trans. Big Data (2025). https://doi.org/10.1109/TBDATA.2025.3533891
23. Päßler, J., Aguado, E., Silva, G.R., Tarifa, S.L.T., Corbato, C.H., Johnsen, E.B.: A formal model of metacontrol in maude. In: Leveraging Applications of Formal Methods, Verification and Validation. Verification Principles (2022). https://doi.org/10.1007/978-3-031-19849-6_32
24. Sinreich, D.: An architectural blueprint for autonomic computing. Technical report, IBM (2006). https://web.archive.org/web/20230714193134/https://citeseerx.ist.psu.edu/document?repid=rep1&type=pdf&doi=0e99837d9b1e70bb35d516e32ecfc345cd30e795, (captured with the Wayback Machine)
25. Talasila, P., et al.: Composable digital twins on digital twin as a service platform. Simulation **101**(3), 287–311 (2025). https://doi.org/10.1177/00375497241298653
26. The Apache Software Foundation: Apache Jena (2025). https://jena.apache.org/
27. The Modelica Association: Functional Mock-up Interface (2025). https://fmi-standard.org/
28. The World Wide Web Consortium: SPARQL 1.1 Query Language (2013). https://www.w3.org/TR/sparql11-query/
29. The World Wide Web Consortium, Open Geospatial Consortium: Semantic Sensor Network Ontology (2017). https://www.w3.org/TR/vocab-ssn/
30. Vesse, R., Zettlemoyer, R.M., Ahmed, K., Moore, G., Pluskiewicz, T., Lang, S.: dotNetRDF (2025). https://dotnetrdf.org/
31. Yang, X., Ran, Y., Zhang, G., Wang, H., Mu, Z., Zhi, S.: A digital twin-driven hybrid approach for the prediction of performance degradation in transmission unit of CNC machine tool. Robot. Comput.-Integr. Manufact. (2022). https://doi.org/10.1016/j.rcim.2021.102230

Physics-Informed Neural Networks for SIR Models: Evaluating Data Integration Strategies

Daniel Leto[1(✉)], Roberto C. Alamino[2], Elizabeth Fialho Wanner[1,2], Thais Webber[2], and Diego Souza[2]

[1] Centro Federal de Educação Tecnológica de Minas Gerais, Belo Horizonte, Brazil
daniel.costa@aluno.cefetmg.br

[2] School of Computer Science and Digital Technologies, Aston University, Birmingham, UK
{r.c.alamino,e.wanner1,t.webber,dfons24}@aston.ac.uk

Abstract. Physics-informed neural networks (PINNs) represent a promising idea in deep learning, capable of integrating the robust predictive power of neural networks with the foundational principles of physical laws, often expressed as differential equations. This technique is particularly valuable for scientific discovery in situations where observational data are limited or noisy, offering an alternative to obtain robust and data-efficient solutions for complex forward and inverse problems. In mathematical epidemiology, they can be used as a framework to model disease transmission dynamics, such as those described by the classical Susceptible-Infectious-Recovered (SIR) model, defined by ordinary differential equations. Despite their inherent advantages, training PINNs to capture complex dynamic behaviours accurately poses significant challenges. These difficulties often stem from training pathologies inherent to this technology. This study evaluates two distinct methodologies for employing PINNs to solve the SIR model's equations. The first approach relies purely on minimising the residual of the underlying differential equations. The second, building on recent advances, incorporates observational reference data specifically for the Infected (I) compartment into the loss function, alongside the residuals, simulating scenarios where disease dynamics could be extracted from real-world data. Our empirical findings indicate that, while the residual-only approach exhibits variable accuracy, the strategic integration of observational reference data dramatically enhances model accuracy and stability.

Keywords: Physics-Informed Neural Networks · SIR Modelling · Data Integration · Model Accuracy

1 Introduction

Methods for applying machine learning models, in particular neural networks, to the solution of differential equations were firstly introduced in the 1990s

L. Lestingi et al. (Eds.): DataMod 2025, LNCS 16421, pp. 85–100, 2026.
https://doi.org/10.1007/978-3-032-25552-5_6

[11,16]. However, they only gained widespread attention more recently, following their rediscovery in the form now known as Physics-Informed Neural Networks (PINNs) [7,17]. Since then, they have been used to address a variety of phenomena described by both ordinary and partial differential equations (ODEs and PDEs), including chaotic dynamical systems [2], fluid dynamics [6], and disease spreading [9,14,15], the latter being the main focus of this work.

PINNs are better viewed as an extension of classical collocation and spectral methods for solving PDEs (with ODEs as special cases) [7]. The method uses an artificial neural network (ANN) as a trial parametric solution of the PDE, with its parameters optimized by minimizing a loss function combining (1) observed data points, (2) PDE residuals at chosen collocation points, and (3) boundary conditions of the problem. Additional constraints can be included, though at the cost of increased optimization difficulty. While data may be useful in inverse problems, they are typically unnecessary when solving PDEs directly.

There is growing evidence that PINNs provide several advantages over traditional numerical and statistical methods for solving differential equations in scientific modelling. These include: (1) seamless integration of real-world data into physics [24]; (2) effective treatment of ill-posed and stiff inverse problems [7,23]; (3) improved accuracy and scalability under limited data regimes [6,17,18], and (4) serving as a differentiable surrogate for physical systems [5,18]. However, there are also important limitations that must be considered and addressed to ensure reliable performance and robust model outcomes. The implementation of ANNs, particularly deep architectures, requires careful application of established techniques regarding training protocols, hyper-parameter tuning, and input data quality [12] to properly train such models and achieve effective results. Notably, the construction and minimisation of the loss function specifically for PINNs is a non-trivial problem due to the complex interplay between all the different components, which can affect overall model performance and convergence.

Compartmental models of disease spread, most prominently the SIR model, also known as the Kermack-McKendrick model [8,20], pose specific challenges for PINNs. These models describe disease dynamics in a population by dividing individuals into compartments (e.g., susceptible, infected, recovered, vaccinated, exposed), with each compartment governed by an ODE that captures its rate of change relative to the others based on heuristic epidemiological rules. The total population can be treated as constant in closed models or time-varying in open models [1]. Typically, the dynamics are expressed in terms of the fractions of individuals in each compartment relative to the total population. In such models, PINNs have to solve a coupled system of ODEs subject to the additional constraint that the sum of all compartments equals the total population at each time point. In this study, we focus on the direct problem, comparing solutions of the governing equations with and without the inclusion of additional data, and providing a comprehensive analysis of the results.

To the best of our knowledge, only a few studies have addressed this approach in detail [9,14,15,21]. Millevoi et al. [14], for instance, briefly mention training a separate network for the Infected compartment, referred to as the split approach.

In this work, we conduct an in-depth analysis of this idea and its broader implications. Our goal is to establish a foundational benchmark before introducing real-world complexities such as noise or incomplete system information. By further comparing PINN solutions with classical numerical methods, we highlight the strengths and limitations of PINNs in modelling epidemic dynamics.

The remainder of this paper is organized as follows. Section 2 reviews recent developments in PINNs, with a particular focus on their application in solving SIR models and related compartmental frameworks. Section 3 provides a detailed overview of the SIR model and explains the methodology for solving its governing equations using PINNs. Sections 4 and 5, respectively, describe the experimental setup and present the results obtained from our comparative analyses. Section 6 discusses potential future directions, challenges, and opportunities for advancing PINN-based approaches in epidemiological modelling.

2 Related Work

Despite their conceptual elegance and early empirical successes, PINNs are known to encounter significant challenges, often referred to as training pathologies, which can hinder their practical effectiveness and even lead to erroneous solutions [7,24,25]. These difficulties become particularly pronounced when dealing with systems exhibiting highly non-linear, multi-scale, or chaotic behaviour, such as the Navier-Stokes equations in turbulent regimes or chaotic Lorenz systems [2,23]. Key issues identified in the literature include spectral bias, where networks struggle to learn high-frequency features [26,27], unbalanced backpropagated gradients [25], and causality violation, where conventional PINNs undesirably minimize PDE residuals at later times before accurately solving for earlier times, leading to physically implausible solutions for time-dependent PDEs [23]. Furthermore, PINN performance can degrade with increasing network depth, often suffering from ill-posed initializations and unstable training processes [22].

In mathematical epidemiology, PINNs have been increasingly adopted to model disease transmission dynamics, especially in frameworks such as the classical Susceptible-Infectious-Recovered (SIR) model and its variations (e.g., SEIR, SIRD) [4,14,15]. This application is critical for understanding and forecasting real-world epidemics like COVID-19 and seasonal influenza [15,18], and for estimating key time-varying parameters such as infection rates or effective reproduction numbers [4,5,15]. For instance, Grimm et al. [4] utilized PINNs to estimate time-dependent contact rates in SIR and SEIR models by decomposing the problem into shorter time intervals. Ning et al. [15] applied PINNs to the SEIRD model for COVID-19, not only for parameter estimation and prediction but also for analysing the impact of non-pharmaceutical interventions. Long et al. [5] proposed a data-driven deep learning approach that identifies time-varying parameters of the SIRD model using PINNs and then uses long-term-short-memory networks (LSTMs) for future predictions of infectious cases.

To overcome the training challenges of PINNs and improve their performance, several methodological advancements have been proposed [7]. These include loss re-weighting schemes to balance the optimization process [27] and adaptive sampling strategies for collocation points to enhance accuracy in complex or high-frequency systems. Novel network architectures have also been proposed, such as Fourier feature embeddings, which mitigate spectral bias in standard PINNs [26], and modified Multi-Layer Perceptrons (MLPs) [25], designed to facilitate better gradient flow and representation learning. Causal training strategies have been developed to explicitly enforce physical causality during training, significantly improving accuracy even for chaotic systems [23]. Furthermore, architectures like PirateNets used adaptive residual connections and specialised initialisation schemes [22], to achieve stable and efficient training of deeper PINN models.

A significant recent development, directly relevant to this study, involves hybrid approaches that integrate observational data with physics-informed training [17]. Since purely physics-driven optimization can converge to inaccurate solutions, particularly in stiff or ill-posed problems, researchers have explored anchoring PINNs with data-driven techniques to leverage the strengths of both [7]. For instance, the Epidemiologically Informed Neural Networks (EINNs) framework combines a PINN-based 'time module' to learn latent epidemic dynamics with a 'feature module' (an RNN) that ingests heterogeneous, exogenous data, yielding improved short- and long-term forecasts [19]. Hamiltonian-Dirac Neural Networks (HDNNs) incorporate Dirac constraints and energy conservation as regularization terms in the loss function, and can also learn parametric dependencies by taking problem-specific parameters as inputs [6].

Importantly, recent studies have explored strategies where specific components of a model are learned directly from data to enhance the overall PINN solution. Millevoi et al. [14] investigated 'joint' and 'split' approaches for PINNs in compartmental epidemiological models, with the latter training separate neural networks for individual state variables or parameters. Although their work briefly mentions training a separate network for the Infected compartment, a systematic analysis of the effects and potential advantages of such data-driven hybrid PINN architectures, particularly for the SIR model's forward problem and its parameter sensitivity in stiff regimes, remains largely unexplored.

This study addresses this gap by rigorously comparing a purely physics-informed PINN with a hybrid approach, where the Infected compartment of the SIR model is anchored to synthetic reference data. Through a systematic evaluation across a wide range of epidemiological parameters, including extreme high-transmission scenarios, we reveal how strategically integrating data can substantially enhance the robustness, accuracy, and stability of PINN solutions. These findings provide a foundational framework for developing more reliable and generalizable PINN-based tools for public health decision-making and advance robust, data-informed approaches to inverse problems in epidemiology.

3 PINN Methodology for Solving the SIR Model

We now outline the general procedure for solving PDEs using the PINN methodology, before specializing it to the ODE system governing the SIR model. As our focus is restricted to forward solutions rather than inverse problems, we consider only the governing equations and boundary conditions, without incorporating observational data into the training.

Consider a dynamical phenomenon described by a system of PDEs and boundary conditions given, respectively, by

$$\begin{cases} \mathcal{L}_\nu[\boldsymbol{u}(x)] = \boldsymbol{f}_\nu(x), \\ \mathcal{B}_\mu[\boldsymbol{u}(x_0)] = \boldsymbol{g}_\mu(x_0), \end{cases} \tag{1}$$

where $x \in \Omega$ denotes the free variables, typically representing spatial and time dimensions, $x_0 \in \partial\Omega$ specifies boundary points, $\boldsymbol{u} = (u_1(x), u_2(x), ..., u_m(x))$ are the dependent variables, $\mathcal{L}_\nu$, $\nu = 1, ..., N$ denotes the set of N general partial differential operators characterising each of the N PDEs to be solved, $\mathcal{B}_\mu$, with $\mu = 1, ..., M$ representing the M boundary conditions and $\boldsymbol{f}_\nu$, and $\boldsymbol{g}_\mu$ are general functions of the free variables.

In the PINN framework, the vector function $\boldsymbol{u}(x)$ is approximated by a parametric model $\Phi(x \mid \theta)$, typically an ANN, with trainable parameters θ. The model parameters are optimised by minimizing a loss function composed of two terms: the residuals of the governing equations, evaluated at a set of n^c collocation points (taken identically across all equations for simplicity) and the boundary conditions terms, enforced at n^b_μ points for each condition, which may vary between boundaries. A common measure is the quadratic error, which leads to the loss function:

$$L = L_{PDE} + L_{BC}, \tag{2}$$

$$L_{PDE} = \frac{1}{N}\sum_{\nu=1}^{N} \lambda_\nu^{PDE} \sum_{i=1}^{n_c} \left(\mathcal{L}_\nu[\Phi(x_i|\theta)] - \boldsymbol{f}_\nu(x_i)\right)^2, \tag{3}$$

$$L_{BC} = \frac{1}{M}\sum_{\mu=1}^{M} \lambda_\mu^{BC} \sum_{i=1}^{n_c} \left(\mathcal{B}_\mu[\Phi(x_{0,i}|\theta)] - \boldsymbol{g}_\mu(x_{0,i})\right)^2. \tag{4}$$

The derivatives of the parametric model are computed via automatic differentiation, which applies the chain rule to evaluate derivatives with respect to the inputs at the selected points.

The parameters λ_ν^{PDE} and λ_μ^{BC} control the relative weighting of the equation residuals and boundary condition terms in the loss function and must be selected carefully. Figure 1 graphically represents this concept.

The general framework described is now applied to the Susceptible-Infected-Recovered (SIR) model [8], where $\Omega = \mathbb{R}$. The SIR model consists of three coupled, non-linear ordinary differential equations, with the independent variable x corresponding solely to time t. The dependent variables represent the population fractions in each compartment: Susceptible $S(t)$, Infected $I(t)$, and Recovered $R(t)$.

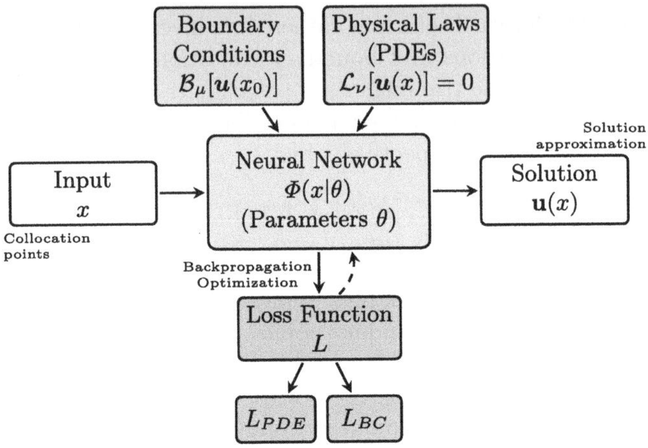

$$L_{total} = \lambda_\nu^{PDE} + \lambda_\mu^{BC} L_{BC}$$

Fig. 1. Conceptual architecture of a Physics-Informed Neural Network (PINN) focused on physics and boundary conditions. The neural network takes spatio-temporal coordinates x as input and outputs the approximate solution $u(x)$. Training is driven by a loss function that incorporates the residual of the differential equations (L_{PDE}) and the initial/boundary conditions (L_{BC}), weighted by coefficients λ_i to balance their relative contribution.

The model is governed by the following system of equations:

$$\begin{aligned} \frac{dS}{dt} &= -\beta S(t) I(t), \\ \frac{dI}{dt} &= \beta S(t) I(t) - \eta I(t), \\ \frac{dR}{dt} &= \eta I(t), \end{aligned} \tag{5}$$

where β is the effective transmission rate and η is the recovery rate. The boundary conditions are given by the initial state of the system at $t = 0$, i.e., $S(0) = S_0$, $I(0) = I_0$, and $R(0) = R_0$.

To construct the PINN loss function, we first define the neural network approximations for each compartment as $\hat{S}(t; \theta_S)$, $\hat{I}(t; \theta_I)$, and $\hat{R}(t; \theta_R)$, where $\theta_S, \theta_I, \theta_R$ are the trainable parameters of three separate neural networks. The SIR equations are then reformulated to define the residuals, which the PINN aims to minimize. These residuals result from the direct application of the operator $\mathcal{L}_\nu[\cdot]$ from Eq. 1 to the SIR dynamics:

$$\begin{aligned}\mathcal{R}_S &:= \frac{d\hat{S}}{dt} + \beta\hat{S}(t)\hat{I}(t),\\ \mathcal{R}_I &:= \frac{d\hat{I}}{dt} - \beta\hat{S}(t)\hat{I}(t) + \eta\hat{I}(t),\\ \mathcal{R}_R &:= \frac{d\hat{R}}{dt} - \eta\hat{I}(t).\end{aligned} \tag{6}$$

The time derivatives of the network outputs, such as $\frac{d\hat{S}}{dt}$, are computed through automatic differentiation. During training, the optimizer iteratively updates the network parameters θ to minimize the residuals, enforcing the SIR equations as accurately as possible througout the temporal domain.

The final loss function is constructed by incorporating these specific residuals and the initial conditions into the general form of Eqs. 3 and 4. The equation loss, L_{ODE}, is not the ODE loss and corresponds to the mean squared error of the residuals evaluated across all collocation points. The boundary condition loss, L_{BC}, is defined as the mean squared error between the network predictions at $t = 0$ and the known initial values for each compartment. Explicitly, $L_{BC} = L_{S_0} + L_{I_0} + L_{R_0}$, where the initial state loss at each compartment C is given by:

$$L_{C,t_0} = (\hat{C}(0) - C_0)^2. \tag{7}$$

By minimizing the total loss $L = L_{ODE} + L_{BC}$, the PINN is trained to learn a function that simultaneously satisfies the dynamical laws of the SIR model and its initial state, yielding a solution to the system.

4 Experimental Design

The study was designed to evaluate a PINN framework for solving the SIR epidemiological model. The methodology first details the setup for a single training run, followed by an overview of the comprehensive experimental scope.

Regarding network architecture, the state of each compartment in the SIR model (Susceptible, Infected, and Recovered) was approximated by a dedicated, fully connected neural network. All three networks shared an identical architecture, featuring four hidden layers with 256 neurons each. The hyperbolic tangent ($tanh()$) was used as the activation function, as it provides better performance for its differentiability properties [24]. Network weights were initialized using the Xavier Uniform scheme to facilitate stable training [3]. An absolute value operation was applied to the network's output to enforce the physically necessary constraint of non-negative population counts [13,20].

For the loss function and causal training of the PINNs, optimization was guided by a physics-informed loss that relies solely on the initial condition, without direct use of additional data points. This loss function is composed of two main terms, with the same weights from Eq. 2. The first, the initial condition loss, explicitly penalizes the model if its predictions at the start time deviate from the known initial values, ensuring training stability and properly modelling the system's behaviour [7,15,17]. The second and main component, the physics residual loss, measures how well the network outputs satisfy the governing differential equations of the SIR model.

A crucial aspect of our method is the implementation of a causal training strategy, an approach shown to be vital for the successful training of PINNs on time-dependent problems [23]. Instead of treating all points in time equally, our method respects the natural, forward progression of time by weighting the physics residual loss at each time step based on the cumulative error from all previous steps. The weight w_i at the time step t_i is given by

$$w_i = \exp\left(-\epsilon \sum_{k=1}^{i-1} L_{ODE}(t_k, \theta)\right), \tag{8}$$

where ϵ is a causality parameter that governs how strictly the loss shrinks. In this study, we set $\epsilon = 1$. This process forces the optimizer to first find an accurate solution for earlier time points before proceeding to later ones, preventing the model from converging to physically implausible solutions.

For optimization, the network parameters were updated using the Adam optimizer via backpropagation [10,12] with a constant learning rate of 1×10^{-3}, which is the default value. Each model was trained for a total of 1000 epochs, following best research practices [24]. Figure 2 illustrates the whole training process for a PINN that tries to solve a SIR model.

To evaluate the framework's performance and robustness, we designed a large-scale experiment spanning a wide range of scenarios. For the SIR model, a 6×6 grid search was conducted over the transmission (β) and recovery (η) rates, with values evenly spaced within the range $[0, 0.5]$. This setup allows us to systematically assess the model's behaviour under different epidemiological dynamics, particularly in regimes where $\beta/\eta \gg 1$. Such high-transmission scenarios are especially important to consider, as they closely resemble real-world dynamics [13] and make the problem less well-posed [20]. Ensemble training was employed to ensure robustness: for each of the 36 parameter sets, 30 independent models were trained. This approach, totalling 1080 unique training runs per configuration, enables a comprehensive assessment of training stability and provides a means to quantify uncertainty in the model's predictions.

Finally, two comparative training configurations were investigated. The first, a fully physics-informed approach ('Residual I'), trained the networks for all three compartments exclusively using the physics-based loss. The second, a hybrid approach ('External I'), began by training a standard neural network on synthetic data for the Infected compartment, generated by solving the ODEs with a 4th-order Runge-Kutta method. This pre-trained network was then used as a fixed parametric function of T ($\hat{I}(t) = \mathcal{N}_I(t; \theta_I)$) to train the Susceptible and Recovered compartments as PINNs. This dual-configuration experiment allows for a direct comparison between a purely physics-driven approach and a hybrid method that is partially anchored to reference data. Figure 3 illustrates this process in detail. Figure 4 presents the overall experimental design.

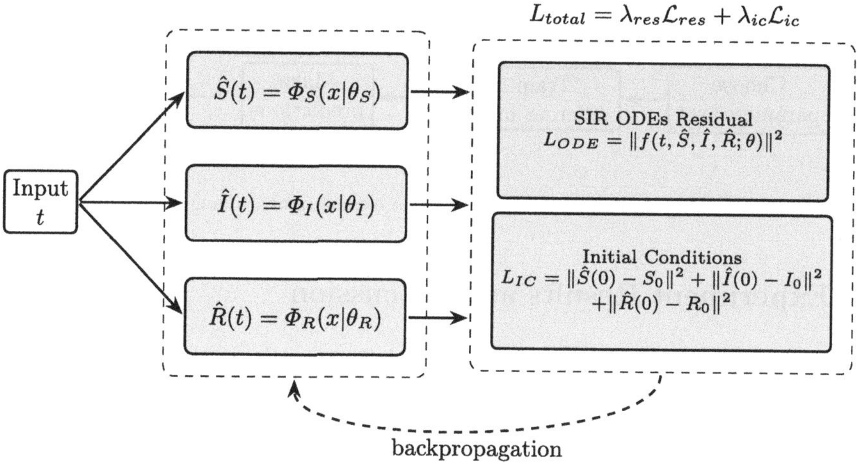

Fig. 2. Conceptual diagram of the PINN used to approximate the solution of the SIR model using only the equations. Three distinct neural networks, each with its own parameters $(\theta_S, \theta_I, \theta_R)$, receive time t as input and output the state of the corresponding compartment. Training is performed via backpropagation to minimize a composite loss function, L_{total}, which is a weighted sum of two terms: the residual of the governing ODEs ($\mathcal{L}_{res}$) and the error at the initial state ($\mathcal{L}_{ic}$).

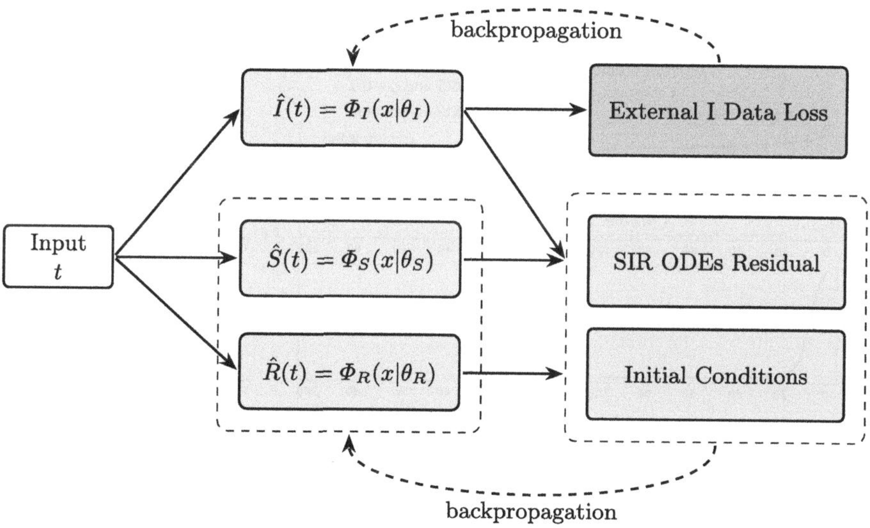

Fig. 3. Conceptual diagram of the PINN used to approximate the solution of the SIR model using the equations and external infection data. The network for the I compartment (θ_I) is optimised using reference data obtained through a classical solution method. Parameters (θ_S, θ_R) are optimized using the equations as previous. L_{total} is calculated using the three compartments, but backpropagation only affects S and R compartments.

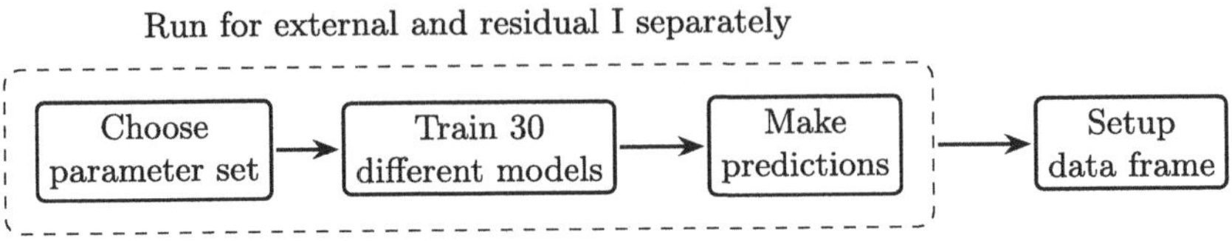

Fig. 4. Diagram depicting the experimental design.

5 Experiment Results and Discussion

To assess the performance of the proposed framework, we present the results from the numerical experiments outlined in the previous section. We begin with a representative case to highlight the differences between the two training configurations, and then extend the analysis to the full parameter grid.

Figure 5 presents a direct comparison between the fully physics-informed (Residual I) and the hybrid (External I) approaches for a challenging high-transmission scenario with parameters $\beta = 0.5$ and $\eta = 0.1$. This regime, where $\beta/\eta \gg 1$, is known to be particularly challenging for both numerical solvers and PINN models [20]. The plots display the median predictions from an ensemble of 30 trained models alongside the ground truth solution obtained via a 4th-order Runge-Kutta method.

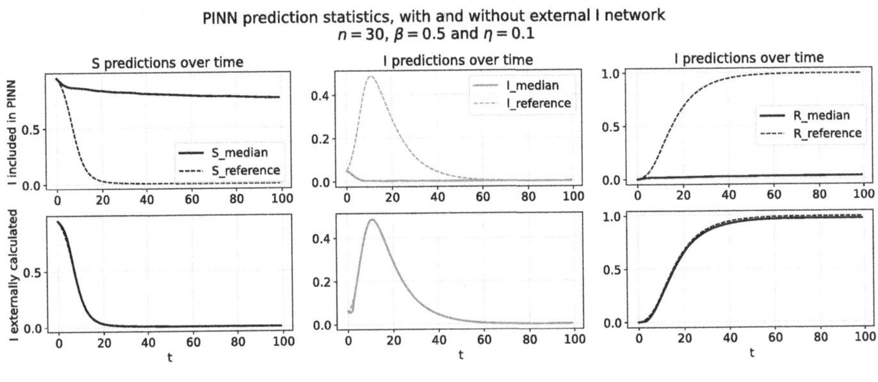

Fig. 5. Comparison of prediction statistics for the two training configurations with parameters $\beta = 0.5$ and $\eta = 0.1$. The top row shows median predictions from the fully physics-informed approach, where all compartments were learned solely from the SIR equations. The bottom row shows median predictions from the hybrid approach, in which the Infected (I) compartment was learned from external data. Each median is computed across an ensemble of 30 independent runs.

The results reveal clear performance differences between the two methods for this parameter set. The External I approach (bottom row of Fig. 5), achieves high accuracy, with median predictions for the Susceptible, Infected, and Recovered compartments closely matching their reference curves across the time domain. This indicates that anchoring the model with reliable data for even a single compartment, enables the PINN framework to effectively leverage the physical equations to accurately infer the dynamics of the remaining states.

In contrast, the fully physics-informed Residual I approach, shown in the top row, struggles to reproduce the correct dynamics. Although the initial conditions are satisfied, the median prediction for the Infected compartment underestimates the epidemic peak and exhibits a temporal shift. Consequently, the Susceptible curve declines too slowly, while the Recovered curve rises much more slowly than ground truth. This illustrates that in high-transmission scenarios, a purely self-supervised, physics-driven optimization can converge to an incorrect solution.

This example strongly suggests that in ill-posed or challenging parameter regimes, the hybrid approach offers a clear advantage in both accuracy and stability. Anchoring part of the model with data helps regularize the training process, steering the optimizer toward the correct solution where the fully physics-informed method fails. Previous studies have shown that gradient pathologies can arise during PINN training due to the stochastic nature of neural networks and problem stiffnesses [7,14,24–26], which can sometimes be mitigated using strategies such as gradient clipping.

To further investigate this behaviour, we analyse a second case with less stiff dynamics. Figure 6 shows the results for parameters $\beta = 0.5$ and $\eta = 0.4$. In this scenario, the ratio β/η is much closer to one, producing a milder epidemic curve with fewer individuals in the Infected compartment and a better-posed problem from a mathematical perspective.

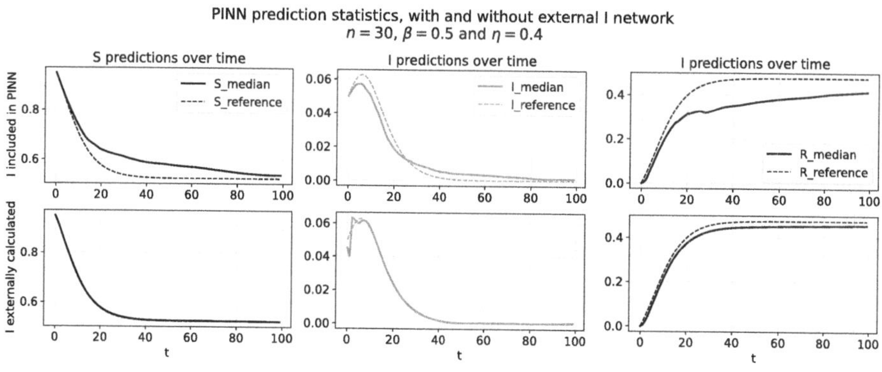

Fig. 6. Comparison of prediction statistics for a non-stiff problem ($\beta = 0.5$, $\eta = 0.4$). The top row shows the fully physics-informed (Residual I) approach, whose performance is visibly improved. The bottom row shows the hybrid (External I) approach, which remains highly accurate.

In this non-stiff scenario, the fully physics-informed Residual I model (top row of Fig. 6) demonstrates a markedly improved performance, capturing the overall epidemic dynamics and timing across all compartments, with only minor deviations from the reference. The hybrid External I approach (bottom row) remains highly accurate, showing near-perfect alignment with the reference data.

These two examples strongly suggest that the stiffness of the underlying differential equations, largely determined by parameter rations, is a critical factor in the success of a purely physics-informed approach. Anchoring the model with external data for even a single compartment provides a robust solution across both stiff and non-stiff regimes. In contrast, the fully physics-informed model remains highly sensitive to problem's characteristics: it performs well in non-stiff scenarios but struggles in more challenging, stiff cases. This highlights the importance of data-driven regularization when applying PINNs to challenging inverse problems.

To generalize these findings, we performed a statistical analysis across the full 36-point parameter grid. The results, presented as heatmaps of the median error for each compartment, confirm the trends observed in the representative cases and emphasize the performance differences between the two training configurations. Figure 7 displays the median errors for the fully physics-informed Residual I configuration, where performance is highly dependent on the system parameters.

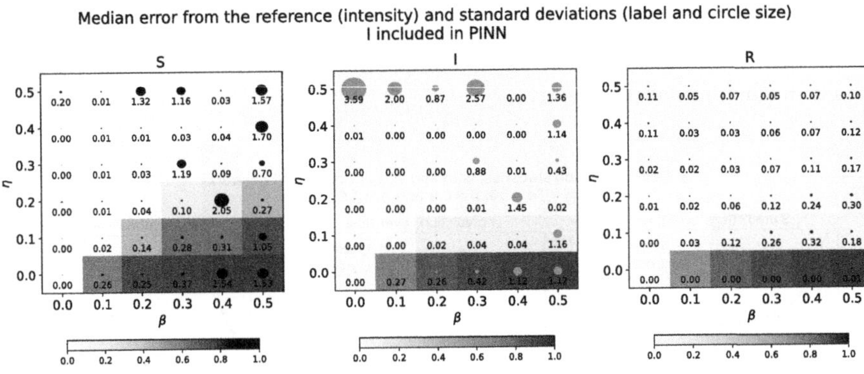

Fig. 7. Median error heatmaps for the fully physics-informed (Residual I) configuration across the $\beta - \eta$ parameter grid. The label indicates the average standard deviation of the predictions. High errors in the bottom-right quadrant show the model's failure in stiff, high-transmission scenarios.

For non-stiff problems with similar value of β and η (upper-left region), the model performs well with low errors. However, as stiffness increases (toward the bottom-right, where $\beta \gg \eta$), accuracy deteriorates dramatically. Median errors for the Susceptible and Infected compartments exceed 1.0 in the most challenging cases, indicating a complete failure to capture the dynamics. The Recovered compartment follows the same trend, though with smaller error magnitudes. Notably, no clear relationship is observed between parameter values and the standard deviation of predictions across compartments (as indicated by labels and circle sizes). The gradient overflow may also contribute to this behaviour, a hypothesis that warrants further investigation.

In contrast to the variable performance of the fully physics-informed model, the hybrid External I configuration demonstrates remarkable stability and accuracy, as shown in Fig. 8. Median errors remain exceptionally low across the parameter space for all three compartments. For both Susceptible and Infected compartments, the median error is consistently at or near zero, with only negligible deviations in isolated cases. The Recovered compartment shows slightly higher but still minimal errors, generally below 0.05. These results demonstrate the robustness of the hybrid approach: anchoring the Infected compartment with data enables the PINN framework to reliably reconstruct the other states regardless of the problem stiffness.

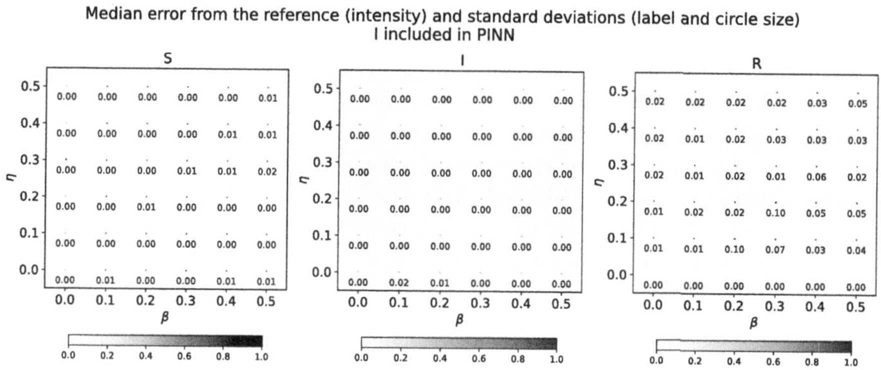

Fig. 8. Median error heatmaps for the hybrid (External I) configuration across the $\beta - \eta$ parameter grid. The labels indicate the average standard deviation of the 30-model ensemble predictions for each parameter set. The consistently low error values demonstrate high accuracy and stability.

Collectively, these results show that while a purely physics-informed PINN can solve the SIR model under certain conditions, its performance lacks robustness across parameter regimes. Its susceptibility to failure in stiff scenarios exposes a significant limitation. In contrast, the hybrid approach emerges as a highly effective and stable alternative, demonstrating that even limited data-driven anchoring can substantially enhance the reliability and accuracy of PINNs for solving complex epidemiological models.

6 Conclusion

This study establishes that while purely physics-informed PINNs are promising, their successful application to epidemiological models depends critically on the system's mathematical characteristics. We demonstrated that anchoring the SIR model with observational data for a single compartment yields robust and accurate solutions in high-transmission regimes where purely physics-driven models fail. This finding highlights a fundamental principle: for PINNs to be reliable in epidemiology, a hybrid, data-informed approach is essential to handle real-world disease dynamics.

Furthermore, a review of the literature reveals a frequent reliance on heuristics and 'rules of thumb' for training hyperparameters, network architectures, and loss function weighting. Such choices, though practical, are rarely validated for epidemiological models, whose frequent non-linear dynamics and potential stiffness may invalidate generic assumptions. By detailing and justifying our experimental protocol, this work argues that systematic elucidation of tuning rules is crucial. Establishing such guidelines will enable a PINN framework for SIR models that is not only accurate but also reproducible and reliable. This transition to data-anchored models marks a paradigm shift, especially as focus moves from forward prediction to inverse problems, such as inferring time-varying transmission rates. In this context, the traditional machine learning goal of generalization aligns with the scientific goal of high-fidelity data assimilation. A model that perfectly fits the observed time series is no longer 'overfitted'; it becomes a powerful, differentiable surrogate for the discrete and noisy measurements. The accuracy of discovered parameters, such as a time-varying $\beta(t)$, is directly contingent on how precisely this surrogate and its derivatives capture the true dynamics. Therefore, the demonstrated ability of our hybrid model to achieve near-perfect fits validates its role as a robust foundation for parameter discovery in complex systems.

Future work will build on this foundation by addressing the observed gradient pathologies in purely physics-informed models and formalizing our ensemble method into a principled Uncertainty Quantification (UQ) framework. This will yield confidence intervals for predictions and inferred parameters, a critical step for translating model outputs into actionable public health insights. With this framework, we will tackle real-world inverse problems using epidemiological data (e.g., the COVID-19 pandemic data) to estimate time-varying transmission rates.

The long-term vision extends beyond parameter inference towards data-driven equation discovery. Using the flexibility of the PINN framework, we aim to identify new functional terms that better describe transmission dynamics than classical SIR-based models [7]. Ultimately, this work contributes to the development of a new generation of epidemiological models that dynamically integrate mechanistic principles with real-time data, promising a more agile and accurate response to future public health crises.

References

1. Cooper, I., Mondal, A., Antonopoulos, C.G.: A sir model assumption for the spread of covid-19 in different communities. Chaos Solitons Fractals **139**, 110057 (2020). https://doi.org/10.1016/j.chaos.2020.110057. https://www.sciencedirect.com/science/article/pii/S0960077920304549

2. Elabid, Z., Chakraborty, T., Hadid, A.: Knowledge-based deep learning for modeling chaotic systems (2022). https://doi.org/10.48550/arXiv.2209.04259. https://arxiv.org/abs/2209.04259
3. Glorot, X., Bengio, Y.: Understanding the difficulty of training deep feedforward neural networks. In: Teh, Y.W., Titterington, M. (eds.) Proceedings of the Thirteenth International Conference on Artificial Intelligence and Statistics. Proceedings of Machine Learning Research, vol. 9, pp. 249–256. PMLR, Chia Laguna Resort, Sardinia, Italy (2010). https://proceedings.mlr.press/v9/glorot10a.html
4. Grimm, V., Heinlein, A., Klawonn, A., Lanser, M., Weber, J.: Estimating the time-dependent contact rate of sir and seir models in mathematical epidemiology using physics-informed neural networks. Electron. Trans. Numer. Anal. **56**, 1–27 (2022). https://doi.org/10.1553/etna_vol56s1. https://etna.math.kent.edu/volumes/2021-2030/vol56/abstract.php?pages=1-27
5. Jie Long, A.Q.M.K., Furati, K.M.: Identification and prediction of time-varying parameters of covid-19 model: a data-driven deep learning approach. Int. J. Comput. Math. **98**(8), 1617–1632 (2021). https://doi.org/10.1080/00207160.2021.1929942
6. Kaltsas, D.A.: Constrained hamiltonian systems and physics-informed neural networks: Hamilton-Dirac neural networks. Phys. Rev. E **111**(2) (2025). https://doi.org/10.1103/physreve.111.025301
7. Karniadakis, G.E., Kevrekidis, I.G., Lu, L., Perdikaris, P., Wang, S., Yang, L.: Physics-informed machine learning. Nat. Rev. Phys. **3**(6), 422–440 (2021). https://doi.org/10.1038/s42254-021-00314-5
8. Kermack, W.O., McKendrick, A.G., Walker, G.T.: A contribution to the mathematical theory of epidemics. Proc. Roy. Soc. London Ser. A Containing Pap. Math. Phys. Character **115**(772), 700–721 (1927). https://doi.org/10.1098/rspa.1927.0118. https://royalsocietypublishing.org/doi/abs/10.1098/rspa.1927.0118
9. Kim, M., Kim, Y., Kim, Y.: Physics-informed neural networks for optimal vaccination plan in sir epidemic models. arXiv preprint arXiv:2502.19890 (2025)
10. Kingma, D.P., Ba, J.: Adam: a method for stochastic optimization (2014). https://arxiv.org/abs/1412.6980
11. Lagaris, I.E., Likas, A., Fotiadis, D.I.: Artificial neural networks for solving ordinary and partial differential equations. IEEE Trans. Neural Netw. **9**(5), 987–1000 (1998). https://doi.org/10.1109/72.712178
12. Lecun, Y., Bottou, L., Bengio, Y., Haffner, P.: Gradient-based learning applied to document recognition. Proc. IEEE **86**(11), 2278–2324 (1998). https://doi.org/10.1109/5.726791
13. Leto, D., Wanner, E., Alamino, R., Webber, T.: Modelling covid-19 with a sir variant using real-world data: a case study in Brazil. In: Czekster, R.M., Milazzo, P. (eds.) From Data to Models and Back, pp. 34–51. Springer, Cham (2025). https://doi.org/10.1007/978-3-031-87908-1_3
14. Millevoi, C., Pasetto, D., Ferronato, M.: A physics-informed neural network approach for compartmental epidemiological models. PLOS Comput. Biol. **20**(9), 1–29 (2024). https://doi.org/10.1371/journal.pcbi.1012387
15. Ning, X., Guan, J., Li, X.A., Wei, Y., Chen, F.: Physics-informed neural networks integrating compartmental model for analyzing COVID-19 transmission dynamics. Viruses **15**(8), 1749 (2023). https://doi.org/10.3390/v15081749
16. Psichogios, D.C., Ungar, L.H.: A hybrid neural network-first principles approach to process modeling. AIChE J. **38**(10), 1499–1511 (1992). https://doi.org/10.1002/aic.690381003

17. Raissi, M., Perdikaris, P., Karniadakis, G.: Physics-informed neural networks: a deep learning framework for solving forward and inverse problems involving nonlinear partial differential equations. J. Comput. Phys. 686–707 (2019). https://doi.org/10.1016/j.jcp.2018.10.045
18. Rama, M., Santin, G., Cencetti, G., Tizzoni, M., Lepri, B.: Forecasting seasonal influenza epidemics with physics-informed neural networks. arXiv preprint arXiv:2506.03897 (2025)
19. Rodríguez, A., Cui, J., Ramakrishnan, N., Adhikari, B., Prakash, B.A.: EINNs: epidemiologically-informed neural networks. In: Proceedings of the AAAI Conference on Artificial Intelligence, vol. 37, pp. 14453–14460 (2023). https://doi.org/10.1609/aaai.v37i12.26690
20. Wacker, B., Schlüter, J.: Time-continuous and time-discrete sir models revisited: theory and applications. Adv. Differ. Eqn. **2020**(1), 556 (2020). https://doi.org/10.1186/s13662-020-02995-1
21. bin Waheed, U., Haghighat, E., Alkhalifah, T., Song, C., Hao, Q.: Pinneik: Eikonal solution using physics-informed neural networks. Comput. Geosci. **155**, 104833 (2021). https://doi.org/10.1016/j.cageo.2021.104833
22. Wang, S., Li, B., Chen, Y., Perdikaris, P.: Piratenets: physics-informed deep learning with residual adaptive networks (2024). https://arxiv.org/abs/2402.00326
23. Wang, S., Sankaran, S., Perdikaris, P.: Respecting causality for training physics-informed neural networks. Comput. Methods Appl. Mech. Eng. **421**, 116813 (2024). https://doi.org/10.1016/j.cma.2024.116813
24. Wang, S., Sankaran, S., Wang, H., Perdikaris, P.: An expert's guide to training physics-informed neural networks (2023). https://arxiv.org/abs/2308.08468
25. Wang, S., Teng, Y., Perdikaris, P.: Understanding and mitigating gradient flow pathologies in physics-informed neural networks. SIAM J. Sci. Comput. **43**(5), A3055–A3081 (2021). https://doi.org/10.1137/20M1318043
26. Wang, S., Wang, H., Perdikaris, P.: On the eigenvector bias of fourier feature networks: from regression to solving multi-scale PDEs with physics-informed neural networks. Comput. Methods Appl. Mech. Eng. **384**, 113938 (2021). https://doi.org/10.1016/j.cma.2021.113938
27. Wang, S., Yu, X., Perdikaris, P.: When and why PINNs fail to train: a neural tangent kernel perspective. J. Comput. Phys. **449**, 110768 (2022). https://doi.org/10.1016/j.jcp.2021.110768

Low-Cost Embedded PSO for Decentralized, Scalable and Sustainable Hydroelectric Dispatch

Keila L. de Oliveira[1], Diego F. P. de Souza[2], Thais Webber[2], Elizabeth Fialho Wanner[2(✉)], and Carolina Gil Marcelino[1]

[1] Instituto de Computação, Universidade Federal do Rio de Janeiro (UFRJ), Rio de Janeiro, Brazil
keila.oliveira@ufrj.br, carolina@ic.ufrj.br

[2] School of Computer Science and Digital Technologies, Aston University, Birmingham, UK
{dfons24,t.webber,e.wanner1}@aston.ac.uk

Abstract. The increasing demand for electrical energy highlights the need for efficient operation of power generation systems. This study presents an embedded optimization device for hydroelectric dispatch developed on low-cost hardware. The proposed device introduces control strategies that conserve water resources while reliably meeting energy demands through a portable and efficient Particle Swarm Optimization (PSO) algorithm, adapted for micro- and resource-constrained hydroelectric applications. To validate its effectiveness, a Hydroelectric Power Plant (HPP) dispatch simulation model and the PSO algorithm were implemented and tested on embedded platforms (Arduino Mega 2560 and Raspberry Pi 3 Model B), with performance benchmarked against a high-performance computing machine. Results show that, despite computational limitations, embedded systems can effectively support hydroelectric dispatch planning, providing a cost-effective, scalable, decentralized, and sustainable alternative to traditional control solutions.

Keywords: Embedded Optimization · Micro Hydroelectric Dispatch · Particle Swarm Optimization · Low-Cost Hardware · Edge Computing

1 Introduction

The persistent rise in energy demand underscores the urgent need for innovative strategies that can both enhance efficiency and drive sustainability in power generation. Meeting this challenge is complex, requiring the modernization of the ageing energy infrastructure, the integration of variable renewable sources, the deployment of effective energy storage solutions, and regulatory and economic frameworks that can support the transition toward low-carbon systems. A recent report by CNN Brazil (November 8, 2024) [5], projects a 25% increase in national energy demand over the next decade, highlighting the magnitude of this emerging

L. Lestingi et al. (Eds.): DataMod 2025, LNCS 16421, pp. 101–118, 2026.
https://doi.org/10.1007/978-3-032-25552-5_7

challenge. Furthermore, historic consumption peak of 106,532 MW, reported by the Brazilian National Electric System Operator (ONS) on February 26, 2025 [6,7], shows both the growing stress on the grid and the urgent need for more robust, adaptive operational strategies. In this context, our study investigates the operational challenges of hydroelectric power (i.e., hydropower) generation and proposes a novel dispatch optimization approach. While empirically evaluated in the Brazilian system (characterized by high hydropower dependency and rising demand), the methodology is transferable to regions with similar resource and operational constraints. To address efficiency challenges inherent in hydropower generation, we introduce an embedded optimization device implemented on a low-cost hardware platform, specifically designed to support decision-making and enhance resource management during the energy operation planning stage.

Electrical dispatch is a process that determines which generating units (GUs) should operate, and under what conditions, to meet demand while minimizing cost and environmental impact [7]. In hydroelectric systems, this is a mathematically complex task due to nonlinearities and single/multi-objective constraints. Metaheuristic methods have been widely applied with satisfactory performance [12,13,18]. In our study, we develop a low-cost electrical dispatch controller using energy-efficient embedded platforms, especially the Raspberry Pi 3 and the Arduino Mega 2560, to implement the Particle Swarm Optimization (PSO) algorithm [10]. These platforms, widely available and accessible microcontrollers/computers, provide affordability, low power consumption, sensor/actuator integration, and suitability for real-time embedded applications. By executing optimization routines directly on minimal hardware (particularly the Arduino Mega 2560), this work demonstrates the feasibility of complex dispatch optimization in hydroelectric power plants (HPP). This approach enhances both electricity generation and water resource management while providing a sustainable and scalable alternative for future energy control systems.

Although HPP capacity nomenclature varies widely in the literature and between countries [17], there is a wide recognition that classification schemes must be adapted to reflect the specific characteristics and operational contexts under investigation [14]. From a capacity point of view, Reddy et al. [16] divide them as pico ($\leq$5KW), micro ($>$5 KW and $\leq$100 KW), mini ($>$100 KW and $\leq$2 MW), small ($>$2 MW and $\leq$25MW), and large ($>$25 MW) systems. Smaller power plants provide benefits such as lower construction costs, decentralization, and reduced environmental impact. When operating in isolation, these smaller plants have minimal effect on the grid; however, when thousands of them are deployed, it amplifies considerations of equipment cost and the need for distributed optimization. This work contributes to this spectrum of hydroelectric dispatch by demonstrating that the same optimization algorithm applied to large power plants on high-performance computers can also be effectively executed on resource-constrained platforms, such as those representative of *pico*-scale systems. This approach provides a cost-effective alternative for the micro-dispatch problem and establishes the foundation for developing a distributed and scalable dispatch system.

The remainder of this paper is organized as follows. Section 2 reviews the relevant literature on embedded optimization and dispatch in hydroelectric systems, with emphasis on heuristic approaches and controller implementations on low-cost hardware. Section 3 details the techniques used in this work, the optimization algorithm, and better contextualizes the hydroelectric dispatch problem. Section 4 presents the HPP dispatch simulation model and the optimization algorithm used to tune its parameters. Section 5 discusses the results, benchmarking computational feasibility and dispatch effectiveness relative to a high-performance computing platform. Section 6 concludes with insight into scalability, real-world applicability, and directions for future work in sustainable, decentralized hydroelectric dispatch solutions.

2 Related Work

The literature includes studies investigating population-based algorithms on microcontrollers, particularly ATMega, to demonstrate their viability for embedded optimization tasks. In [20], a variation of the *Differential Evolution* population algorithm was proposed, whose implementation on the Arduino Mega 2560 to control algorithm parameters and execute optimization routines, demonstrating the feasibility of performing simulations and practical experiments on resource-constrained hardware. Beyond these general approaches, several studies address specific applications. In [11], a *Finite Impulse Response* filter was implemented using the *Cuckoo Search* algorithm. The Arduino platform was used to generate input signals, control, and measure the outputs of the implemented digital filter. Similarly, [9] used the Arduino within a polymer-electrolyte fuel-cell monitoring system to enable real-time data acquisition and signal processing.

In the context of electrical systems, [19] presents an adaptive over-current protection system for microgrids, assisted by a look-up table (LUT). The objective is to increase the efficiency and reliability of microgrid operation by dynamically adjusting to changes in system parameters and operating conditions, in addition to improving fault detection and protection. In [15], a hybrid photovoltaic/wind system for controlling a microinverter connected to the electrical grid is described. The proposed algorithm adjusts the input voltage of the microinverter, based on the measurement of the voltage of the hybrid system, using an Arduino Mega to manage the operation of the system.

Population-based algorithms have also been widely applied to controller optimization in engineering domains. In [8], a *Proportional-Integral-Derivative* (PID) controller for Buck converters was designed using heuristic optimization techniques—specifically, the PSO and Artificial Bee Colony (ABC) algorithms, to enhance converter efficiency. The ATMega2560 microcontroller was used in both the development and testing phases of the controller.

Building on this foundation, the present work proposes the use of the Arduino Mega 2560 platform as a low-cost and accessible solution to implement heuristic optimization algorithms. In particular, PSO is adopted as the core control strategy, with the objective of maximizing hydroelectric power generation efficiency while minimizing the dependence on high-performance computational infrastructure. This approach emphasizes the potential of embedded systems in facilitating intelligent, resource-efficient control in energy applications. To the best of our knowledge, the algorithms and methodologies discussed in the literature have not yet been applied to the development of an optimization-based control system using Arduino microcontrollers specifically for HPPs. Applications for social good focus on using technology to address pressing environmental and societal challenges. Implementing an optimal dispatch system for HPPs using low-cost hardware contributes to this goal by promoting efficient energy use and reducing water waste. Furthermore, the simplicity of the embedded system reduces CO2 emissions by avoiding high-power computing, offering a sustainable, accessible solution for clean energy management. The results obtained in this study demonstrate that the Arduino Mega 2560 platform is capable of executing simulation routines that yield realistic dispatch strategies for GUs within time frames compatible with operational requirements. These findings highlight the viability of employing low-cost embedded systems for real-time optimization tasks in hydroelectric energy management.

3 The Hydroelectric Dispatch Optimization Problem

Fundamentally, optimization is a broad scientific discipline focused on maximizing or minimizing the value of a so-called objective function, subject to relevant constraints. Thus, objective functions serve as mathematical models that seek to represent a system on a scale, and this system will be optimized, adjusting system parameters to minimize or maximize these functions, within physical or technological limitations. Optimization problems are typically classified by scenario features such as linearity, variable types, permissible values, determinism, and the number of objectives involved.

Based on insights from prior research, it was hypothesized that integrating an optimization model aligned with a simulation model of the HPP would represent an effective strategy to solve the Hydroelectric Dispatch Problem. This section describes the optimization problem, in general terms, the optimization algorithm used, and the dispatch problem, which the optimization algorithm was applied to. Due to their straightforward operations and low memory footprint, such a solution would be well-suited for implementation on embedded platforms.

3.1 Particle Swarm Optimization

In this work, PSO was selected for the optimization task due to its demonstrated effectiveness in complex dispatch problems in hydroelectric GUs, as evidenced by [12]. PSO is particularly well-suited because it is a population-based metaheuristic algorithm that does not require gradient-based methods or differentiation techniques, making it less computationally intensive than other optimization algorithms. This characteristic is especially advantageous for embedded systems and resource-constrained applications, where computational efficiency is essential. Moreover, PSO has been widely recognized for efficiently exploring large, multidimensional search spaces and yielding near-optimal solutions, even in the presence of nonlinearities and constraints typical of real-world energy systems.

First introduced in [10], PSO is inspired by the social behavior of bird flocks searching for food or resting places. The method creates a swarm of particles, each representing a potential solution, dispersed throughout the search space. Each particle is characterized by a D-dimensional vector describing its velocity and position. As particles move through the search space, they adjust their trajectories based on their own experiences and those of their neighbors. Thus, the PSO algorithm seeks the optimal solution by adjusting the trajectory of the individuals in its population by updating the velocity and position of each particle according to Equations (1) and (2), respectively. All the parameters used in this work are defined in Table 1 (please refer to Sect. 4).

$$v_{k+1} = \omega v_k + c_1 r_1 (p_{best_k} - x_k) + c_2 r_2 (g_{best} - x_k), \tag{1}$$

$$x_{k+1} = x_k + v_k. \tag{2}$$

The population initialization should be uniform when the search space is well-defined, with upper and lower bounds used for random initialization as appropriate. Fitness evaluation relies on a predefined objective function, which dictates both the search space and its complexity, while the stopping criteria may be set in advance or determined by a specified number of iterations. Algorithm 1 outlines the standard PSO procedure.

Algorithm 1 PSO Operationalization

```
Initialize a population of k individuals with dimension D
Determine the values of the constants
Evaluate the fitness of each particle
while Stopping criterion not met do
    Draw random numbers for r1 and r2
    Determine the best global and individual positions
    Update the velocity of the particles
    Update the position of the particles
end while
End
```

3.2 Hydroelectric Dispatch Problem

Electric dispatch determines which GUs should be activated to meet the system demand, ensuring efficiency and safety. This process is embedded in the electric power system scheduling, which accounts for the predicted load, energy resources availability, reservoir levels, and the operational characteristics of GUs.

Further details on the scope and responsibilities of the ONS in Brazil are provided in [7]. This work focuses on power system operation planning, a stage preceding real-time operation that defines the detailed dispatch scheduling programming. Planning relies on the energy demand forecasts and on the availability of generation (at the power plants), with particular attention to hydroelectric plants whose output depends on reservoir levels. The process employs optimization models to meet energy demand at minimal cost while maintaining system safety. At this stage, plant operating conditions, GU capacities, and reserve requirements for stability are evaluated. Therefore, the objective is to maximize resource utilization and minimize costs, respecting physical and operational limitations. The production must comply with the operational limits of the GUs, expressed through the following constraints:

1. Power balance – the injected power into the grid must match (i.e., be approximately equal to) the dispatch demand within a tolerance of $\varepsilon = 0.5\%$;
2. Flow limits – the calculated water flow of each GU must remain within its minimum and maximum capacity;
3. Generation limits – the generated power (output of each GU) must remain within its minimum and maximum capacity (i.e., operational bounds);
4. Operation zone – each GU may operate in only one zone.

Given these constraints, the proposed solution comprises two primary contributions: the HPP simulation and the PSO algorithm. Both were designed to operate on either embedded hardware or a high-performance reference machine. The following section presents the methodology, including the simulation and optimisation models, along with key implementation considerations.

4 Methodology and Implementation Considerations

This section details the methodology for the embedded hydroelectric dispatch system, composed of three core components: the Hydraulic Loss Model, the Power Production Model, and the PSO algorithm. Together, these components form a hardware-integrated system that performs the optimisation process and links system inputs and outputs, as shown in Fig. 1.

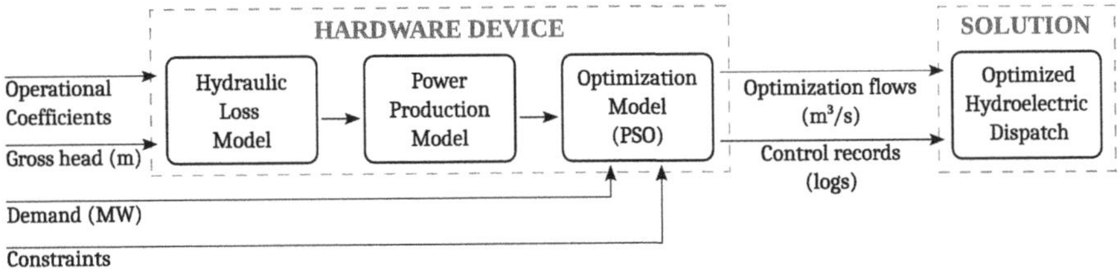

Fig. 1. Schematic of the Embedded PSO device for hydroelectric dispatch optimization, illustrating the interactions among models, input and output variables.

The Hydraulic Loss Model accounts for distributed losses caused by friction along the penstocks and local losses due to singularities such as bends and junctions. The Power Production Model describes the conversion of hydraulic energy into electrical energy by relating generated power to turbine discharge, net head, and turbine efficiency. Finally, the PSO algorithm integrates both models (the loss and power models) to adjust the turbine discharges of each GU, maximizing hydraulic productivity and meeting the required power demand, while the operational constraints ensure that discharge and power remain within physical limits and that each unit operates within a single active zone.

4.1 Hydroelectric Power Plant (HPP) Simulation Model

In HPPs, a GU can be mathematically modeled to represent the dynamic behavior of energy production. This behavior depends on the constructive and functional characteristics of the GU, primarily influenced by flow rate and net head. The model is expressed through a system of equations that incorporates the relevant mechanical and electrical phenomena. The following presents the mathematical model of a GU, as described in [13]. Equation (3) expresses power production in megawatts (MW). Table 1 summarizes the parameters and notation for the PSO algorithm and the hydroelectric power GU model.

$$
\begin{aligned}
ph_{jt} = g.[\rho_{0j} + \rho_{1j} hl_{jt} + \rho_{2j} q_{jt} + \rho_{3j} hl_{jt} q_{jt} \\
+ \rho_{4j} hl_{jt}^2 + \rho_{5j} q_{jt}^2].[Hb_{jt} - \Delta_{H_{jt}}].q_{jt}.
\end{aligned}
\tag{3}
$$

4.2 Optimization Model

The optimization model aims to maximize the electrical energy produced by the set of GUs in the HPP. It is a simplified adaptation of the model in [13], which estimates the plant's output given the available water volume and all operating GUs. The practical goal is to maximize this function, i.e., generate more power with reduced water flow, while meeting the energy demand established for each operating period. The decision variables correspond to the water discharge (q_{jt}) of each GU, gathered in the vector defined by Eq. 4:

$$
x = [q_{1t}, q_{2t} \dots q_{jt}]. \tag{4}
$$

The power demand (D) is the central parameter of the problem, representing the electrical power required at each time stage and ensuring the balance between load and generation.

$$
Maximize\ F(x) = \frac{\sum_{j=1}^{J(r)} ph_{jt}}{\sum_{j=1}^{J(r)} q_{jt}}, \tag{5}
$$

subject to:

Table 1. Model parameters and notation used for the PSO algorithm and hydroelectric power GU representation.

Parameter	*Description*
v_k	velocity of particle (k)
x_k	position of particle (k)
ω	inertia coefficient
p_{best_k}	best position known by the particle (k)
g_{best}	best position known among all particles
c_1	individual acceleration constant (cognitive coefficient)
c_2	global acceleration constant (social coefficient)
r_1 e r_2	random numbers drawn from the interval $[0, 1]$
hl_{jt}	net head at GU (j) at time stage (t)
Hb_{jt}	gross head at GU (j) at time stage (t)
$\Delta_{H_{jt}}$	total losses at GU (j) at time stage (t)
η_{jt}	efficiency of GU (j) at time stage (t) (%)
ph_{jt}	power generated by GU (j) at time stage (t)
g	acceleration due to gravity
$\rho_{0j} \dots \rho_{5j}$	operating coefficients of GU (j)
hl_{jt}	net head at GU (j) at time stage (t)
q_{jt} and q_{jt}	turbine flow rate at GU (j) at time stage (t)
Δ_{Hd}	pipe head losses (m)
Δ_{Hl}	head losses in bends (m)
$J(r)$	generating unit (j)
ε	tolerance (%)
Z_{jk}	operational zone (k) of GU (j)
p	penalty weigh

$$D(1-\varepsilon) \le \sum_{j=1}^{J(r)} ph_{jt} \le D(1+\varepsilon), \tag{6}$$

$$q_{jt}^{min} \le q_{jt} \le q_{jt}max, \tag{7}$$

$$ph_{jk}^{min} \sum_{k=1}^{\emptyset_j} Z_{jk} \le ph_{jt} \le ph_{jk}^{max} \sum_{k=1}^{\emptyset_j} Z_{jk}, \tag{8}$$

$$and\ Z_{jk} \in \{0,1\}, \sum_{k=1}^{\emptyset_j} Z_{jk} \le 1. \tag{9}$$

The objective function, Eq. 5, must incorporate specific characteristics of energy production through a set of constraints. The first constraint, Eq. 6, addresses operational demand, requiring the total power generated by all operating GUs (j *to* $J(r)$) to equal the dispatch demand (D) within a tolerance of $\pm 0.5\%$. The second constraint, Eq. 7, enforces flow limits, constraining water discharge (i.e., the calculated water flow) within each GU's minimum and maximum capacity. The third constraint, Eq. 8, restricts the generated power to the minimum and maximum capacity limits (i.e., operational bounds) of each GU. Lastly, the fourth constraint, Eq. 9, requires each GU to operate within a single operational zone, as defined by the binary variables Z_{jk}. To enforce these constrains, a penalty factor is included in the objective function, yielding the final fitness function expressed by the Eq. 10, where p represents the penalty weight applied to solutions that violate the demand satisfaction constraint, as follows:

$$f' = p \sum_{i}^{n} \max \left[0, \frac{ph_{jt}}{q_{jt}} \right]^2. \tag{10}$$

4.3 Implementation Considerations

A crucial aspect of this study is the selection of hardware to implement both the PSO algorithm and the HPP model. The decision prioritized commercial availability, low acquisition cost, and adequate memory and processing capabilities to meet project requirements. Given the restrictions, three platforms were selected for their technological maturity and market adoption, which ensure reliability and long-term availability, essential for project continuity and scalability. The platforms are detailed below.

- Arduino Mega 2560 (**Arduino2560**) [4]: equipped with an embedded microcontroller, the 8-bit ATMega2560 [1], which balances processing speed and energy consumption. It provides 256 KB flash memory, 8 KB RAM, 16 MHz clock, with firmware compiled using Arduino IDE 2.3.4. This platform is the primary focus of this research, as it represents the most resource-constrained scenario and serves as a reference for future microcontroller selection.
- Raspberry Pi 3 (**RPi3-BCM2837**) [3]: selected as an intermediate platform (slightly more expensive), offers greater computational power while maintaining energy efficiency. It features a 64-bit quad-core ARM Cortex-A53 (1.2 GHz), 1 GB LPDDR2 RAM, and runs Raspberry Pi OS with native C++ and mathematical libraries. Its larger memory and multicore processor enable execution of more complex and parallel models in future applications.
- Personal Computer (**Intel i7-10510U**) [2]: the reference machine is a high-performance personal computer used to execute the algorithm in its original development environment. It contains a 64-bit quad-core, octa-thread Intel Core i7-10510U CPU (1.8 GHz base, up to 4.9 GHz boost), 16 GB DDR4 RAM, and runs Windows 11. This system serves as the benchmark high-performance machine against which the embedded platforms are compared.

5 Experimental Analysis

Validation of the proposed methodology entails verifying the execution of the optimization algorithm, checking its consistency against the reference high-performance machine, and assessing the efficiency of final energy usage. To achieve this, three distinct analyses were conducted as detailed in this section. The first experiment validates the PSO implementation using a canonical optimization benchmark, the Rosenbrock function, enabling cross-platform comparison (Sect. 5.1). Subsequently, two HPP Dispatch scenarios were examined to reflect typical operational challenges encountered by the algorithm (Sect. 5.2). One scenario with hourly and the other with daily dispatch demand. Finally, the analysis concludes with comparative assessment of the energy consumption required to solve these problems across all platforms (Sect. 5.3).

5.1 Algorithm Validation and Hardware Performance Testing

Before integrating the optimization method into the HPP simulation, a preliminary experiment was carried out to assess the ability of the PSO algorithm to produce consistent results without risking harm to the hardware. For this purpose, the PSO method was used to optimize the Rosenbrock function, which is known as a benchmark due to its well-defined characteristics. This is a nonlinear multimodal function, presenting a global minimum located in a flat, narrow, parabolic-shaped valley. This approach allowed for a rigorous evaluation of the algorithm performance under controlled conditions.

The global minimum of the Rosenbrock function occurs at the point $(x, y) = (a, a^2)$, where $f(x, y) = 0$ at the specific point $(1, 1)$. The function is differentiable everywhere except at the origin, where continuity and the derivative are not defined. Its non-convex topology results from the characteristic narrow valley extending from the origin to the minimum, making optimal convergence challenging despite easy identification of the valley. This property tests the optimization algorithm's ability to finely tune parameters to traverse the valley towards the global minimum. The Rosenbrock function is defined by: $f(x, y) = (a - x)^2 + b(y - x^2)^2$, where $a = 1$ and $b = 100$.

The implementation was carried out in C++ and remains consistent across all platforms, with only minor modifications in the microcontroller code to display the output results via the serial communication channel. Using a common code base enabled a comparative analysis from a hardware performance perspective. The parameters used to configure the algorithm were as follows: population size (50), search interval ($[-5.0, 5.0]$), dimensionality (n), iterations (100), inertia factor ($w = 0.5$), cognitive coefficient ($c1 = 1.5$), social coefficient ($c2 = 1.5$), particle position range ($[-5.0, 5.0]$), and particle speed range ($[-1.0, 1.0]$). The objective function was evaluated through five tests configured for 2, 5, 10, 20, and 30 dimensions, respectively. Each configuration was executed 100 times, with 100 iterations per run.

Table 2 presents the average value of *gBest* for each platform and its average execution time across all runs. Preliminary tests confirmed the feasibility of using

Table 2. Average *gBest* and execution time (s) over 100 executions with a population of 50 particles. *D* denotes the problem dimensionality.

D	i7-10510U		RPi3-BCM2837		Arduino2560	
	gBest	time (s)	*gBest*	time (s)	*gBest*	time (s)
2	0.0000	0.1436	0.0000	1.4392	0.0000	399.4670
5	0.6990	0.3469	0.9483	3.7834	0.6952	1026.4720
10	11.5815	0.6569	6.7797	7.7698	6.5226	2082.3090
20	40.1886	1.2229	53.9271	16.3830	–	–
30	100.6960	1.7991	65.2183	23.4121	–	–

the Arduino2560 as a suitable hardware platform for this project. The device executed the PSO algorithm for problems of up to 10 dimensions but produced an 'insufficient memory' error for 20 and 30 dimensions. During preloading, global variables consumed 11,362 bytes of RAM, exceeding the platform limit of 8,192 bytes (138%). Thus, the program lacked sufficient space to allocate additional variables. Considering that the Hydroelectric Dispatch Problem studied has a dimensionality of 6, and the platform performed reliably at 10, the hardware meets the minimum requirements for this work.

The algorithm execution time results were as expected across platforms. The RPi3-BCM2837 CPU is about one order of magnitude slower than the high-performance CPU, whereas the Arduino2560 is roughly two orders slower than the RPi3-BCM2837. Comparing Intel i7-10510U to the RPi3-BCM2837, the former offers frequency boost, a clock up to 4.08× faster, higher RAM bandwidth (DDR4 vs. LPDDR2), and likely more optimized CPU instructions benefiting from greater energy availability. Comparing the RPi3-BCM2837 to the Arduino2560, the former provides a clock 75× faster and a more advanced memory architecture. Moreover, the Arduino2560 is an 8-bit CPU, so executing floating operations with 4-byte precision requires it to break operations into multiple instructions as it lacks a more advanced FPU. Overall, the observed performance differences are justifiable.

5.2 Dispatch Optimization in Hydroelectric Power Plants

This section discusses the application and validation of the optimization method in two typical HPP scenarios: hourly and daily dispatch. The hourly problem is a standard optimization task in hydroelectric operations, involving distribution of demand among the available GUs, keeping operational safety and resource requirements. In practice, this means determining the water volume allocated to each unit. From an optimization standpoint, the goal is to maximize energy production while minimizing water use and respecting operational constraints.

The operational parameters of each GU were determined by [13]: $\rho_0 = 0.1463$, $\rho_1 = 0.018076$, $\rho_2 = 0.0050502$, $\rho_3 = -0.000035254$, $\rho_4 = -0.00012337$, and $\rho_5 = -0.000014507$. To validate the correctness of the algorithms and their

Table 3. Optimization Results for the Hourly Dispatch Problem

Intel i7-10510U				
GU	$ph_{jt}(MW)$	$q_{jt}(m^3/s)$	$hl_{jt}(m)$	$\Delta H_{jt}(m)$
1	52.45717750	106.25004553	53.99872077	0.001279
2	53.37186550	108.08576130	53.99893217	0.001068
3	54.03337097	109.44565150	53.99890300	0.001097
4	53.59468733	108.56291327	53.99895887	0.001041
5	53.08615583	107.54837283	53.99897730	0.001023
6	53.45565783	108.27879847	53.99892607	0.001074
Total	319.998915	648.171543		
Difference	−0.001085	−6.878457		
RPi3-BCM2837				
GU	$ph_{jt}(MW)$	$q_{jt}(m^3/s)$	$hl_{jt}(m)$	$\Delta H_{jt}(m)$
1	52.45717750	106.25004553	53.99872077	0.001279
2	53.37186550	108.08576130	53.99893217	0.001068
3	54.03337097	109.44565150	53.99890300	0.001097
4	53.59468733	108.56291327	53.99895887	0.001041
5	53.08615583	107.54837283	53.99897730	0.001023
6	53.45565783	108.27879847	53.99892607	0.001074
Total	319.998915	648.171543		
Difference	−0.001085	−6.878457		
Arduino2560				
GU	$ph_{jt}(MW)$	$q_{jt}(m^3/s)$	$hl_{jt}(m)$	$\Delta H_{jt}(m)$
1	52.45717697	106.25004503	53.99872040	0.001280
2	53.37186497	108.08576070	53.99893157	0.001068
3	54.03337037	109.44565100	53.99890253	0.001097
4	53.59468690	108.56291270	53.99895850	0.001041
5	53.08615533	107.54837247	53.99897693	0.001023
6	53.45565743	108.27879803	53.99892553	0.001074
Total	319.998912	648.171540		
Difference	−0.001088	−6.878460		

portability, Table 3 consolidates the optimization results for each platform. Since all platforms use the same *Random Number Generator* (RNG) and initial seed, their execution and optimization results are expected to coincide.

The calculated net head values show minor energy losses in each unit, an expected effect of hydraulic and mechanical inefficiencies [13]. Overall, the optimization results are satisfactory, as the solution remains within acceptable operational limits. When comparing the Arduino2560 with the other platforms, deviations occur only on the order of $\sim 10^{-6}$ precision. This behavior is consistent with the absence of a floating-point unit (FPU) in its 8-bit processor, requiring arithmetic on 4-byte floating-point numbers to be decomposed into multiple steps and approximated.

The graphical behavior of the optimization outcomes for each platform is shown in Fig. 2, which complements the results in Table 3. The surface plots depict the relationship between Turbine Flow, GUs, and Power Generated, revealing smooth and continuous profiles.

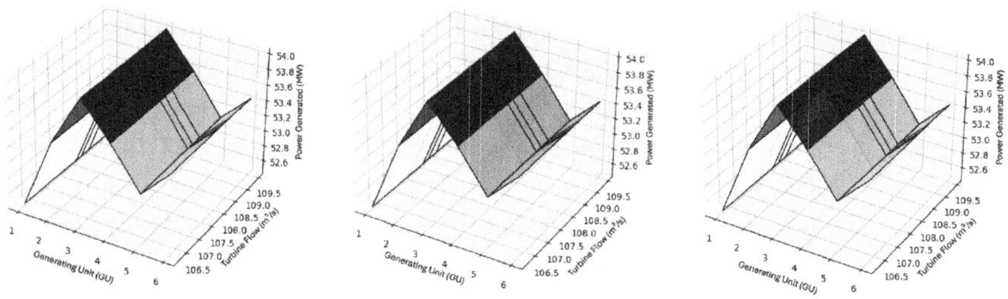

Arduino Mega 2560 | Raspberry Pi 3B | Intel Core i7

Fig. 2. Relationship between Turbine Flow, GUs, and Power Generated.

The results show that the power generation increases with turbine flow until stabilizing near 54 MW, reflecting consistent performance of the optimization process. The algorithm tends to allocate higher flow rates to the most efficient GUs, respecting the flow and power limits of each machine. This behavior is expected, since the model aims to maximize the ratio between generated power and turbine discharge, which naturally favors units with higher hydraulic efficiency. The nearly identical surface profiles highlight the reproducibility of the optimization process across heterogeneous hardware, which confirms that the proposed algorithm and model produce quality optimized solutions, independent of computational resources. To further validate the approach, a more realistic operational scenario was used to assess the suitability of the embedded platforms. In this scenario, the daily dispatch problem demands power changes throughout the day (every hour), which requires the algorithm to continuously compute new solutions The same initial seed and hourly demand values were applied across all platforms. After each iteration, the algorithm adjusted the output flow of each GU, meeting requirements and minimizing the use of water resources.

Table 4 reports the hourly dispatch results for all platforms under the Daily Hydroelectric Dispatch scenario. As expected, the RPi3-BCM2837 produced results identical to the reference machine, while the Arduino2560 showed only minor deviations around the 6th decimal place, are negligible in practical terms and did not affect the overall quality of the solutions. In all cases, generated power remained within the limits required by the Brazilian ONS throughout the 24-hour period, confirming not only the consistency and robustness of the model but also the reliability of embedded devices for dispatch optimization.

Table 4. Daily Hydroelectric Dispatch Optimization Results for Each Platform

Power Generation per Hour (per Platform)							
Hour	Demand	Intel i7-10510U		RPi3-BCM2837		Arduino2560	
	$p(MW)$	$ph_{jt}(MW)$	$q_{jt}(m^3/s)$	$ph_{jt}(MW)$	$q_{jt}(m^3/s)$	$ph_{jt}(MW)$	$q_{jt}(m^3/s)$
00	350	349.9909983	710.1814554	349.9909983	710.1814554	349.9909953	710.1814526
01	345	344.9949326	699.7043991	344.9949326	699.7043991	344.9949292	699.7043957
02	345	344.9938045	699.5519602	344.9938045	699.5519602	344.9938016	699.5519572
03	345	344.9969598	699.7333292	344.9969598	699.7333292	344.9969568	699.7333263
04	345	345.0010758	699.7073317	345.0010758	699.7073317	345.0010728	699.7073284
05	345	344.9966449	699.7877368	344.9966449	699.7877368	344.9966419	699.7877337
06	345	344.9961258	699.6649983	344.9961258	699.6649983	344.9961229	699.6649953
07	355	354.9983808	720.8961901	354.9983808	720.8961901	354.9983774	720.8961876
08	355	354.9980937	720.7240102	354.9980937	720.7240102	354.9980908	720.7240069
09	355	354.9971231	720.8452908	354.9971231	720.8452908	354.9971202	720.8452882
10	355	354.9907742	720.6955888	354.9907742	720.6955888	354.9907714	720.6955860
11	355	354.9934846	720.7836418	354.9934846	720.7836418	354.9934812	720.7836391
12	355	354.9993015	720.7060721	354.9993015	720.7060721	354.9992981	720.7060690
13	320	319.9943131	648.2310625	319.9943131	648.2310625	319.9943102	648.2310599
14	320	319.9978484	648.2489295	319.9978484	648.2489295	319.9978456	648.2489267
15	320	320.0009962	648.1553645	320.0009962	648.1553645	320.0009933	648.1553619
16	320	320.0018065	648.2949466	320.0018065	648.2949466	320.0018038	648.2949432
17	320	319.9991941	648.2946373	319.9991941	648.2946373	319.9991914	648.2946343
18	320	319.9970946	648.2212128	319.9970946	648.2212128	319.9970916	648.2212097
19	350	349.9969884	710.1432728	349.9969884	710.1432728	349.9969852	710.1432698
20	350	349.9881703	710.3264055	349.9881703	710.3264055	349.9881672	710.3264023
21	350	349.9954768	710.1488396	349.9954768	710.1488396	349.9954739	710.1488369
22	350	349.9968898	710.1269992	349.9968898	710.1269992	349.9968867	710.1269961
23	350	349.9951462	710.2431799	349.9951462	710.2431799	349.9951437	710.2431768
Total	8220	8219.911624	16673.41685	8219.911624	16673.41685	8219.911552	16673.41678

It is worth noting that the implementation strategy successfully demonstrated the ability to simulate the HPP and optimize its operations. Results from the embedded platforms were comparable to those of the reference machine, with the floating-point precision of the Arduino2560 remaining satisfactory. This confirms that, even with limited hardware resources, HPP operation can be embedded in a low-cost platform without compromising efficiency. Meanwhile, the RPi3-BCM2837 provided a more balanced solution, reproducing the reference machine's results while also reducing energy usage and cost.

5.3 Comparative Analysis of Energy Consumption

An important factor in selecting embedded platforms for production environments is their energy consumption during operation, which determines both project feasibility and environmental impact. Low-cost platforms such as the Arduino2560 and RPi3-BCM2837 offer advantages in efficiency (Performance/Watt) and accessibility compared to more power-hungry alternatives.

This section evaluates energy consumption across platforms during optimization and dispatch operations in two distinct scenarios. The first analysis estimates energy per unit of time, while the second measures execution time of the optimization algorithm. A USB power meter was used to record the electric current (I) and voltage (U), from which average power (P) was calculated using $P = U \cdot I$, where P is Power in watts (W), U is Voltage in volts (V), and I is the electric Current in amperes (A). Based on this methodology, the energy required to power the RPi3-BCM2837 was $U = 4.869\,\text{V}$, $I = 0.547\,\text{A}$ and $P = 2.663\,\text{W}$; and the energy required to power the Arduino2560 was $U = 5.194\text{V}$, $I = 0.071\,\text{A}$ and $P = 0.369\,\text{W}$, respectively.

The results indicate the Arduino2560 consumes about 7.2× less energy per unit of time than the RPi3-BCM2837. Thus, if both systems operated continuously for a full day, the Arduino2560 would require significantly less energy, contributing to the sustainability goals of this work. This difference reflects the substantial architectural gap between the platforms. Subsequently, the energy required per processing time is measured by multiplying the average energy consumption of each platform by the time needed to complete the task. This value represents the energetic cost of executing the algorithm once.

Table 5 summarizes the measured power consumption across the optimization problems considered in this study. The execution time difference between platforms was substantial. Nevertheless, since the system has ample time to optimize dispatch and reconfigure itself, both platforms were deemed adequate. The execution time, however, directly impacts the accumulated energy required by each platform. The most critical scenario was the Daily Dispatch, where the Arduino2560 required 3.38 h and the RPi3-BCM2837 completed the task in only 0.0123 h. This corresponded to 1.2466 Wh for the Arduino2560 versus 0.0328 Wh for the RPi3, about 38× more energy to complete the optimization.

In large scale, or cloud scenarios, such as backend servers processing thousands of requests per second for multiple HPPs, optimizing response time and absolute energy consumption becomes essential. In an edge scenario, where an embedded platform calculates the dispatch problem only a few times per day while remaining powered on, it is reasonable to accept longer execution times as the total energy usage remains low. Considering these conditions, the Arduino2560 platform offers advantages over the RPi3, providing a sustainable, low-cost alternative, and still enabling decentralized processing at the edge.

Table 5. Execution Time and Energy Consumption of Tasks

Task	RPi3-BCM2837		Arduino2560	
	Time $[h]$	Energy $[Wh]$	Time $[h]$	Energy $[Wh]$
Rosenbrock 2D	0.000400	0.001065	0.110963	0.040920
Rosenbrock 5D	0.001051	0.002799	0.285131	0.105149
Rosenbrock 10D	0.002158	0.005748	0.578419	0.213306
Rosenbrock 20D	0.004551	0.012120	–	–
Rosenbrock 30D	0.006503	0.017321	–	–
Hourly Dispatch	0.001082	0.002881	0.139756	0.051539
Daily Dispatch	0.012322	0.032817	3.380444	1.246620

6 Conclusion

Preliminary tests revealed that high-dimensional problems challenge all platforms in processing performance. Yet, the feasibility of implementing PSO on embedded platforms such as the Arduino Mega 2560 and Raspberry Pi 3 was successfully demonstrated. Although heuristic-based mathematical models typically demand high memory, satisfactory results were achieved across all platforms in terms of efficient flow rates, even when a constrained and low-cost hardware was used. These findings confirm that high-cost hardware is not strictly necessary to ensure the essential functionality of the system. More affordable solutions can be effective for resource optimization, cost reduction, and lowering the energy demanded by the system.

Both energy-efficient platforms demonstrated potential for different deployment models. They could support centralized dispatch control in large HPPs or distributed dispatch systems involving thousands of pico plants operating in parallel (or in cooperation). The Arduino Mega 2560 is economically accessible compared to traditional computers, offering low energy consumption and extending applicability to small, mini, micro, and pico plants. The Raspberry Pi 3, which is also economically accessible and still energy efficient compared to the reference machine, provides greater computational power and flexibility, making it suitable for scenarios requiring more connections or concurrent tasks.

In conclusion, this work demonstrates that embedded preliminary planning with well-defined dispatch conditions can enhance the efficiency of hydroelectric power generation. With an approach that considers sustainability, decentralization, and efficiency, the proposed solution shows that the dispatch problem can be addressed in alignment with both economic and environmental goals.

Acknowledgments. This work was partially funded by the Brazilian research agencies: CNPq-Conselho Nacional de Desenvolvimento Científico e Tecnológico (Grant nb. 403964/2023-7), FAPERJ - Fundação Carlos Chagas Filho de Amparo à Pesquisa do Estado do Rio de Janeiro (Grants nb. E-26/210.057/2024, E-26/210.549/2024, E-26/210.101/2025), CAPES-Coordenação de Aperfeiçoamento de Pessoal de Nível Superior (Grant nb. 23038.006308/2021-70), and UFRJ ALV Grant. The authors thank IC-UFRJ and Aston University for the infrastructure used to conduct this work.

References

1. ATmega2560 Microcontroller. https://www.microchip.com/en-us/product/atmega2560. Accessed 20 Aug 2025
2. Specification of the Intel i7-10510U CPU. https://www.intel.com/content/www/us/en/products/sku/196449/intel-core-i710510u-processor-8m-cache-up-to-4-90-ghz/specifications.html. Accessed 20 Aug 2025
3. Specification of the Raspberry Pi 3 Model B. https://www.raspberrypi.com/products/raspberry-pi-3-model-b/. Accessed 20 Aug 2025
4. The Arduino Mega 2560: Technical Specifications and Features. https://www.arduino.cc/en/Main/ArduinoBoardMega2560. Accessed 26 Feb 2025
5. CNN Brasil: Energy demand will increase by 25% by 2034, says government (2024). https://www.cnnbrasil.com.br/economia/macroeconomia/demanda-por-energia-aumentara-25-ate-2034-diz-governo/. Aaccessed 15 Mar 2025
6. Gov.br: Energy demand reaches new record, and the electrical system maintains stability (2025). https://www.gov.br/mme/pt-br/assuntos/noticias/demanda-de-energia-bate-novo-recorde-e-sistema-eletrico-mantem-estabilidade. Aaccessed 15 Mar 2025
7. ONS Activities (2025). https://www.ons.org.br/paginas/sobre-o-ons/atuacao. Aaccessed 15 Mar 2025
8. Ahmed, M.N., Mohammed, I.K., Younis, A.T.: Design and implementation of PSO/ABC tunned PID controller for buck converters. Periodicals Eng. Nat. Sci. (PEN) **9**(4), 643–656 (2021). https://doi.org/10.21533/PEN.V9I4.2411
9. Calderón, A.J., González, I., Calderón, M., Segura, F., Andújar, J.M.: A new, scalable and low cost multi-channel monitoring system for polymer electrolyte fuel cells. Sensors **16**(3), 349 (2016). https://doi.org/10.3390/s16030349
10. Kennedy, J., Eberhart, R.: Particle swarm optimization. In: Proceedings of ICNN 1995 - International Conference on Neural Networks, vol. 4, pp. 1942–1948. IEEE (1995). https://doi.org/10.1109/ICNN.1995.488968
11. Kumar, A., Agrawal, N., Sharma, I.: Design of finite impulse response filter with controlled ripple using cuckoo search algorithm. In: Chaudhuri, B.B., Nakagawa, M., Khanna, P., Kumar, S. (eds.) Proceedings of 3rd International Conference on Computer Vision and Image Processing. AISC, vol. 1024, pp. 471–482. Springer, Singapore (2020). https://doi.org/10.1007/978-981-32-9291-8_37
12. Liu, S., Li, X.: Hydroelectric unit commitment by enhanced PSO. In: 2010 International Conference on E-Product E-Service and E-Entertainment, pp. 1–4. IEEE (2010), https://doi.org/10.1109/ICEEE.2010.5661259
13. Marcelino, C.G., Camacho-Gómez, C., Jiménez-Fernández, S., Salcedo-Sanz, S.: Optimal generation scheduling in hydro-power plants with the coral reefs optimization algorithm. Energies **14**(9), 2443 (2021). https://doi.org/10.3390/en14092443
14. Nababan, S., Muljadi, E., Blaabjerg, F.: An overview of power topologies for micro-hydro turbines. In: 2012 3rd IEEE International Symposium on Power Electronics for Distributed Generation Systems (PEDG), pp. 737–744. IEEE (2012). https://doi.org/10.1109/PEDG.2012.6254084

15. Özçelik, M.A.: A micro hybrid wind-PV based on grid energy system with enhanced efficiency. Eur. J. Tech. (EJT) **7**(2), 109–118 (2017). https://dergipark.org.tr/en/pub/ejt/issue/34562/395115
16. Reddy, V.R., Uitto, J.I., Frans, D.R., Matin, N.: Achieving global environmental benefits through local development of clean energy? The case of small hilly hydel in India. Energy Policy **34**(18), 4069–4080 (2006). https://doi.org/10.1016/j.enpol.2005.09.026
17. Sachdev, H.S., Akella, A.K., Kumar, N.: Analysis and evaluation of small hydropower plants: a bibliographical survey. Renew. Sustain. Energy Rev. **51**(1018), 1013–1022 (2015). https://doi.org/10.1016/j.rser.2015.06.065
18. Sharifi, M.R., Akbarifard, S., Madadi, M.R., Qaderi, K., Akbarifard, H.: Optimization of hydropower energy generation by 14 robust evolutionary algorithms. Sci. Rep. **12**(1), 7739 (2022). https://doi.org/10.1038/s41598-022-11915-0
19. Swathika, O.G.: LUT assisted adaptive overcurrent protection of reconfigurable microgrids. Int. J. Smart Grid-ijSmartGrid **2**(1), 13–26 (2018). https://doi.org/10.20508/IJSMARTGRID.V2I1.6.G7
20. Tiwari, P., Mishra, V.N., Parouha, R.P.: Enhancing global optimization for sustainable development using modified differential evolution. In: Whig, P., Silva, N., Elngar, A.A., Aneja, N., Sharma, P. (eds) ICSD 2023. CCIS, vol. 1939, pp. 307–318. Springer, Cham (2023). https://doi.org/10.1007/978-3-031-47055-4_26

On the Relationship Between Neural Gradients and Model Reasoning

Jéssica Richards[1](✉), Carlos Eduardo Pedreira[1], Elizabeth Fialho Wanner[2], and Carolina Gil Marcelino[3]

[1] Systems and Computing Department, Federal University of Rio de Janeiro (UFRJ), Rio de Janeiro, Brazil
{nascj,pedreira}@cos.ufrj.br

[2] Aston Centre for Artificial Intelligence Research and Application, Aston University, Birmingham B4 7ET, UK
e.wanner1@aston.ac.uk

[3] Institute of Computing, Federal University of Rio de Janeiro (UFRJ), Rio de Janeiro, Brazil
carolina@ic.ufrj.br

Abstract. As machine learning increasingly shapes decisions that directly impact people's lives, the demand for transparency and accountability has grown. Explainable Artificial Intelligence (XAI) has emerged as a field dedicated to making the reasoning of autonomous decision systems clearer and more interpretable. Among the many approaches to XAI, gradient-based explanations use a model's internal gradients to highlight feature importance. In this work, we investigate whether a model's gradients reveal consistent patterns that reflect its reasoning process. To keep the problem tractable, given the exponential growth in neural network dimensionality and corresponding gradients, we conducted our experiments using a Multilayer Perceptron as a controlled, toy example. For statistical analysis, we applied the Mantel and Energy tests. Our results indicate that gradient patterns emerge as intrinsic properties of the model's architecture and the dataset on which it is trained.

Keywords: Explainable Artificial Intelligence · Gradients · Multilayer Perceptron

1 Introduction

Decisions made by autonomous and intelligent systems are increasingly shaping the lives of the general population, driven by the growing adoption of Artificial Intelligence (AI). The need for understanding such decisions becomes even more critical in contexts involving power imbalances, for example, when the state employs AI models for diagnosis and treatment planning in public healthcare [1].

There is growing evidence that Machine Learning (ML) can amplify existing inequalities [2], and as new social groups emerge, such unfair treatment

L. Lestingi et al. (Eds.): DataMod 2025, LNCS 16421, pp. 119–126, 2026.
https://doi.org/10.1007/978-3-032-25552-5_8

may result in even greater discriminatory impacts [3]. The industrialization and widespread use of arbitrary decisions pose significant risks to individual rights, particularly in sensitive domains such as the legal system. When an autonomous system makes decisions that directly affect an individual's life, the need for accountability becomes undeniable. Enhancing transparency into the internal workings of these systems offers a potential path toward ensuring such accountability [4,5].

Systems that humans cannot interpret or understand are, by definition, incomprehensible. Explainable Artificial Intelligence (XAI) is a research field dedicated to making such systems more transparent and interpretable [6]. As the adoption of AI expands, transparency in autonomous decision-making becomes increasingly essential, not only to foster trust, but also to support industry self-regulation [7].

Understanding how a machine reasons can help identify when an autonomous or intelligent system fails [8], or assist in debugging issues in computer vision models. Gradient-based explanation methods, such as Integrated Gradients [9], employ gradient information to associate input features with model outputs, thereby revealing aspects of the model's decision-making process. Building on this foundation, our work investigates whether the gradients themselves exhibit patterns that reflect the model's internal reasoning. By analysing these patterns, our experiments offer a new perspective on knowledge discovery and data modelling within autonomous systems. The remainder of this paper is organised as follows: Sect. 2 reviews related work, Sect. 3 describes the experimental setup, Sect. 4 presents the results, and Sect. 5 concludes the paper.

2 Context in Literature

Algorithms such as backpropagation and stochastic gradient descent update a model's weights using the gradient of the loss function between predicted and expected outcomes [10]. These methods have been fundamental to advancing the usability and accuracy of modern neural networks, enabling them to approximate complex functions effectively. Beyond training, the gradients themselves—representing the network's internal information can be exploited to assess the importance of input features relative to the output.

In the context of XAI, gradient-based explanations are widely used to estimate feature importance by analysing the partial derivatives of the output with respect to each input dimension [11]. Some approaches, such as Integrated Gradients by Sundararajan et al. [9], combine input features with model gradients to derive feature attributions. Others, like Grad-CAM [12], use gradient information from convolutional layers to generate saliency maps that highlight the most relevant regions of an image.

Visual analyses, such as those presented in FullGrad [13], indicate that gradient-based methods frequently identify comparable regions of importance across images, despite relying on different mathematical principles. From the end-user's perspective, the primary differences among these approaches typically concern two aspects: the manner in which results are visualised and the fidelity of the resulting saliency maps. While prior studies have demonstrated that gradients can highlight features influential to a model's output, this work seeks to address the following question: do gradients encode consistent patterns that reflect the model's underlying reasoning process?

3 Experimental Design

This work investigates whether analysing gradients can uncover structural differences or clustering patterns within a model. To guide our experiments, we formulated the following research questions:

- **Q1:** In a trained model, do gradients naturally cluster according to the predicted class?
- **Q2:** Are gradients computed on the test set internally consistent?
- **Q3:** Are gradients computed on the training set internally consistent?
- **Q4:** Do the gradient distributions from the training and test sets (per predicted class) exhibit similarity or divergence?

To address these research questions, we designed a controlled toy experiment focused on image classification using the MNIST dataset [14]. The dataset consists of 70,000 grayscale images of handwritten digits, each sized 28×28 pixels (784 input dimensions). We implemented a simple two-layer neural network with 784 input neurons, 50 hidden neurons, and 10 output neurons. The hidden layer employed ReLU activation [16], while the output layer used softmax activation. The model was trained for 5 epochs.

We used the TensorFlow library [17] to train the model and compute gradients with respect to the predicted class. For statistical analysis, the test set contains approximately 1,400 images per class. However, due to the curse of dimensionality, some hypothesis tests could not be reliably applied given the available sample size. Specifically, gradients of the output with respect to input pixels lie in a high-dimensional space $\mathbb{R}^{784}$, whereas gradients with respect to the hidden layer parameters lie in a lower-dimensional space $\mathbb{R}^{50}$. To ensure the robustness of our statistical tests, we restricted our analysis to the lower-dimensional gradients, which we consider a proxy for the model's internal reasoning.

All experiments were implemented in Python 3.12. The model was built and trained using TensorFlow 2.19. For statistical analysis, we employed the Hyppo library [15] to perform the Energy test and scikit-bio [19] for the Mantel test. The dataset was partitioned into 80% training (56,000 images) and 2% testing (14,000 images). To assess robustness, we trained 50 independent models, each initialized with a unique random seed ranging from 0 to 49. These seeds were consistently applied across all libraries requiring random initialization.

4 Results

To investigate whether gradients reveal consistent patterns, we organized the computed gradients into 1,000 groups, each represented as a tuple *(label, input set, model)*. The *label* corresponds to the model's predicted class for an image, the *input set* indicates whether the image belongs to the training or test set, and *model* identifies the trained model. This grouping allows us to examine patterns within each group and assess their consistency across different input sets, aiming to uncover recurring structures in the model's reasoning.

We first evaluated the internal consistency of gradients within the test set (*Q2*). For this statistical analysis, we employed the Energy Test, which determines whether two samples originate from the same underlying distribution. This non-parametric, distance-based method assesses similarity between samples by analysing how far apart their data points are, on average, within the multidimensional feature space. Unlike parametric tests, it does not assume normality and can be effectively applied to high-dimensional data. These properties make the Energy Test particularly suitable for our objective of determining whether gradient samples are drawn from the same distribution [18].

As the Energy Test operates on two distributions, we randomly partitioned each group into two equally sized subsets and applied the test to evaluate their statistical similarity. For 100 repetitions, the null hypothesis was rejected in only one case, while in the remaining splits it was not rejected. Many splits returned a p-value of 1.0, likely due to the relatively small sample size per subset (506 samples) compared to the 50-dimensional gradient space. These results, while inconclusive, suggested that gradients within the same group might originate from the same distribution.

Next, we examined whether gradients from different predicted classes follow the same distribution while keeping the input set and model constant. We applied the Energy test to all pairwise combinations among the 10 labels, excluding self-comparisons, yielding 45 comparisons per model. This procedure was repeated across all 50 trained models. In every comparison, the null hypothesis was strongly rejected, indicating that gradients from different predicted classes follow distinct distributions. These findings reinforce the notion that gradients within the same group are highly likely drawn from the same distribution.

To further evaluate consistency across input sets, we compared gradients between the training and test sets. For each group, we randomly sampled a number of gradients equal to the size of the smaller group before applying the Energy test. Table 1 summarizes these results. The column *Input Set* indicates which sets were compared: "training" and "testing" for within-set comparisons, and "training-testing" for across-set comparisons. The column *% of Tests with No Significant Difference* reports the proportion of comparisons where the null hypothesis was not rejected, further highlighting the internal consistency of gradients within groups.

Although the null hypothesis of the Energy Test states that two samples are drawn from the same underlying distribution, the fact that it was not rejected for the majority of random splits provides strong evidence that gradients within the same predicted class follow a similar distribution. Conversely, gradients belonging to different classes exhibit distinct distributions, thereby supporting our conclusions for questions (Q2)–(Q4).

Table 1. comparisons between gradients and it's results

input set	% of Tests with No Significant Difference
testing set	0.936
training set	0.956
testing-training set	0.968

The results in Table 1 address questions *Q2*, *Q3*, and *Q4*, leaving *Q1*: Do gradients exhibit discernible patterns across predicted classes?

For addressing (Q1), we computed correlation matrices to analyse the relationships among gradients produced by each model for a given input set. Each matrix corresponds to a specific(*model, input set*) pair and captures the pairwise correlations between gradients grouped by their predicted class. Gradients were sampled per class, and correlations were calculated across all pairs within these groups. Figure 1 presents the resulting correlation matrix for the test set, constructed using 200 gradients per class. Classes are arranged in ascending order from 0 to 9.

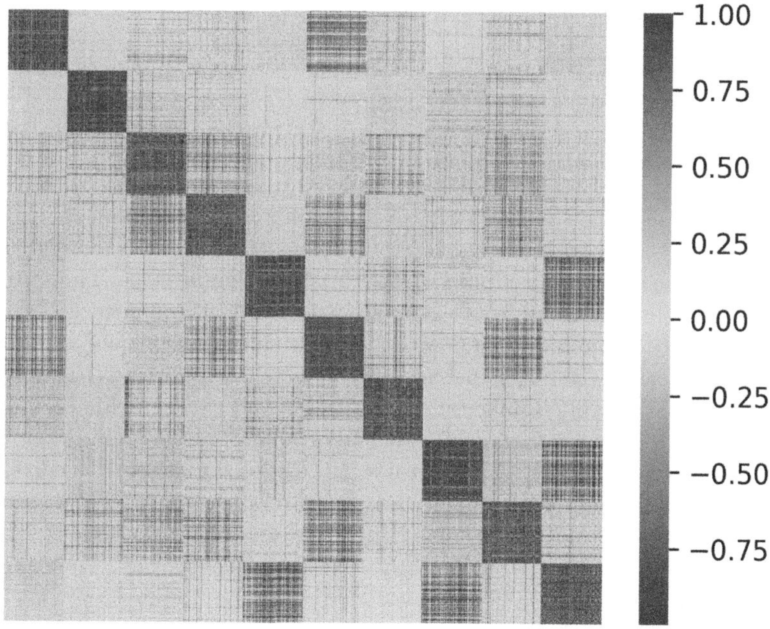

Fig. 1. Correlation matrix of gradients from the test set for a single trained model. Each block shows the pairwise correlation between gradients grouped by their predicted class (0–9).

As shown in Fig. 1, gradients from the same predicted class exhibit high correlation, while gradients from different classes show low correlation. This provides visual evidence that gradients encode information related to the model's final decisions.

Next, we investigated whether this characteristic is preserved when using the same model across different input sets. Specifically, we compared correlation matrices computed from the training and test sets. The goal is to assess whether the model maintains consistent decision patterns when dealing with training data, where gradients are adjusted during learning, versus test data, where the model has no prior exposure beyond the training set.

To assess whether the distinct separation of gradients is preserved across different input sets, we employed the Mantel test for statistical analysis. The Mantel test quantifies the correlation between two matrices representing either distances or similarities across samples. Specifically, it evaluates the correlation of corresponding elements between the matrices and compares this observed correlation against a distribution obtained through permutation, testing whether the observed relationship is stronger than expected by chance [20].

This approach is particularly suitable for our task, as it determines whether the structural relationships among gradients are consistent across input sets, while accommodating high-dimensional data and relaxing assumptions of normality. The Mantel test formulates the following hypotheses:

- Null hypothesis (H_0): The similarity between correlation matrices arises from random chance, indicating no true structural consistency.
- Alternative hypothesis (H_1): There exists a significant relationship between the matrices that is not attributable to random chance.

Using a significance threshold of 0.05, we computed correlation matrices for each input set of all 50 trained models, resulting in 100 matrices. Pairwise Mantel tests across these matrices produced 4,950 statistical comparisons. This extensive set of comparisons was necessary to evaluate whether decision patterns were consistent within the same model and across models sharing the same architecture and task. In all cases, the null hypothesis was rejected, supporting the conclusion that the matrices exhibit significant similarity beyond random chance.

These results suggest that, while specific gradient values may differ across models, the structural patterns of gradients—as captured by the correlation matrices—are consistent for a given task and architecture. This indicates the presence of a shared, underlying "reasoning" pattern within the model.

5 Final Remarks

In this work, we develop a proof-of-concept framework to investigate whether neural network gradients exhibit structural patterns that reflect the underlying reasoning of the model. Using a controlled experiment, we applied both the Energy and Mantel tests to assess the internal consistency of gradients within and across predicted classes, input sets, and trained models. Our analysis shows that gradients within the same predicted class are highly consistent, while gradients from different classes follow distinct distributions. Furthermore, correlation analyses and Mantel tests reveal that the structural patterns of gradients are preserved across training and test sets, indicating that the model applies consistent decision rules for a given task and architecture. These results indicate that gradient information extends beyond feature attribution, encoding meaningful insights into the model's decision-making process. In particular, gradients reveal internal consistency, reasoning stability, and cross-model invariances—properties that are crucial for assessing whether different models, or the same model under distribution shifts, rely on consistent decision mechanisms.

These findings suggest that a model's internal representations have the potential to serve as a powerful tool for knowledge discovery, as the observed patterns may provide insights into the decision-making rules of a black-box model. In future work, we plan to investigate whether this phenomenon persists in larger, more complex models and across different tasks. A key challenge will be identifying datasets with sufficient sample sizes to accommodate the high dimensionality of the problem. Additionally, we aim to examine whether these patterns emerge during early stages of training and to develop methods for integrating gradient information comprehensively, thereby providing a more complete explanation of the model's internal decision logic.

Acknowledgments. This work was partially funded by the Brazilian research agencies: CNPq (Grant Number 403964/2023-7), FAPERJ - Fundação Carlos Chagas Filho de Amparo à Pesquisa do Estado do Rio de Janeiro (Grant Numbers E-26/210.057/2024, E-26/210.549/2024, E-26/210.101/2025), CAPES (Research founds Grant Number - 23038.006308/2021-70), FAPEMIG and UFRJ ALV Grant. The authors thank PESC-UFRJ, IC-UFRJ, and Aston University for the infrastructure used to conduct this work.

References

1. Ploug, T., Holm, S.: Right to contest AI diagnostics. In: Lidströmer, N., Ashrafian, H. (eds.) Artificial Intelligence in Medicine, pp. 227–238. Springer, Cham (2022). https://doi.org/10.1007/978-3-030-64573-1_267
2. Sikstrom, L., Maslej, M.M., Hui, K., Findlay, Z., Buchman, D.Z., Hill, S.L.: Conceptualising fairness: three pillars for medical algorithms and health equity. BMJ Health Care Inform. **29**(1), e100459 (2022). https://doi.org/10.1136/bmjhci-2021-100459
3. Ott, T., Dabrock, P.: Transparent human - (non-) transparent technology? The Janus-faced call for transparency in AI-based health care technologies. Front. Genet 13, (2022)
4. Barclay, I., Taylor, H., Preece, A., Taylor, I., Verma, D., Mel, G.: A framework for fostering transparency in shared artificial intelligence models by increasing visibility of contributions (2021). arXiv preprint arXiv:2103.03610. https://doi.org/10.48550/arXiv.2103.03610

5. Adamson, G.: Can we use non-transparent artificial intelligence technologies for legal purposes? In: Proceedings of the 2020 IEEE International Symposium on Technology and Society (ISTAS), pp. 43–52. IEEE (2020). https://doi.org/10.1109/ISTAS50296.2020.9462204
6. Verhagen, R.S., Neerincx, M.A., Tielman, M.L.: A two-dimensional explanation framework to classify AI as incomprehensible, interpretable, or understandable. In: Calvaresi, D., Najjar, A., Winikoff, M., Främling, K. (eds.) EXTRAAMAS 2021. LNCS (LNAI), vol. 12688, pp. 119–138. Springer, Cham (2021). https://doi.org/10.1007/978-3-030-82017-6_8
7. Rivas, P.: AI orthopraxy: towards a framework that promotes fairness. In: Proceedings of the 2020 IEEE International Symposium on Technology and Society (ISTAS), pp. 80–84. IEEE (2020). https://doi.org/10.1109/ISTAS50296.2020.9462167
8. Winfield, A., et al.: IEEE P7001: a proposed standard on transparency. Front. Robot. AI **8**, Article 665729 (2021). https://doi.org/10.3389/frobt.2021.665729
9. Mukund S., Ankur T., and Qiqi Y.: Axiomatic attribution for deep networks. In: Proceedings of the 34th International Conference on Machine Learning (ICML 2017), vol. 70, pp. 3319–3328. JMLR.org (2017). https://doi.org/10.5555/3305890.3306024
10. Bishop, C.M.: Pattern Recognition and Machine Learning. Springer, New York (2006)
11. Haiyan, Z., et al.: Explainability for large language models: a survey. ACM Trans. Intell. Syst. Technol. **15**, 2–40 (2024). https://doi.org/10.1145/3639372
12. Selvaraju, R.R., Cogswell, M., Das, A., Vedantam, R., Parikh, D., Batra, D.: Grad-CAM: visual explanations from deep networks via gradient-based localization. In: 2017 IEEE International Conference on Computer Vision (ICCV), pp. 618–626. IEEE (2017). https://doi.org/10.1109/ICCV.2017.74
13. Srinivas, S., Fleuret, F.: Full-gradient representation for neural network visualization. In: Proceedings of the 33rd International Conference on Neural Information Processing Systems, pp. 4124–4133. Curran Associates Inc, Red Hook (2019)
14. LeCun, Y., Bottou, L., Bengio, Y., Haffner, P.: Gradient-based learning applied to document recognition [MNIST Database of Handwritten Digits]. IEEE (1998)
15. Panda, S.: hyppo: a multivariate hypothesis testing python package, (2019)
16. Nair, V., Hinton, G.E.: Rectified linear units improve restricted Boltzmann machines. In: Fürnkranz, J., Joachims, T. (eds.) ICML 2010. LNCS, vol. 632, pp. 807–814. Omnipress (2010)
17. Abadi, M.: TensorFlow: Large-scale machine learning on heterogeneous systems. Software available from tensorflow.org, (2015)
18. Barter, W., Burr, C., Parkes, C.: Calculating p-values and their significances with the Energy Test for large datasets. J. Instrum. **13**(04), P04011–P04011 (2018)
19. The scikit-bio development team: scikit-bio: a bioinformatics library for data scientists, students, and developers. Version 0.5.5 (2020). http://scikit-bio.org
20. Manly, B.F. J.: Randomization, Bootstrap and Monte Carlo Methods in Biology, Chapman and Hall/CRC (2007). https://doi.org/10.1201/9781315273075. 3rd edn

Taylor's DAgger: Verified Integration for Efficient Imitation-Learning of an MPC

Stijn Bellis, Kasper Engelen, Thomas Gueutal, Ramesh Krishnamurthy(✉), and Guillermo A. Pérez

University of Antwerp – Flanders Make, Antwerp, Belgium
stijn.bellis@uantwerpen.be, ramesh.rnsit@gmail.com

Abstract. We address the challenge of enabling formal verification of Model Predictive Control (MPC) by learning a surrogate in the form of a neural network (NN). While this approach simplifies questions of latency and allows the application of NN-verification techniques, it crucially relies on effectively training the NN to imitate the MPC, a process known as imitation learning. Recognizing the difficulties in learning with nonholonomic constraints and unstable dynamics, we build upon the Dataset Aggregation (DAgger) approach, which iteratively collects data by querying the expert (MPC) on states reached by the learned model. Our main contribution is our proposal to use verified integration methods, specifically Taylor models, to obtain a conservative overapproximation of reachable states in a dynamical system. This allows for the generation of more data points per simulation along an NN-controlled trajectory and facilitates the consideration of small perturbations to control actions after retraining. Our hypothesis is that these extensions will lead to a more efficient learning of the MPC surrogate, which is empirically evaluated on an autonomous truck-with-trailer navigation problem.

Keywords: Model predictive control · Imitation learning

1 Introduction

Model predictive control (MPC) is an optimal control technique. That is, it can be used to find a control for a dynamical system that minimizes some cost function and satisfies constraints on the state variables. One of the characteristic properties of MPC is that it relies on a model of the system, unrolled up to a finite horizon, to determine control values for the next timestep. Many academic and commercial MPC solvers are being applied to a plethora of real-world problems.

Some questions regarding the formal guarantees of using MPC are immediate:

1. How *far from* an *optimal* (minimal-cost) solution is the MPC?
2. How *safe* are trajectories consistent with the MPC?

This work was supported by the "DIRAC" Flanders Make and "SynthEx" (G0AH524N) FWO projects.

L. Lestingi et al. (Eds.): DataMod 2025, LNCS 16421, pp. 127–144, 2026.
https://doi.org/10.1007/978-3-032-25552-5_9

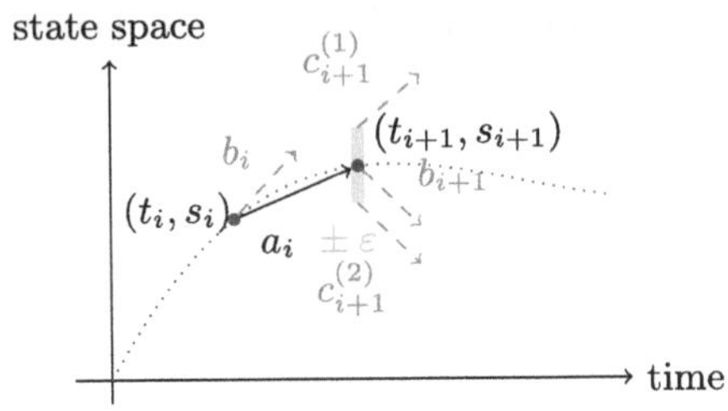

Fig. 1. Illustration of overapproximated successor states used for Taylor-augmented DAgger.

3. What is its worst-case *latency* (the time before a control value is chosen)?

Formal verification of MPC-controlled dynamical systems is hard to automate because MPC solves instances of mathematical programming problems in an online fashion. This is particularly the case when the dynamics or cost functions are not linear. Some works have proposed to circumvent this by learning a surrogate of the MPC in the form of a (deep) neural network (NN) [2,14]. Indeed, the safety and near-optimality questions can be approached using recent tools and techniques to analyze NN-controlled dynamical systems [9,13,17]. The crucial step enabling this framework is that of training a NN to imitate the MPC well enough, a task known as *imitation learning.*

Assuming the dynamical system is known and given in the form of a system of ordinary differential equations, one can generate training data by using numerical integration methods and querying the MPC controller to guide the learning of a neural network (NN) policy. In [16], the authors argue that following the (learned) model and then querying an expert (MPC or otherwise) to collect data about "what the expert would do" in situations reached by the surrogate leads to more efficient learning than collecting a data set based solely on simulations following the expert. This approach is known as Data Set Aggregation (DAgger).

Unfortunately, learning in the presence of *nonholonomic constraints* (i.e., constraints over velocity, angles, or other quantities that are generally history-dependent, instead of just positions in space-time) is known to be particularly hard. Lagrangian neural networks and their extensions for nonholonomic constraints can mitigate this problem [10]. An arguably bigger problem is that DAgger does not account for *unstable dynamics* where a small change in control actions produces a vastly different state. It seems reasonable that in such cases one should stop following the learned model, retrain, and restart from the next iteration. However, this may result in smaller dataset extensions after every simulation since they are "cut short". Moreover, one should consider the fact that simulating[1] the (neural-network controlled) environment is mostly done using numerical methods, e.g., forward Euler or Runge-Kutta (see, for instance, [11]).

[1] In fact, optimization is usually also done numerically on a discretized version of the original optimal control problem.

Our contribution. We extend the DAgger approach to learn a surrogate of a given MPC in the form of an NN. Importantly, we treat the MPC as a black box and, beyond implementing the early simulation exits based on large-distance deviations from MPC-consistent trajectories, we propose to use *verified integration* methods to obtain more states from which to query the MPC along a single NN-controlled trajectory. That is to say, after following the NN to obtain a sequence of states and control actions (i.e. a trajectory), to each state-action pair (s, a) we associate a hyperrectangle $D_{s,a}$ of successor states of (s, a) after $t_{i+1} - t_i$ units of time, given the dynamics, obtained via verified (Taylor-model) integration methods (see Fig. 1 for a graphical depiction of the Taylor-augmented rollout and reachable set construction). Such methods provide a conservative overapproximation of the solution to initial value problems (given an initial state and a dynamical system in the form of a system of ordinary differential equations). In addition to increasing the number of data points obtained per simulation (even if truncated), the method also allows us to introduce small perturbations to a so that $D_{s,a}$ contains states reached after retraining (assuming that the new action a' prescribed by the NN from s is not too far off from a). Our hypothesis is that both of these extensions to DAgger, together, will contribute to more efficiently learning a surrogate of the MPC. We empirically evaluate this hypothesis on a case study from a truck-with-trailer autonomous navigation problem.

The implementation and data for the experiments is available on Zenodo [4].

2 MPC for a Truck with One Trailer

Here, we present a case study based on the autonomous parking of a truck with a single trailer. More precisely, the truck is supposed to park the trailer in a specified parking spot. Our presentation of the dynamics of the system follows closely [7], where the authors also describe the MPC framework and tools we employ (as a black box) later. We will use the case study as a running example to introduce, one by one, all elements of our imitation learning framework.

2.1 Dynamics of the System

The kinematic model of the truck and trailer is given as a set of nonlinear ordinary differential equations (ODEs), expressed as $\dot{\boldsymbol{s}} = \boldsymbol{f}(\boldsymbol{s}, \boldsymbol{u})$, where $\boldsymbol{s}$ is the *state vector* and $\boldsymbol{u}$ is the *control input.*

The system includes the truck (vehicle 0) and the trailer (vehicle 1). The state vector is represented as $\boldsymbol{s} = [x, y, \theta_0, \theta_1]^\intercal \in \mathbb{R}^4$, where $[x, y]^\intercal$ gives the position of the axle of the trailer, θ_0 and θ_1 are the orientations of the truck and trailer, respectively, with respect to a "world frame". The control input vector $\boldsymbol{u} = [v_0, \omega_0]^\intercal$ consists of the truck's longitudinal velocity v_0 and its angular velocity ω_0. The ODEs that govern the behavior of the system are as follows:

$$\dot{x} = v_1 \cdot \cos(\theta_1) \qquad \dot{y} = v_1 \cdot \sin(\theta_1)$$

$$\dot{\theta}_0 = \omega_0 \qquad \dot{\theta}_1 = \frac{v_0}{L_1} \cdot \sin(\beta_{01}) - \frac{M_0}{L_1} \cdot \cos(\beta_{01}) \cdot \omega_0$$

Table 1. Initial and target states, values of constants, and constraints on the path. All numbers are given in SI units (particularly, angles are in radians).

Initial state	$x = 0.0$, $y = 0.25$, $\theta_0 = \theta_1 = 1.571$
Target state	$x = -1.188$, $y = 0.743$, $\theta_0 = \theta_1 = 4.189$
Constants	$L_0 = 0.3375, M_0 = 1, L_1 = 0.3, M_1 = 0.06$
Velocity bounds	$-0.2 \leq v_0 \leq 0.2$ m/s
Acceleration bounds	$-1.0 \leq \dot{v_0} \leq 1.0$ m/s^2
Yaw rate bounds	$-\frac{\pi}{10} \leq \dot{\theta_0} \leq \frac{\pi}{10}$ rad/s^2
Hitch angle bounds	$-\frac{\pi}{4} \leq \beta_{01} \leq \frac{\pi}{4}$ rad

where v_1 stands for the velocity of the trailer and it is determined by:

$$v_1 = v_0 \cdot \cos(\beta_{01}) + M_0 \cdot \sin(\beta_{01}) \cdot \omega_0,$$

and $\beta_{01} = \theta_0 - \theta_1$ is the relative angle between the truck and the trailer. The constants L_i represent the distance between the steering wheel and the axle center (or hitching point and axle center); and M_i, the distance between the axle center and the hitching point for vehicle i.

2.2 Constrained Reachability Problem

Our optimal control problem (OCP) consists of choosing control input values so that, from a given initial state, the system reaches a target final state. Throughout the path followed from the initial to the target state, a number of *path constraints* also need to be satisfied. See Table 1 for the concrete initial and target states, as well as the aforementioned constraints, that we use in our experiments. These are taken from code[2] provided by the authors of [7].

In [7], the authors describe a framework for obtaining an MPC that relies on a sequence of two *corridors* to guide the truck from its initial state to its target state. The OCP is split into three stages: In the first stage, both the truck and the trailer are entirely within the first corridor. The second stage involves one vehicle in the first corridor and the other in the second corridor. In the third stage, both vehicles are in the second corridor. See Fig. 2 for a graphical depiction of a simulation of the MPC solution. The dashed lines in Fig. 2 define *corridors* that guide the MPC from the truck's initial state to the target. In the final configuration, both truck and trailer are within the second (diagonal) corridor, corresponding to the third stage of the split OCP.

3 Standard DAgger for Learning to Imitate the MPC

This section describes a deep learning framework based on examples obtained from the MPC for the truck-trailer system given in [7]. Importantly, the MPC

[2] Source file on GitLab: truck_trailer_multistage_3stages.py.

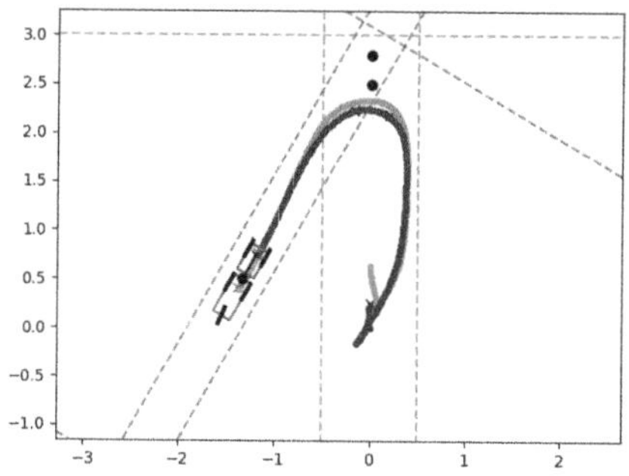

Fig. 2. Simulation of the truck-and-trailer system reaching its target state. Visualization generated using the Rockit tool [12].

Table 2. Bounds used for hyperparameter tuning.

Hyperparameter	Lower bound	Upper bound
No. of layers	1	3
No. of neurons per layer	16	96
Learning rate	10^{-5}	0.1

implements a piecewise constant control function $\boldsymbol{u}(t)$ with a sampling time of 0.5s. That is, the value of the control parameters v_0 and ω_0 is changed precisely every 0.5s based on the output of the MPC given the current state. Hence, we chose to train a NN to implement a function $f : \mathbb{R}^4 \to \mathbb{R}^2$ that assigns a value of the longitudinal velocity v_0 and the angular velocity ω_0 to each state.

Below, we describe our approach to train a baseline NN. In this section, we focus on clearly explaining the baseline obtained using DAgger only. Later, we will extend the approach as described in the introduction. We split the description into the following: NN architecture, training scheme (DAgger), and validation metrics. The implementation of all these elements is done using the Supervised Learning Workflow Management (SLWM) library described in [3].

3.1 Choice of Architecture of the NN

We now describe the architecture for our NN surrogate of the MPC. The input to the NN corresponds to the state $\boldsymbol{s} \in \mathbb{R}^4$ of the truck-with-trailer system. In particular, and as explained in Sect. 2.1, the state includes the trailer's position (x, y) and the orientations (θ_0, θ_1) of the truck and trailer, respectively. The output of the NN corresponds to its prediction of the control actions required from the current state. Concretely, these are velocity v_0 and yaw rate ω_0.

Hyperparameter tuning is applied to optimize parameters such as the number of layers and neurons per layer (see Table 2 for the concrete bounds we used in our experiments). To be precise, we create the NN using the functional API of TensorFlow 2.13.0. Regarding the activation functions of each layer, we use

ReLU, a common choice compatible with NN-verification tools. For the output layer, we fix a linear activation function. Then, we use the Keras 2.13.1 *hyperband* algorithm to determine the number of hidden layers and the number of neurons per layer. We fix the sampling time to 0.5 s across all training and validation phases, consistent with the control update frequency of the MPC.

To ensure reproducibility, all experiments are conducted using a fixed set of 10 random seeds: 1, 2, 3, 4, 5, 21, 23, 24, 25, and 37. These seeds are applied uniformly across all stochastic components of the learning pipeline. Specifically, we initialize the random number generators for TensorFlow, NumPy, and Python's random module using the same seed value for each run. This ensures that the data shuffling, weight initialization, and any sampling-based procedures are synchronized across repeated runs, allowing us to attribute observed variations in performance to the model behavior rather than randomness in training conditions. Each seed is used to run a full 10-iteration DAgger schedule, allowing us to analyze convergence trends, training variability, and outlier behavior under controlled conditions. The outputs of each seed are stored separately for post hoc analysis of both training metrics and closed-loop simulation traces.

3.2 DAgger Training Scheme

The training strategy we follow proceeds in rounds. To bootstrap the process we first gather an initial set of data. The initial dataset is generated from expert simulations using the Rockit tool. The expert trajectories, representing the truck-and-trailer's ideal path and control actions, are saved for an initial training round of the NN. For our choice of timestep (0.5 s), we start 100 simulations from evenly spaced initial positions (and the same angles as specified in Table 1) from a 10×10 grid around the initial location. Each simulation has a maximum length of 50 steps. Hence, we get 5K pairs of states and control values.

The rest of the training consists of repeatedly performing data aggregation and retraining the NN for a number of rounds. In short, we use the current dataset to tune hyperparameters that determine the NN architecture and the learning rate. Then, we proceed to training. Next, we use the NN to collect more data by simulating the truck-and-trailer system as before, but this time controlled by the NN and not the MPC, while storing all 5K states reached during the simulation. Following the DAgger approach, we then ask the MPC expert for actions to label all states with its recommended action. We *aggregate* this new data, i.e., append it to the original dataset, and repeat. A detailed step-by-step description of the training and retraining workflow, including dataset splits and hyperparameter tuning protocol, is provided in [15].

Outlier Filtering. Unstable dynamics may result in (early versions of) the NN-controlled simulations to veer far off the reference expert traces. We can set a threshold to filter out such states. This does mean that some (early) iterations may add fewer data points for retraining. In our experiments, we set a threshold of at most 0.1 on the Euclidean distance between positions[3] of the trailer.

3.3 Loss and Validation Metrics

We use the mean squared error (MSE) as the loss function during training. To precisely define the function, we need to introduce some notation. Let $D = \{(\boldsymbol{s}^{(i)}, \boldsymbol{a}^{(i)}) \mid i \in I\}$ be a (data)set of states $\boldsymbol{s}^{(i)}$ labeled with (true) control actions $\boldsymbol{a}^{(i)}$. Our NN N labels each state $\boldsymbol{s}^{(i)}$ with a predicted action $\boldsymbol{b}^{(i)}$. If the control actions have cardinality d, the mean squared error of N over D is defined as $\mathrm{MSE}(D, N) = \frac{1}{|D|d} \sum_{i \in I} \sum_{j=0}^{d-1} \left(a_j^{(i)} - b_j^{(i)}\right)^2$.

Using mean squared error as a loss function is fine when looking at imitation learning as a regression task. That is to say, when we learn a function from states to control actions. However, it does not accurately represent how far a NN-controlled trajectory would be from an expert-controller trajectory as a whole. Because of this, we also use the *accumulated squared error* as a metric between trajectories. Again, some notation is needed to make this precise. Let $t = \boldsymbol{s}^{(0)}\boldsymbol{a}^{(0)} \ldots \boldsymbol{a}^{(n-1)}\boldsymbol{s}^{(n)}$ be a trajectory obtained by simulating the expert. The corresponding trajectory obtained by simulating the NN from $\boldsymbol{s}^{(0)}$ is $N(t) = \boldsymbol{q}^{(0)}\boldsymbol{b}^{(0)} \ldots \boldsymbol{b}^{(n-1)}\boldsymbol{q}^{(n)}$. Then, the accumulated squared error of $N(t)$ and t, with respect to component k, is defined as follows.

$$\mathrm{ASE}_k(N, t) = \sum_{i=0}^{n-1} \left(s_k^{(i)} - q_k^{(i)}\right)^2$$

Given a set T of trajectories, the value $\mathrm{ASE}_k(N, T)$ is just the average of $\mathrm{ASE}_k(N, t)$ over all $t \in T$. (Recall that we have a number of initial states that we use to obtain multiple simulated trajectories.) We posit that the accumulated squared error gives a better indication of the performance of the NN and use it to visualize progress during the training process.

3.4 Experiments and Discussion

We now evaluate our learning-based controller through a series of closed-loop simulations across 10 random seeds. The results are organized into five parts: ASE trends, test loss, the role of outlier filtering, training data distribution, and trajectory comparisons between the learned and expert policies.

ASE. To evaluate closed-loop performance of the learned policy, we use the *ASE* metric introduced in Sect. 3.3. Figures 3a and 3b show the distribution of ASE values for the trailer's coordinates x_1 and y_1 across 10 DAgger iterations, with 10 different random seeds per iteration. Each box plot reflects the ASE over 50-step simulated trajectories from a fixed grid of initial states.

[3] Based on initial experiments, we determined that a threshold on the angles of the vehicles did not make much of a difference. Hence, we focus on the positions only.

Overall, we observe a downward trend in both the median and interquartile spread of ASE values as DAgger iterations progress. By iterations 9 and 10, the median ASE for x_1 drops below 1.0, indicating improved closed-loop tracking. However, for y_1, although the median steadily decreases, the first quartile remains above 1.0, suggesting residual error in some trajectories.

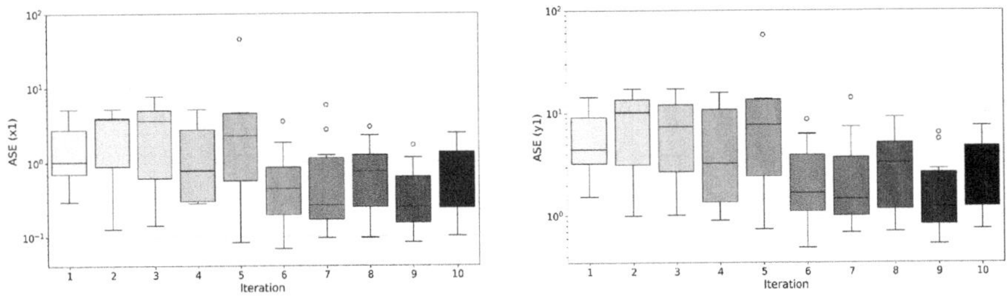

(a) ASE for x_1

(b) ASE for y_1

Fig. 3. Distribution of ASE across 10 DAgger iterations (10 seeds per iteration) for the trailer's coordinates x_1 and y_1.

Iteration 5 in both plots contains one or two prominent outliers above 10^1 or even 10^2 in squared-error units (m^2). On closer inspection, these originate from only two random seeds (seed 5 and seed 25). Per-seed analysis confirms that these spikes arise due to a highly imbalanced dataset collected in that particular iteration (e.g., points clustered near the start of the trajectory). Importantly, the ASE recovers in subsequent iterations, and such events occur in only 2 out of 100 runs. This suggests these outliers are isolated cases of *unlucky sampling*, not indicative of, for example, instability or implementation bugs.

Note that these results validate the outlier filtering scheme applied to each batch of collected data. Despite removing 15–25% of samples per round, the retained points are sufficient to support stable training, and ASE improves over time without runaway errors (i.e., errors that grow over time during simulation). Without filtering, such spikes would likely be more frequent and more extreme.

MSE as Test Loss. In addition to closed-loop metrics, we assess pointwise prediction accuracy using the mean squared error (MSE) on the external test set, as defined in Sect. 3.3. Figure 4 shows the test loss over 10 DAgger iterations, averaged across 10 seeds. For each iteration, we display the mean and standard deviation, along with per-seed trajectories.

The test loss remains low throughout all iterations, with values below 0.06 and typically in the range of 0.01 to 0.03. This indicates that the DNN accurately reproduces the expert's control actions for unseen test data. There is no evidence of overfitting to the growing training dataset, despite the fact that the network architecture is reselected at each iteration via hyperparameter tuning.

Although the mean test loss shows a mild upward trend over the first few iterations (likely due to the growing complexity of the aggregated dataset), it remains largely stable from iteration 4 onwards. The spread across different seeds remains moderate and stable, suggesting that the networks generalize well to unseen data regardless of random initialization and training variability.

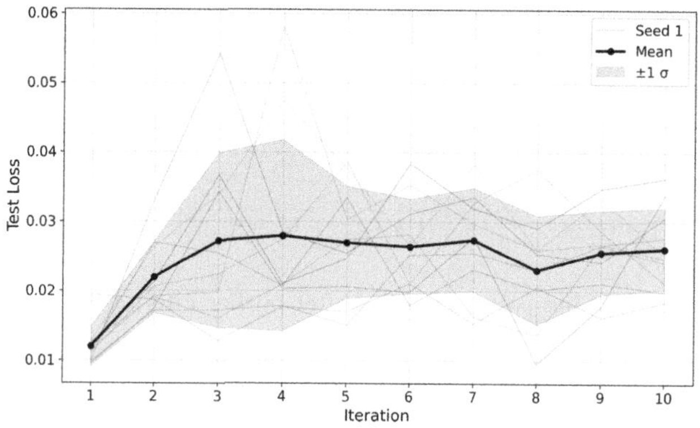

Fig. 4. Test MSE loss over ten DAgger iterations.

Outlier Filtering. As described in Sect. 3.2, we apply outlier filtering to the collected data at each DAgger iteration. This step removes samples whose control labels deviate significantly from the local average, helping to suppress spurious training gradients caused by noise or sparsely visited regions.

Figure 5 shows the number of training points retained after filtering, for all 10 seeds and 10 DAgger iterations. Each iteration begins with a maximum of 5000 newly collected points (dashed purple line), but only a subset of these is retained based on a Euclidean distance threshold (at most 0.1) between the NN-predicted and expert trailer positions (x_1, y_1). The solid black curve shows the mean across seeds, with the shaded region denoting one standard deviation.

Across all iterations, the number of retained samples remains well above 1500, even in the worst-case seeds. The average retention stabilizes between 2000 and 2700 samples by later iterations, indicating that the majority of the data passes the filtering criterion. This affirms that our filtering strategy is conservative: it eliminates harmful outliers without discarding too much of the useful data.

Fewer retained points also reduce the computational overhead of expert relabeling, since only the retained subset needs to be passed through the expert (MPC) to obtain reference actions. Outlier filtering thus removes potentially misleading samples while also speeding up the relabeling pipeline. As seen in Fig. 3, the closed-loop accuracy (ASE) continues to improve steadily across iterations, validating the effectiveness of this trade-off.

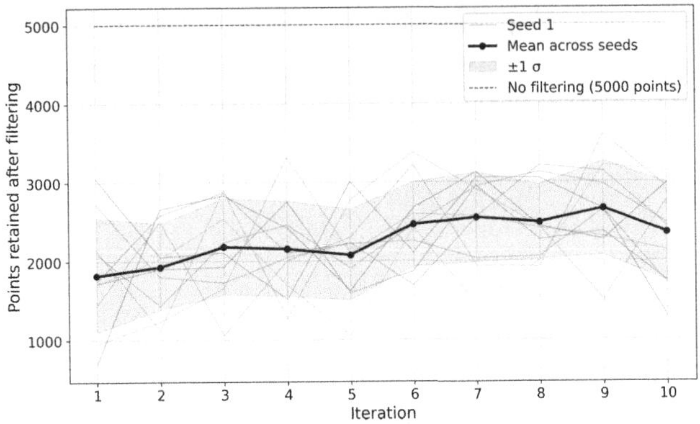

Fig. 5. Number of training points retained after outlier filtering per DAgger iteration (mean across seeds $\pm 1\sigma$).

Distribution of Training Data. We briefly analyze how the training data evolves across DAgger iterations to get an insight into how data coverage and filtering affect policy improvement.

Across iterations, we observe that the training set initially contains dense clusters near the early segments of the trajectory, while later regions are covered more sparsely. This imbalance often leads to inconsistent learning behavior and occasional spikes in rollout error, especially when the neural network encounters parts of the state space that are poorly represented in the training data. By iteration 5, however, the distribution improves both in terms of spatial coverage and through the removal of redundant or erratic samples (i.e., outliers), leading to more stable learning in later rounds.

Closed-loop DNN Trajectory vs MPC. To evaluate how well the learned policy reproduces expert behavior in closed-loop simulation, we overlay trajectories from the neural network (NN) controller and the MPC expert for a selected seed (seed 23). Figure 6 shows results for iterations 5 and 10.

The thin light red line indicates the desired trajectory (which is, incidentally, always followed by the depiction of the truck and trailer). The dark red line formed by a sequence of thick dots of the same color is the trajectory of the NN-controlled truck, while the gray line is that of the trailer.

The trajectory at iteration 5 exhibits noticeable deviation from the expert path. The DNN fails to track the full arc and veers early, reflecting the limited coverage and poor generalization of the initial model. In contrast, by iteration 10, the DNN reliably tracks the expert trajectory through the corridor, with a near-exact match in both path shape and final position. This confirms that learning stabilizes after the initial few iterations.

Visual trends in intermediate iterations show how trajectory quality improves incrementally, with early rollouts occasionally terminating prematurely due to insufficient forward velocity. These terminations are caused by suboptimal speed profiles rather than divergence from the expert and disappear after iteration 5.

These observations correlate with the quantitative improvements reported earlier: ASE steadily decreases across iterations (Fig. 3), and test loss remains low and stable (Fig. 4).

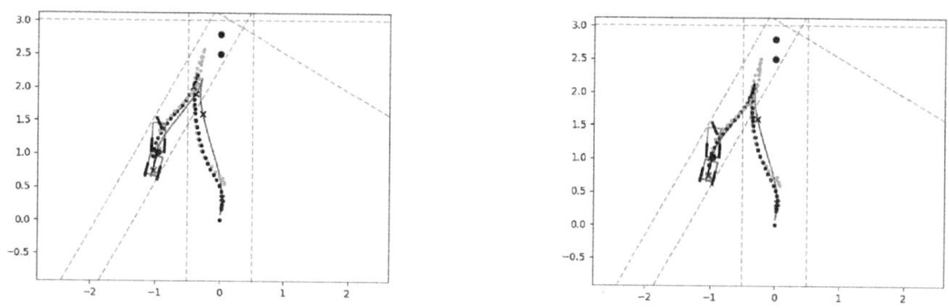

(a) Iteration 5 (b) Iteration 10

Fig. 6. Comparison of closed-loop trajectories from the learned DNN policy (truck in dotted dark red; trailer in dotted gray) and the desired MPC trajectory (thin solid red).

4 Taylor's DAgger: More Efficient Learning

In the previous section, we introduced DAgger and outlier filtering. Here, we are interested in minimizing the number of DAgger rounds while obtaining a surrogate with performance comparable to the results of the previous section. To achieve this, we propose another type of data aggregation based on verified integration of the dynamics of the system. Intuitively, we want to follow a trajectory that would be used in a further DAgger round, and aggregate, for each state-control action pair along it, additional states contained in an overapproximation of the states guaranteed[4] to be reached in the next timestep. Usually, such overapproximations take the form of convex polytopes from which we could sample the desired additional points. (See Fig. 1 for a more visual version of this intuition.)

Below, we first give a short recollection of verified integration and point to sources on Taylor-model integration, our choice of verified integration technique. Then, we briefly dwell on our implementation of the technique and some design choices. Finally, we present experimental results regarding the proposed *Taylor aggregation*, continuing with our truck-and-trailer case study.

[4] Recall our use of the Rockit tool for simulations to enable DAgger. The tool, as many others, uses Runge-Kutta methods to simulate trajectories.

4.1 Taylor Model-based Integration of ODEs

In order to predict the next-state-values based on a current state and control input, we use verified integration to simulate the dynamics until a specified time horizon. As noted earlier in Sect. 2.1 our truck-with-trailer dynamical system is described as a system of ODEs. Various numerical techniques exist to approximate the value $y(t)$ of a dynamical system f at time t from initial condition x_0, such as Runge-Kutta. However, we wish to obtain an interval $Y(t)$ such that the exact solution $y(t)$ is guaranteed to be in the interval $Y(t)$.

Definition 1 (Verified integration). *Let $\boldsymbol{f}(\boldsymbol{y})$ be an ODE, and let Y_0 be an interval of initial values at time-step t_0. A verified integration procedure produces a sequence of intervals $(Y_t)_{t>t_0}$ such that $\forall y_0 \in Y_0, t_i \in T : y(t_i, y_0) \in Y_{t_i}$, where $y(t_i, y_0)$ is the solution to an initial-value problem evaluated at time t_i.*

Note that this integration procedure allows for uncertainty in the initial value, since Y_0 can be a set of initial values.

One such verified integration technique manipulates *Taylor models*, i.e., multivariate polynomials paired with remainder hypercubes, to compute the set Y. This technique was proposed by Berz and Makino [5] and versions of it have been implemented in JuliaReach [6], flow* [8] and CORA [1], to name a few. We use the TMJets algorithm from JuliaReach.

4.2 Augmenting DAgger Using Verified Integration

We will now consider how to incorporate verified integration into DAgger. Let $(x, y, \theta_0, \theta_1)$ be a state from the dataset and let (v_0, ω_0) be the action obtained using the MPC expert. We first perturb (v_0, ω_0) into $[v_0 - \varepsilon_v, v_0 + \varepsilon_v] \times [\omega_0 - \varepsilon_\omega, \omega_0 + \varepsilon_\omega]$, with $\varepsilon_v = 0.001\,\text{m/s}$ and $\varepsilon_\omega = 0.05\,\text{rad/s}$. Together, this results in a set of initial conditions $Y_0 = \{(x, y, \theta_0, \theta_1)\} \times [v_0 - \varepsilon_v, v_0 + \varepsilon_v] \times [\omega_0 - \varepsilon_\omega, \omega_0 + \varepsilon_\omega]$. We then use the verified integration technique to solve the system of ODEs described in Sect 2.1 together with the set of initial values Y_0 up to a horizon $h = 0.5s$. The result is a set of states $Y_h = X \times Y \times \Theta_0 \times \Theta_1$. Note that the exact state of the system after the horizon h is guaranteed[5] to be in the set Y_h, due to the properties of the verified integration algorithm. The set Y of successors is thus an overapproximation of what happens when a control action (v_0, ω_0) is taken from a state-space point $(x, y, \theta_0, \theta_1)$. From Y we obtain 4 additional states by considering 4 combinations of extremal values of X and Y combined with the midpoints for Θ_0 and Θ_1. These additional states are added to the dataset, resulting in an augmented dataset.

[5] We mean here the *real* successor as per the dynamics and not the subsequent state along the current trajectory. This is again due to Runge-Kutta or other numerical methods being used for simulations while, based on the choice of timestep, they could be off from the actual function defined by the ODEs and initial value.

4.3 Experiments and Discussion

We now evaluate the effectiveness of Taylor aggregation in accelerating learning. As before, we assess performance using ASE, test loss, and closed-loop trajectory comparisons.

ASE. We analyze the impact of Taylor aggregation on the accuracy of the learned policy by comparing the ASE across iterations, both with and without Taylor aggregation. Figures 7a and 7b illustrate the distribution of ASE values for state components x_1 and y_1, respectively, computed across five random seeds per iteration. These box plots provide a visual comparison of the variability, central tendency, and presence of outliers in each training configuration.

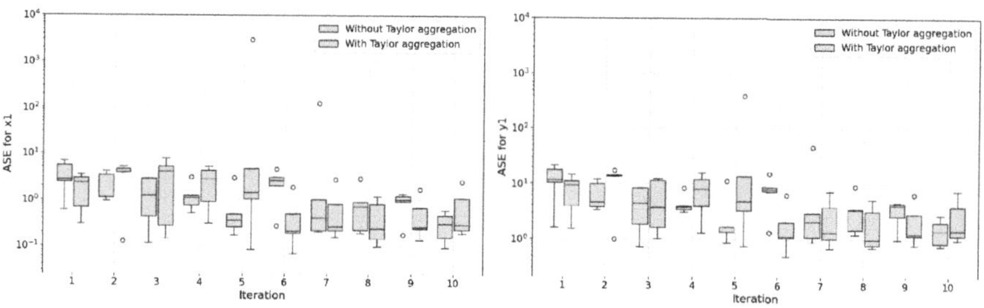

(a) ASE for x_1 (b) ASE for y_1

Fig. 7. Comparison of ASE for x_1 and y_1 across 10 DAgger iterations (5 seeds per iteration), with and without Taylor aggregation.

For the longitudinal component x_1, both configurations show noticeable variability in early iterations (1–3), reflecting the instability of the initial learning rounds. From iteration 4 onward, Taylor aggregation yields tighter box plots and fewer outliers, indicating more consistent performance across seeds. However, the median ASE is not always lower with aggregation, particularly in iterations (6–10), where the non-aggregated models occasionally achieve slightly better medians. Nevertheless, the blue boxes (with Taylor) remain visibly more compact, highlighting reduced variance and more predictable model quality across random initializations.

For the lateral component y_1, both configurations show steady improvement across iterations, with most trajectories converging by iteration 10. In mid-stage iterations, particularly 4, 5, and 6, the blue boxes (Taylor aggregation) are noticeably tighter and contain fewer outliers than their non-aggregated counterparts, indicating lower variability across seeds. As with x_1, the median ASE occasionally favors the non-aggregated models (e.g., iterations 8–10), but the differences are modest. Overall, Taylor aggregation promotes more consistent training outcomes: it reduces variance and suppresses extreme errors, even when it does not yield the lowest median.

Taken together, these results support the conclusion that Taylor aggregation enhances training stability in DAgger. The aggregated models show more consistent behavior across random seeds, even if their median accuracy is not always superior. This is particularly important in real-world settings, where one typically cannot select a favorable seed and instead relies on reliable performance across different training runs.

MSE as Test Loss. Fig. 8 presents a comparison of the test loss for models trained with and without Taylor aggregation. For each DAgger iteration, the plot shows the mean MSE across five random seeds (bold lines), along with shaded regions indicating $\pm 1\sigma$ standard deviation. Thin, transparent lines correspond to the individual seed-wise traces.

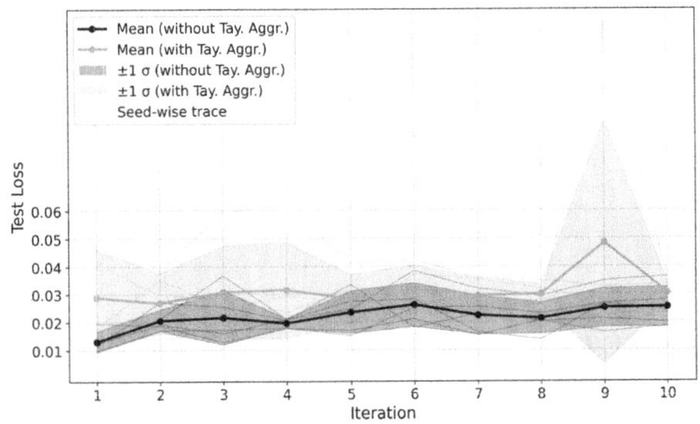

Fig. 8. Test loss (MSE) across 10 DAgger iterations (5 seeds per iteration). We compare training with and without Taylor aggregation. Bold lines denote the mean, shaded areas show $\pm 1\sigma$, and transparent lines show individual seeds.

As discussed in Sect. 3.4, the configuration without Taylor aggregation exhibits a smooth and relatively stable trend in test loss, with modest variance across seeds. In contrast, the test loss for DNNs with Taylor aggregation starts higher in the initial iterations and displays greater fluctuation, particularly around iterations 4–6 and iteration 9. These fluctuations coincide with wider shaded regions, indicating larger seed-to-seed variability. Despite the noise, the overall trend does not indicate systematic improvement over the baseline. In fact, the Taylor aggregation models tend to exhibit slightly higher mean test loss at nearly every iteration compared to their non-aggregated counterparts.

This result contrasts with the improved ASE performance observed earlier, highlighting a discrepancy between test loss and closed-loop rollout behavior. One explanation lies in how Taylor aggregation modifies the expert labels during DAgger, enriching the dataset around states visited by the current policy and their local successors. This shift nudges the training distribution toward the on-policy distribution, helping the model behave more reliably in closed-loop settings where each output recursively affects future inputs. However, the test loss is computed on a fixed set of expert state-action pairs, evaluated independently of rollout dynamics. As a result, models trained with Taylor aggregation may generalize better under sequential execution, even if their predictions on static test inputs yield slightly higher MSE.

In summary, while test loss remains a useful metric for generalization, it is not always predictive of closed-loop performance. The higher variance and slightly elevated average loss observed under Taylor aggregation do not contradict the improved ASE trends; rather, they highlight the limitations of static validation metrics when evaluating imitation learning under distribution shift.

4.4 Closed-Loop DNN Trajectory Vs MPC

We now evaluate the impact of Taylor aggregation on learning efficiency by comparing closed-loop trajectories obtained from NNs trained with and without Taylor aggregation.

Figure 9 shows representative rollouts of the truck-and-trailer system, where the control inputs are generated by the NN trained using Taylor-augmented DAgger (left) versus standard DAgger (right). All NNs are trained with ReLU activations and outlier filtering. These rollouts use seed 23.

Panels (a) and (b) depict rollouts from different training regimes: iteration 2 with Taylor aggregation, and iteration 6 without. Despite being an earlier round, the trajectory in panel (a) already aligns well with the expert reference, whereas the trajectory in panel (b) still shows residual deviation. This qualitative comparison supports our hypothesis: Taylor aggregation accelerates learning by enriching the dataset with verified reachable states.

These observations align with the trends in Fig. 7, where models trained with Taylor aggregation show lower ASE and fewer outliers across seeds. While the test loss (Fig. 8) does not consistently improve, the superior closed-loop behavior seen here reinforces that Taylor aggregation enhances policy robustness under sequential execution, even if static metrics are inconclusive.

Importantly, both training regimes ultimately converge to well-aligned trajectories in later iterations. This implies that Taylor aggregation does not degrade final policy quality but *enables faster convergence in earlier rounds.*

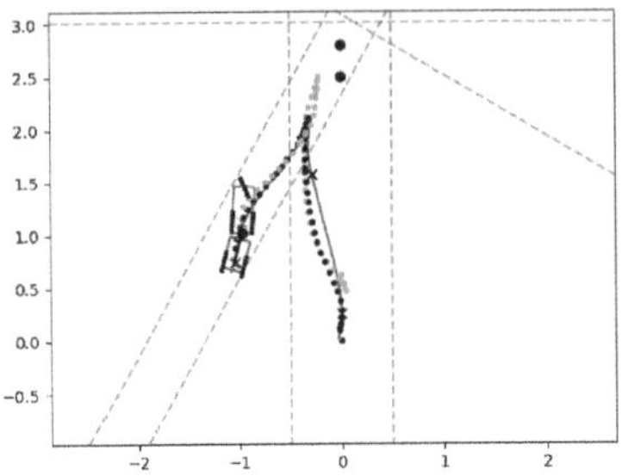

(a) With Taylor aggregation, iteration 2

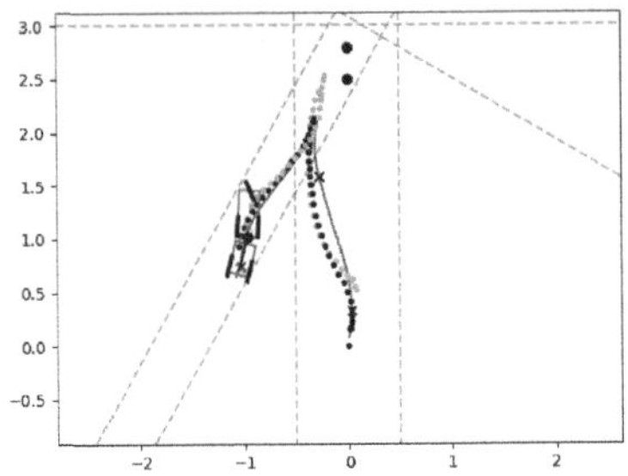

(b) Without Taylor aggregation, iteration 6

Fig. 9. Representative closed-loop trajectories of the truck-trailer system using NNs trained with and without Taylor aggregation.

5 Conclusion

Training surrogate models for MPC has emerged as a strategy that enables formal verification of complex hybrid systems. In this work, we have focused on how to obtain such surrogates in the form of neural networks. Our proposed method, Taylor aggregation, brings together formal reachability analysis and imitation learning by using verified integration to enrich expert demonstrations within DAgger. Our experiments with a truck-and-trailer case study show that this approach improves training efficiency and robustness: models trained with Taylor aggregation achieve better closed-loop behavior and lower trajectory error (ASE) in fewer training rounds. More importantly, they exhibit reduced variance and outlier sensitivity across random seeds, leading to more consistent performance. Although test loss (MSE) did not consistently improve, this highlights the limitations of static metrics in capturing sequential decision-making quality. As a direction for future work, we hypothesize that combining Taylor aggregation with targeted data cleaning strategies may further improve stability and performance during training.

References

1. Althoff, M., Grebenyuk, D., Kochdumper, N.: Implementation of Taylor models in CORA 2018. In: Frehse, G., Althoff, M., Bogomolov, S., Johnson, T.T. (eds.) ARCH18. 5th International Workshop on Applied Verification of Continuous and Hybrid Systems, ARCH@ADHS 2018, Oxford, UK, July 13, 2018. EPiC Series in Computing, vol. 54, pp. 145–173. EasyChair (2018). https://doi.org/10.29007/ZZC7
2. Bellis, S., et al.: A framework for the competitive analysis of model predictive controllers. In: Bournez, O., Formenti, E., Potapov, I. (eds.) Reachability Problems - 17th International Conference, RP 2023, Nice, France, October 11-13, 2023, Proceedings. Lecture Notes in Computer Science, vol. 14235, pp. 141–154. Springer (2023. https://doi.org/10.1007/978-3-031-45286-4_11

3. Bellis, S., Denil, J., Krishnamurthy, R., Pérez, G.A.: SLWM: a library for implementing complex training workflows for surrogates of MPC's. In: Ding, W., et al. (eds.) IEEE International Conference on Big Data, BigData 2024, Washington, DC, USA, December 15-18, 2024. pp. 4139–4144. IEEE (2024). https://doi.org/10.1109/BIGDATA62323.2024.10825275
4. Bellis, S., Engelen, K., Gueutal, T., Krishnamurthy, R., Perez, G.: Code for Taylor's DAgger: Verified Integration For Efficient Imitation-learning of an MPC (2025). https://doi.org/10.5281/zenodo.18059976
5. Berz, M., Makino, K.: Verified integration of odes and flows using differential algebraic methods on high-order Taylor models. Reliable Comput. **4**, 361–369 (1998). https://api.semanticscholar.org/CorpusID:9145342
6. Bogomolov, S., Forets, M., Frehse, G., Potomkin, K., Schilling, C.: Juliareach: a toolbox for set-based reachability. In: Ozay, N., Prabhakar, P. (eds.) Proceedings of the 22nd ACM International Conference on Hybrid Systems: Computation and Control, HSCC 2019, Montreal, QC, Canada, April 16-18, 2019. pp. 39–44. ACM (2019). https://doi.org/10.1145/3302504.3311804
7. Bos, M., Vandewal, B., Decré, W., Swevers, J.: MPC-based motion planning for autonomous truck-trailer maneuvering. IFAC-PapersOnLine **56**(2), 4877–4882 (2023)
8. Chen, X., Sankaranarayanan, S., Ábrahám, E.: Flow* 1.2: more effective to play with hybrid systems. In: Frehse, G., Althoff, M. (eds.) 1st and 2nd International Workshop on Applied Verification for Continuous and Hybrid Systems, ARCH@CPSWeek 2014, Berlin, Germany, April 14, 2014 / ARCH@CPSWeek 2015, Seattle, WA, USA, April 13, 2015. EPiC Series in Computing, vol. 34, pp. 152–159. EasyChair (2015). https://doi.org/10.29007/1W4T
9. Fan, J., Huang, C., Chen, X., Li, W., Zhu, Q.: ReachNN*: A Tool for Reachability Analysis of Neural-Network Controlled Systems. In: Hung, D.V., Sokolsky, O. (eds.) ATVA 2020. LNCS, vol. 12302, pp. 537–542. Springer, Cham (2020). https://doi.org/10.1007/978-3-030-59152-6_30
10. Finzi, M., Wang, K.A., Wilson, A.G.: Simplifying Hamiltonian and Lagrangian neural networks via explicit constraints. In: NeurIPS (2020)
11. Martinez, A.J.F., Vigoya, A.A., Decré, W., Swevers, J., Gillis, J.: Impact: a toolchain for fast specification, prototyping, and deployment of model predictive control. In: 42nd Benelux Meeting on Systems and Control, Date: 2023/03/21-2023/03/23, Location: Elspeet, The Netherlands, p. 96 (2023)
12. Gillis, J., Vandewal, B., Pipeleers, G., Swevers, J.: Effortless modeling of optimal control problems with rockit. In: 39th Benelux Meeting on Systems and Control, Date: 2020/03/10-2020/03/12, Location: Elspeet, The Netherlands (2020)
13. Ivanov, R., Carpenter, T., Weimer, J., Alur, R., Pappas, G., Lee, I.: Verisig 2.0: Verification of Neural Network Controllers Using Taylor Model Preconditioning. In: Silva, A., Leino, K.R.M. (eds.) CAV 2021. LNCS, vol. 12759, pp. 249–262. Springer, Cham (2021). https://doi.org/10.1007/978-3-030-81685-8_11
14. Ivanov, R., Weimer, J., Alur, R., Pappas, G.J., Lee, I.: Verisig: verifying safety properties of hybrid systems with neural network controllers. In: Ozay, N., Prabhakar, P. (eds.) Proceedings of the 22nd ACM International Conference on Hybrid Systems: Computation and Control, HSCC 2019, Montreal, QC, Canada, April 16-18, 2019. pp. 169–178. ACM (2019). https://doi.org/10.1145/3302504.3311806
15. Krishnamurthy, R.: Formal analysis tools for nonlinear model-predictive control: formal verification techniques for real-world MPC. Ph.D. thesis, University of Antwerp (2025)

16. Ross, S., Gordon, G.J., Bagnell, D.: A reduction of imitation learning and structured prediction to no-regret online learning. In: Gordon, G.J., Dunson, D.B., Dudík, M. (eds.) Proceedings of the Fourteenth International Conference on Artificial Intelligence and Statistics, AISTATS 2011, Fort Lauderdale, USA, April 11-13, 2011. JMLR Proceedings, vol. 15, pp. 627–635. JMLR.org (2011). http://proceedings.mlr.press/v15/ross11a/ross11a.pdf
17. Tran, H., et al.: Safety verification of cyber-physical systems with reinforcement learning control. ACM Trans. Embed. Comput. Syst. **18**(5s), 105:1–105:22 (2019). https://doi.org/10.1145/3358230

From Transformers to Weighted Automata: Towards the Verification of Large Language Models

Smayan Agarwal[1(✉)], Aslah Ahmad Faizi[2], Shobhit Singh[1], and Aalok Thakkar[1]

[1] Ashoka University, Sonipat, India
{smayan.agarwal_ug25,shobhit.singh,aalok.thakkar}@ashoka.edu.in
[2] Patna, India

Abstract. Large language models (LLMs) are increasingly deployed in safety-critical settings, yet their black-box nature makes it difficult to provide formal guaranties about their behavior. Existing verification approaches rely primarily on empirical probing and testing, leaving open the question of how to reason rigorously about general-purpose transformer architectures.

In this work, we establish a principled bridge between transformers and weighted automata, a classical model from formal language theory. This connection enables us to transfer verification tools from automata theory to the analysis of LLMs. Our contributions are twofold: First, we develop a formal correspondence between transformer architectures and weighted automata over reals, showing how distributional properties of LLMs can be captured within this framework. Second, we introduce an identity testing algorithm for weighted automata that provides a statistical method for distinguishing whether two stochastic models define the same distribution up to a tolerance threshold.

This work provides the first formal bridge between modern neural sequence models and classical automata theory, clarifying both the potential and the computational challenges for rigorous LLM verification.

Keywords: Large Language Models · Transformers · Weighted Automata · Verification · Identity Testing · Formal Methods

1 Introduction

The success of transformer-based language models has created an urgent need for principled methods to understand and verify their behaviour. As these models are deployed in safety-critical applications, ranging from medical diagnosis to legal reasoning, the black-box nature of their decision-making processes poses fundamental challenges for certification and reliability guarantees.

A.A Faizi — Independent Researcher.

L. Lestingi et al. (Eds.): DataMod 2025, LNCS 16421, pp. 145–162, 2026.
https://doi.org/10.1007/978-3-032-25552-5_10

Theoretical results from formal language theory offer an alternative approach. By establishing systematic correspondences between transformer variants and well-characterized computational models, we can leverage automata theory, circuit complexity, and descriptive logic to obtain predictive accounts of capabilities and limitations for specific architectural choices.

1.1 The Gap Between Benchmarks and True Capabilities

Large Language Models (LLMs) perform well on benchmarks, and yet fail on general tasks. Recent work demonstrates that even state-of-the-art models collapse when faced with simple inductive reasoning problems [5,15]. Furthermore, these models often rely on superficial neighbour-based heuristics rather than generalization [18].

Current evaluation practices systematically inflate performance estimates while obscuring true model capabilities. A critical issue is *benchmark data contamination*, where test items appear in training corpora. Studies show that GPT-4 achieves over 50% accuracy on contaminated MMLU items, fundamentally violating the train–test split principle [10,28]. This contamination operates alongside preference leakage, where evaluator LLMs exhibit systematic bias toward models sharing training data or architectural relationships, creating circular evaluation systems that measure memorization rather than understanding.

Recent frameworks expose these limitations. Cohen-Inger et al.'s C-BOD analysis demonstrates that high-performing models rely on "superficial memorization of benchmark cues" [7]. Similarly, Shojaee et al.'s examination of Large Reasoning Models reveals "complete accuracy collapse beyond certain complexities" and "counterintuitive scaling limits" where reasoning effort paradoxically decreases on challenging problems despite adequate computational resources [24]. These highlight a need for formal guarantees.

1.2 The Verification Challenge

Formal verification of neural models faces a fundamental computational barrier. For a model $M : \Sigma^* \to \mathcal{Y}$, and a property R, verification requires establishing the universal claim $\forall w \in D : R(M(w)) = 1$. This is only tractable when the input domain D admits symbolic specification (e.g., as a regular language or logical constraint). When D is defined extensionally by length bounds $D = \Sigma^{\leq n}$, the domain size becomes $\Theta(|\Sigma|^n)$. Any sound black-box verifier then faces a worst-case $\Omega(|D|)$ query lower bound, making universal verification computationally infeasible for even modest n.

Practical verification therefore requires structured domains D that admit finite abstraction through techniques like product constructions or model checking, rather than exhaustive enumeration of all token sequences up to length n.

1.3 Why Global Constraints Are Insufficient

While enforcing global constraints, such as K-Lipschitz bounds, appears attractive for certification, this approach fundamentally mismatches capability requirements. Lipschitz constraints depend on continuous embedding metrics rather than discrete string functions, compound pessimistically across layers, and force low-contrast attention that prevents the sharp routing needed for algorithmic behaviors. Empirically, global Lipschitz training trades accuracy for minimal certified radii, over-regularizing the selective attention mechanisms that give Transformers their power while providing certificates too weak to justify the capability loss [9,11,16,17,20,22,27,29].

1.4 Automata-Theoretic Foundations

Recent theoretical advances have begun mapping transformer expressivity to classical computational models. Notably, Angluin et al. [1] proved that rightmost hard-attention encoders with strict causal masking recognize exactly the star-free languages (first-order logic over strings). Adding periodic positional predicates upgrades this class to FO[MOD], while arbitrary monadic predicates yield FO[Mon]. These precise equivalences reveal that transformers align with well-studied fragments of logic and automata theory. Similarly, architectural variants map naturally to circuit complexity classes: unique and averaging hard-attention encoders correspond to AC^0 and TC^0 respectively [12,25]. Such characterizations suggest that transformer expressivity analysis can be grounded in established frameworks rather than relying solely on empirical exploration.

1.5 Weighted Finite Automata as an Abstraction Layer

While the above results apply to restricted transformer variants, modern LLMs use soft attention mechanisms that compute distributions over sequences. This motivates our focus on Weighted Finite Automata (WFA) over reals as a natural model for stochastic sequence generation that generalizes both classical finite automata and hidden Markov models. WFA provide several advantages for LLM analysis:

1. Compositional structure: Unlike neural networks, automata admit modular analysis through product constructions and closure properties.
2. Algorithmic foundation: Classical algorithms exist for equivalence testing, minimization, and property verification.
3. Statistical learning theory: Spectral methods enable provable recovery of automata from sample data [2,14].

1.6 Technical Approach and Contributions

The key two insights of our work are reflected in the two-step reduction:

Step 1: Transformer to WFA. We prove that the self-attention mechanism in decoder-only transformers can be exactly computed by a structured RNN that maintains running accumulators for the attention normalization. We then apply spectral learning to the RNN's induced function, using Hankel matrix analysis to extract a finite-state weighted automaton approximation. We discuss this in Sect. 3.

Step 2: Identity Testing of WFA. We develop the first identity testing procedure for rational stochastic languages on infinite domains. This technique can be applied to the WFA obtained in Step 1 to provide formal guarantees about a restricted transformer architecture. We discuss this in Sect. 4.

Through these, our work makes two primary contributions toward verification and explainability of LLMs:

1. **Formal reduction theorem:** We prove that decoder-only transformers are equivalent to structured RNNs, which can be approximated by WFA with controlled error bounds.
2. **A black-box algorithm for identity testing.** We design an algorithm that, given only sample access to an unknown distribution over strings (e.g., LLM outputs), tests whether this distribution is ε-close to some WA with confidence $1 - \delta$. This test serves as a *certificate of abstraction*: whenever it accepts, one can meaningfully reason about the black-box model via the corresponding WA. This enables (a) verification of safety and correctness properties, (b) improved interpretability through automaton-based explanations of sequential behavior, and (c) applicability to proprietary black-box models where internal parameters are inaccessible.

2 Notation and Preliminaries

This section establishes the notation and foundational concepts used throughout the paper. We assume familiarity with basic formal language theory, linear algebra, and probability theory.

2.1 Sets, Alphabets, and Strings

Let Σ denote a finite alphabet. In the context of LLMs, the alphabet Σ typically represents the model's *vocabulary* or *tokenizer*, where each symbol $\sigma \in \Sigma$ corresponds to a unique token. The set of all finite strings over Σ is denoted Σ^*, which includes the empty string ϵ. The length of a string x is denoted $|x|$. The set of all strings of length at most θ is denoted $\Sigma^{\leq \theta}$.

2.2 Distributions and Distances

A distribution P over a countable set $\mathcal{X}$ (in our case, $\mathcal{X} = \Sigma^*$) is a function $P : \mathcal{X} \to [0,1]$ such that $\sum_{x \in \mathcal{X}} P(x) = 1$. We denote the set of all distributions over Σ^* by $\mathcal{S}(\Sigma^*)$, and call them stochastic languages.

The primary distance measure between two distributions P and Q is the ℓ_1 distance (which is twice the total variation distance):

$$\|P - Q\|_1 = \sum_{x \in \Sigma^*} |P(x) - Q(x)|.$$

For a distribution P and a set $S \subseteq \Sigma^*$, we write $P(S) = \sum_{x \in S} P(x)$.

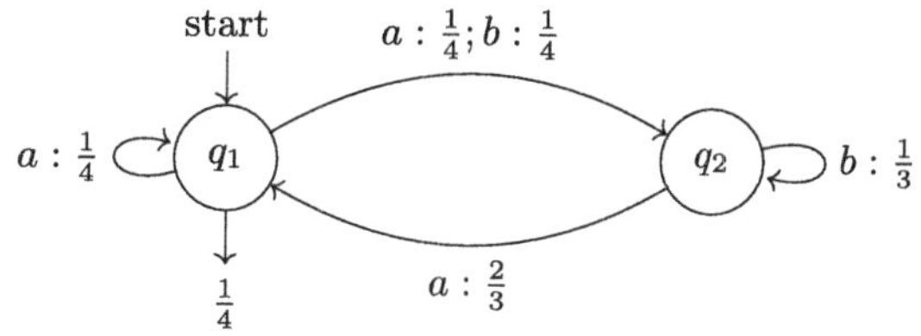

Fig. 1. A weighted finite automaton over the alphabet $\{a, b\}$. State q_1 is both initial and accepting with weight 1. The transition labels indicate the symbol and the weight (probability) associated with each move.

2.3 Weighted Finite Automata and Rational Stochastic Languages

Definition 1 (Weighted Finite Automaton (WFA)). *Let Σ be a finite alphabet. For a given semiring $(K, +, \cdot, 0, 1)$, a weighted finite automaton is a tuple $\mathcal{A} = (\Sigma, Q, \lambda, \mu, \rho)$, where Q is a finite set of states, $\lambda, \mu \in K^Q$ are the initial and final weight functions, and $\rho\colon Q \times \Sigma \times Q \to K$ is the transition weight function. The semantics of $\mathcal{A}$ is the function $f_{\mathcal{A}}\colon \Sigma^* \to K$ given by*

$$f_{\mathcal{A}}(w) = \sum_{q_0,\dots,q_n \in Q} \lambda(q_0) \cdot \rho(q_0, w_1, q_1) \cdots \rho(q_{n-1}, w_n, q_n) \cdot \mu(q_n),$$

for $w = w_1 \cdots w_n \in \Sigma^*$.

Definition 2 (Rational Stochastic Language). *The class of rational stochastic languages over alphabet Σ and field $\mathbb{R}$, denoted $\mathcal{S}^{rat}_{\mathbb{R}}(\Sigma)$, consists of all functions $f\colon \Sigma^+ \to \mathbb{R}$ such that:*

1. *$f = [\![\mathcal{A}]\!]$ for some WFA $\mathcal{A}$ over the semiring* $(\mathbb{R}, +, \cdot, 0, 1)$
2. *f is a stochastic language*

The restricted class $\mathcal{S}^{rat}_{\mathbb{R}+}(\Sigma)$ considers only automata with non-negative weights. When the semiring is clear from context, we write simply $\mathcal{S}^{rat}(\Sigma)$.

Figure 1 shows a WFA over the alphabet $\{a, b\}$. It induces a rational stochastic language over $\{a, b\}^*$. For a detailed discussion on WFA and stochastic languages, see [4].

2.4 Recurrent Neural Networks

Definition 3 (Recurrent Neural Network (RNN)). *A* recurrent neural network (RNN) *is a triple $R = (\alpha, g, \beta)$ where: (i)$\alpha \in \mathbb{R}^d$ is the initial state vector, (ii) $g : \mathbb{R}^d \times \Sigma \to \mathbb{R}^d$ is the recurrent transition function, (iii) $\beta : \mathbb{R}^d \to \mathbb{R}$ is the output function. The RNN processes a sequence $w = w_1 \dots w_n \in \Sigma^*$ by producing a sequence of hidden states:*

$$h_0 = \alpha,$$
$$h_i = g(h_{i-1}, w_i) \quad \text{for } i = 1, \dots, n.$$

The output of the RNN for the sequence is $f_R(w) = \beta(h_n)$. [19]

Intuitively, an RNN maintains a hidden state h_i that serves as a compressed memory of all past inputs up to position i. At each step, the transition function g updates this state based on the previous hidden state and the current input symbol. The initial vector α represents the network's starting memory, and the output function β maps the final hidden state to a scalar value or prediction. In standard neural implementations, g and β are parameterized by weight matrices and nonlinearities such as tanh or ReLU, allowing the RNN to approximate complex sequence-to-value mappings.

2.5 The Spectral Learning Framework

Spectral learning offers a method to learn a finite state representation from i.i.d. samples [2,14]. The *Hankel matrix* $H_f \in \mathbb{R}^{\Sigma^* \times \Sigma^*}$ of a function $f : \Sigma^* \to \mathbb{R}$ is a bi-infinite matrix whose entries are defined for any $(p, s) \in \Sigma^* \times \Sigma^*$ by $H_f[p, s] = f(ps)$, where ps denotes the concatenation of p and s.

A fundamental result [23] states that f is rational (i.e., computable by a WFA of d states) if and only if its Hankel matrix H_f has finite rank d. We discuss this in further detail in Sect. 3.2.

2.6 Transformer Attention

Transformers [26] are the popular LLM design architecture. At a high level, they operate over sequences of discrete symbols from a finite alphabet Σ, which are mapped to sequences of vectors via an embedding layer. Each transformer layer is a length-preserving function on such vector sequences, combining *self-attention*—which retrieves and mixes information from a variable-length history—and *feed-forward networks* applied position-wise. Stacks of these layers, together with input and output projections, yield a powerful sequence model.

For theoretical analysis, it is crucial to treat transformers as operating on inputs of *unbounded length*, rather than fixing a maximum context window. This allows us to compare them with formal language models such as automata, circuits, and logics, and to ask: *what languages can transformers recognize or generate?* Variants of the architecture (encoder, decoder, encoder–decoder), choices of attention mechanism (softmax, hard), and restrictions on precision or positional encodings all impact expressivity [25].

Definition 4 (Decoder-Only Transformer). *Let Σ be a finite alphabet and $d \in \mathbb{N}$. A one-layer decoder-only Transformer is a tuple*

$$\mathcal{T} = (\alpha, W_Q, W_K, W_V, \beta),$$

where

- $\alpha : \Sigma \to \mathbb{R}^d$ *is the embedding map assigning each symbol an embedding vector;*

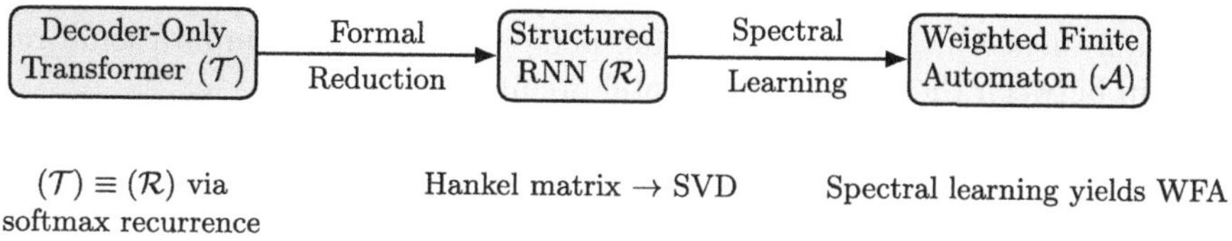

Fig. 2. Pipeline for reducing a decoder-only Transformer $\mathcal{T}$ to a weighted automaton $\mathcal{A}$. Step 1: establish equivalence with a structured RNN $\mathcal{R}$ (Sect. 3.1). Step 2: recover $\mathcal{A}$ from $\mathcal{R}$ via spectral learning on truncated Hankel matrices (Sect. 3.2).

- $W_Q, W_K, W_V \in \mathbb{R}^{d\times d}$ *are the learned query, key, and value projection matrices;*
- $\beta : \mathbb{R}^d \to \mathbb{R}$ *is the output map.*

Given a sequence $w = \sigma_1 \cdots \sigma_n \in \Sigma^*$, *the model first maps it to embeddings* $e_i = \alpha(\sigma_i)$. *At each position* n, *the layer computes a* query *vector* $q_n = W_Q e_n$ *for the current symbol, as well as* key *and* value *vectors* $k_i = W_K e_i$, $v_i = W_V e_i$ *for all previous symbols. The hidden state at position* n *is then obtained by attending to the past:*

$$h_n = \frac{\sum_{i=1}^{n} v_i\, e^{q_n^\top k_i}}{\sum_{j=1}^{n} e^{q_n^\top k_j}},$$

that is, a weighted sum of the values v_i, *where the weights depend on how similar the current query* q_n *is to each past key* k_i. *Finally, the model output on* w *is*

$$f_{\mathcal{T}}(w) := \beta(h_n).$$

Intuitively, a decoder-only Transformer processes a sequence one token at a time, much like an RNN, but instead of maintaining a single recurrent hidden state, it computes a new hidden representation h_n for the current token by looking at all previous tokens simultaneously through the *attention mechanism*. This mechanism allows Transformers to model long-range dependencies more effectively than RNNs, because each token can directly attend to any previous token without being bottlenecked by a single hidden state.

3 From Transformers to Weighted Finite Automata

We reduce a one-layer decoder-only transformer to a WFA via an intermediate RNN. Figure 2 illustrates the pipeline: the transformer $\mathcal{T}$ is first unfolded into an equivalent structured RNN $\mathcal{R}$; then, $\mathcal{R}$ is approximated by a WFA $\mathcal{A}$ through spectral learning.

3.1 Decoder-Only Transformer as a Recurrent Model

We now demonstrate an interesting viewpoint: that the self-attention mechanism in transformers can be computed by a carefully constructed RNN [30].

This equivalence provides a fascinating perspective on the computational relationship between these two fundamental architectures.

Construction. We construct a specific RNN that computes the softmax self-attention mechanism of a decoder-only transformer at position n. Let $\sigma(x) = (1 + e^{-x})^{-1}$ denote the sigmoid function.

For the query vector $q_n \in \mathbb{R}^d$ and a sequence of key-value pairs $\{(k_i, v_i)\}_{i=1}^n$, the goal of the RNN is to compute the value accumulator:

$$f_n = \frac{\sum_{j=1}^n v_j e^{q_n^\top k_j}}{\sum_{j=1}^n e^{q_n^\top k_j}}. \tag{1}$$

We define an RNN whose state $h_i \in \mathbb{R}^{d+1}$ is a composite vector containing two components:

1. $g_i \in \mathbb{R}$: A scalar for the running log-partition function ($\log \sum_{j=1}^i e^{q_n^\top k_j}$).
2. $f_i \in \mathbb{R}^d$: A vector for the running weighted sum of values ($\sum_{j=1}^i v_j e^{q_n^\top k_j}$).

We pack these into a single state vector: $h_i = (g_i, f_i)$.

The initial state, transition function, and output function for this RNN are defined as follows:

$$\begin{aligned}
\alpha = h_0 &= (q_n^\top k_1, v_1), \\
g(h_{i-1}, w_i) &= \begin{pmatrix} \log(e^{g_{i-1}} + e^{q_n^\top k_i}) \\ v_i \cdot \sigma(q_n^\top k_i - g_{i-1}) + f_{i-1} \cdot \sigma(g_{i-1} - q_n^\top k_i) \end{pmatrix}, \\
\beta(h_n) &= \frac{f_n}{e^{g_n}}.
\end{aligned}$$

Here, the input w_i to the RNN at step i is used to retrieve the corresponding key-value pair (k_i, v_i). The output function β performs the final normalization.

Theorem 1 (Equivalence of Attention and RNN). *For any input sequence $(e_1, \ldots, e_n)$ with associated keys and values, the output of the self-attention mechanism at position n (Eq. 1) is equal to the output of the constructed RNN:*

$$h_n^{attention} = \beta(g^*(\alpha, (k_1 v_1, \ldots, k_n v_n))).$$

Proof (Sketch). We prove by induction that after processing the i-th element, the RNN's state contains the correct intermediate values:

$$e^{g_i} = \sum_{j=1}^i e^{q_n^\top k_j}, \qquad f_i = \sum_{j=1}^i v_j e^{q_n^\top k_j}.$$

The base case $i = 1$ holds by the definition of α. For the inductive step:

– The update for g_i is defined as the log-sum-exp of the previous accumulator and the new term, which correctly computes the new log-partition.

– The update for f_i is a weighted sum. Using the identities for the sigmoid function,

$$\sigma(q_n^\top k_i - g_{i-1}) = \frac{e^{q_n^\top k_i}}{e^{g_{i-1}} + e^{q_n^\top k_i}} = \frac{e^{q_n^\top k_i}}{e^{g_i}},$$

$$\sigma(g_{i-1} - q_n^{\top k_i}) = \frac{e^{g_{i-1}}}{e^{g_{i-1}} + e^{q_n^\top k_i}} = \frac{e^{g_{i-1}}}{e^{g_i}}.$$

Substituting these into the transition function shows that:

$$f_i = \frac{e^{q_n^\top k_i}}{e^{g_i}} v_i + \frac{e^{g_{i-1}}}{e^{g_i}} f_{i-1}.$$

By the inductive hypothesis, $f_{i-1} = \sum_{j=1}^{i-1} v_j e^{q_n^\top k_j}$ and $e^{g_{i-1}} = \sum_{j=1}^{i-1} e^{q_n^\top k_j}$. Therefore, this update rule ensures $f_i = \sum_{j=1}^{i} v_j e^{q_n^\top k_j}$.

The output function β then divides f_n by e^{g_n} to produce the final normalized output as in Eq. 1, which is precisely the output of the attention mechanism, completing the proof.

Interpretation. This construction shows that the softmax self-attention mechanism in a transformer layer is not inherently non-recurrent. It can be *exactly* computed by an RNN with a carefully designed state and transition function. The RNN's state maintains two accumulators: one for the normalizing denominator and one for the numerator of the attention-weighted sum. This establishes a formal equivalence between the two models for this specific computation.

3.2 Spectral Learning for RNN Approximation

We now reduce the RNN constructed in the previous section, to a WFA using the spectral learning method [2,3,21]. The core insight is that the function $f_R : \Sigma^* \to \mathbb{R}$ computed by the RNN defines a Hankel matrix H whose rank reveals the intrinsic state complexity of f_R. If this matrix is low-rank, the function can be compactly represented by a WA [23].

A direct application of the spectral method is infeasible for unbounded sequences. To manage this, we introduce a truncation parameter $\theta \in \mathbb{N}$, restricting our analysis to the set of sequences of length at most θ, denoted $\Sigma^{\leq\theta}$. For any function $f : \Sigma^* \to \mathbb{R}$, we write $f_{\leq\theta}$ for its restriction to this finite domain.

Spectral Learning Procedure. The procedure for converting the RNN R to a WA A is formalized in Algorithm 1 and involves the following steps:

1. **Define Prefix and Suffix Sets:** Fix the truncation length θ. Set the prefix set P and the suffix set S to both be $\Sigma^{\leq\theta}$.
2. **Construct the Hankel Matrix:** Form the Hankel matrix $H \in \mathbb{R}^{P\times S}$, where each entry is defined by the output of the RNN:

$$H[p, s] = f_R(ps), \quad \text{for all } p \in P, s \in S. \tag{2}$$

Constructing H requires evaluating the RNN on all concatenations ps where $|p|, |s| \leq \theta$.

Algorithm 1: CONVERT-RNN-TO-WA(R, θ, r)

Input: RNN R, truncation length θ, target rank r.
Output: WA $A = (\nu, \{M_\sigma\}, \tau)$ of dimension r.

Set $P \leftarrow \Sigma^{\leq\theta}$, $S \leftarrow \Sigma^{\leq\theta}$ and index them arbitrarily.
for $p \in P, s \in S$ **do**
  $H[p, s] \leftarrow f_R(ps)$; `// Construct Hankel matrix (Eq. 2)`
end
Compute rank-r truncated SVD: $H \approx U_r \Sigma_r V_r^\top$
Define vectors $\nu \leftarrow U_r \Sigma_r^{1/2} e_\epsilon$ and $\tau \leftarrow (\Sigma_r^{1/2} V_r^\top)^\top e_\epsilon$; `// (Eq. 3)`
for $\sigma \in \Sigma$ **do**
  for $p \in P, s \in S$ **do**
    $H_\sigma[p, s] \leftarrow f_R(p\sigma s)$; `// Construct shifted matrix (Eq. 4)`
  end
  $M_\sigma \leftarrow \Sigma_r^{-1/2} U_r^\top H_\sigma V_r \Sigma_r^{-1/2}$; `// Project to get transitions (Eq. 5)`
end
return $A = (\nu, \{M_\sigma\}, \tau)$

3. **Compute Low-Rank Approximation:** Compute a rank-r truncated Singular Value Decomposition (SVD) of the Hankel matrix:

$$H \approx U_r \Sigma_r V_r^\top,$$

where r is the target dimension of the WA. The matrices U_r and V_r provide orthonormal bases for the column and row spaces of H, respectively, and Σ_r contains the top r singular values.

4. **Extract WA Parameters:** The WA parameters are derived by projecting the Hankel matrix and its shifts into the low-dimensional space defined by the SVD.
   - **Initial and Final Vectors:** Let e_ϵ be the basis vector corresponding to the empty string. The initial vector ν and final vector τ are defined as:

$$\nu = U_r \Sigma_r^{1/2} e_\epsilon, \quad \tau = (\Sigma_r^{1/2} V_r^\top)^\top e_\epsilon. \tag{3}$$

   - **Transition Matrices:** For each symbol $\sigma \in \Sigma$, form the shifted Hankel matrix H_σ, where:

$$(H_\sigma)[p, s] = f_R(p\sigma s). \tag{4}$$

The transition matrix M_σ for symbol σ is then obtained by projection:

$$M_\sigma = \Sigma_r^{-1/2} U_r^\top H_\sigma V_r \Sigma_r^{-1/2}. \tag{5}$$

Outcome. The resulting automaton $A = (\nu, \{M_\sigma\}_{\sigma\in\Sigma}, \tau)$ approximates the behavior of the RNN R on sequences up to length θ. If the Hankel matrix H has exact rank r, the recovery by the WA is exact for all $w \in \Sigma^{\leq\theta}$. Otherwise, the approximation error is bounded by the spectral error of the truncated SVD [8].

3.3 Correctness and Analysis of the Reduction

We now establish the correctness of the conversion procedure outlined in Algorithm 1. The following theorem characterizes the approximation guarantees, separating errors arising from truncation and those from spectral approximation.

Theorem 2 (Approximation Guarantees). *Let R be an RNN with induced function $f_R : \Sigma^* \to \mathbb{R}$. Fix a truncation length $\theta > 0$ and let $f_{R,\leq\theta}$ be its restriction to $\Sigma^{\leq\theta}$. Let H be the Hankel matrix indexed by $P = S = \Sigma^{\leq\theta}$ and let A be the WA returned by Algorithm 1 with target rank r. Then:*

1. ***Exact Recovery:*** *If* $\text{rank}(H) = r$ *and the SVD is computed exactly, then* $f_A(w) = f_R(w)$ *for all* $w \in \Sigma^{\leq\theta}$.
2. ***Approximate Recovery:*** *If H is approximated by a rank-r matrix $\widehat{H}$ such that $\|H - \widehat{H}\|_2 \leq \eta$, then for every $w \in \Sigma^{\leq\theta}$, the pointwise error is bounded by:*
$$|f_A(w) - f_R(w)| \leq C(\theta, |\Sigma|, r) \cdot \eta, \tag{6}$$
where $C(\theta, |\Sigma|, r)$ is a polynomial factor dependent on the truncation length, alphabet size, and target rank.
3. ***Full-Space Guarantee:*** *For a target distribution Q over Σ^*, if the tail mass beyond length θ is bounded ($\sum_{|w|>\theta} Q(w) \leq \delta$) and the approximation error on $\Sigma^{\leq\theta}$ is bounded ($\|f_A - f_R\|_1 \leq \gamma$), then the WA A satisfies:*
$$\|f_A - Q\|_1 \leq \|f_R - Q\|_1 + \gamma + 2\delta. \tag{7}$$
If the RNN itself is an approximation to Q (i.e., $\|f_R - Q\|_1 \leq \epsilon$), then the total error is $\epsilon + \gamma + 2\delta$.

Proof (Proof Sketch). (1) The exact recovery case is a direct consequence of the spectral learning theory for WFA [2,3]. When $\text{rank}(H) = r$, the truncated SVD yields a minimal linear representation for the function $f_{R,\leq\theta}$, which is exactly captured by the constructed WA A.

(2) The approximate case follows from perturbation analysis. The error η in the Hankel matrix approximation propagates to the parameters $(\nu, \{M_\sigma\}, \tau)$ of the WA. Standard bounds on the sensitivity of the SVD [8] imply that this propagation is controlled, leading to a pointwise error that is polynomial in the problem parameters and linear in η.

(3) The full-space guarantee is obtained by a decomposition of the ℓ_1 error:

$$\begin{aligned}\|f_A - Q\|_1 &= \sum_{w\in\Sigma^*} |f_A(w) - Q(w)| \\ &\leq \underbrace{\sum_{|w|\leq\theta} |f_A(w) - f_R(w)|}_{\leq\gamma} + \underbrace{\sum_{|w|\leq\theta} |f_R(w) - Q(w)|}_{\leq\epsilon} + \underbrace{2\sum_{|w|>\theta} Q(w)}_{\leq 2\delta}.\end{aligned}$$

The result follows from applying the bounds for each term.

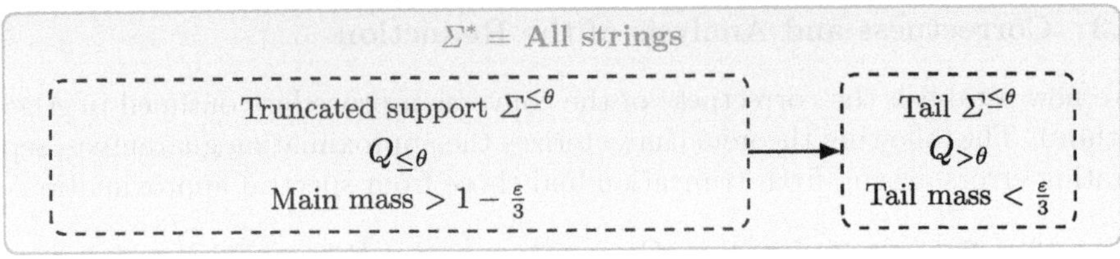

Fig. 3. Schematic of truncation and tail error decomposition. The gray rectangle represents the full domain Σ^*. The blue box is the truncated support $\Sigma^{\leq\theta}$, containing most of the probability mass ($Q_{\leq\theta} > 1-\varepsilon/3$). Truncation ensures the tail mass $Q_{>\theta}$ is bounded by $\varepsilon/3$, and hence contributes minimally. The total ℓ_1 error is decomposed as γ (estimation) $+C\eta$ (spectral) $+\delta$ (tail mass), highlighting that the bulk of the distribution is concentrated in a manageable region while the tail is small and controlled.

Complexity Analysis. The computational complexity of Algorithm 1 is dominated by the construction of the Hankel matrices and the SVD computation. Let $k = |\Sigma^{\leq\theta}| = O(|\Sigma|^\theta)$. The algorithm requires:

- $O(k^2)$ evaluations of f_R, each requiring $O(\theta \cdot T_{\text{step}})$ time, where T_{step} is the cost of one RNN transition.
- $O(k^3)$ time for the SVD of a $k \times k$ matrix.
- $O(|\Sigma| \cdot k^2)$ memory for storing the Hankel and shifted Hankel matrices.

This exponential dependence on θ limits practical application to small truncation lengths, though sampling techniques can mitigate this cost. [13]

Remarks. This reduction demonstrates that the function computed by the RNN (and hence, by Theorem 1, the self-attention mechanism) can be approximated by a WFA. The quality of approximation is governed by the truncation length θ and the spectral rank r of the finite Hankel matrix. This provides a foundational link between transformers and automata theory, enabling the application of formal methods to analyse their behaviour.

4 Identity Testing for Rational Stochastic Languages

A fundamental verification question is whether the distribution P generated by a black-box model (e.g., an LLM) is close to a known, well-understood reference distribution Q. For our purposes, Q is a rational stochastic language, specified by a weighted automaton or a stochastic regular expression (SRE). This motivates the study of *identity testing* (also known as goodness-of-fit testing) for distributions over infinite domains [6].

In this section, we present an identity testing algorithm for rational stochastic languages, which, to our knowledge, is the first to tackle this problem for infinite domains by leveraging the specific structure of rational distributions. The algorithm reduces the infinite-domain problem to a finite one via a tailored truncation strategy (illustrated in Fig. 3), enabling the use of sample-optimal finite-domain testers.

Definition 5 (Identity Testing for Stochastic Languages). *Let Q be a known rational stochastic language, and let P be an unknown distribution over Σ^* accessible only via i.i.d. samples. Given parameters $\varepsilon > 0$ and $\delta \in (0,1)$, an* identity tester *is an algorithm that, with probability at least $1-\delta$, outputs:*

- ACCEPT *if $\|P-Q\|_1 < \varepsilon$, and*
- REJECT *if $\|P-Q\|_1 > \varepsilon$.*

The sample complexity of the tester is the number of samples required from P to achieve this guarantee.

We employ the ℓ_1 distance as it corresponds to the total variation distance, providing a robust and interpretable measure of discrepancy across the entire support. This is preferable to the ℓ_∞ distance, which is very sensitive to pointwise errors, and the KL divergence, which requires absolute continuity.

4.1 Reduction to Finite Support via Truncation

The core of our approach is to truncate the distributions to strings of bounded length, ensuring the tail mass of the reference distribution Q is negligible. This reduction allows us to apply finite-domain identity testers.

Definition 6 (Truncation Length). *θ[)] For a distribution Q, define $\theta(Q,\xi)$ as:*

$$\theta(Q,\xi) = \min_{[\![\mathcal{A}]\!]=Q} \left(|\mathcal{A}_Q| \cdot \max\left\{1, \left\lceil \frac{\log(\xi)}{\log(1-\rho(\mathcal{A}))} \right\rceil \right\} \right)$$

where the minimum is taken over all equivalent WFAs $\mathcal{A}$ that represent Q, $|\mathcal{A}_Q|$ is the number of states, and $\rho(\mathcal{A})$ is the spectral radius (maximum eigenvalue) of the automaton's transition matrix.

Lemma 1. *Let $\varepsilon > 0$ be the target accuracy. For the reference distribution Q, the truncation length $\theta = \theta(Q, \varepsilon/3)$ satisfies:*

$$Q_{>\theta} := \sum_{x \in \Sigma^{>\theta}} Q(x) < \frac{\varepsilon}{3}.$$

Proof. Let $\mathcal{A}$ be a WFA realizing Q that achieves the minimum in the definition of $\theta(Q,\varepsilon/3)$. Let n be its number of states and ρ its spectral radius.

By the spectral properties of WFAs, the probability that a string generated by $\mathcal{A}$ has length greater than L decays roughly as $O(\rho^L)$ in the sense of total mass. More formally, there exists a constant C such that for all $L \geq n$,

$$Q_{>L} \leq C \cdot \rho^{L-n+1}.$$

Choosing $L = \theta$ as defined, we have $\theta \geq n \cdot \max\left\{1, \left\lceil \frac{\log(\varepsilon/3)}{\log(1-\rho)} \right\rceil \right\}$. In particular, $\theta \geq n \cdot \left\lceil \frac{\log(\varepsilon/3)}{\log(1-\rho)} \right\rceil$ when $\rho < 1$.

Algorithm 2: ℓ_1-IDENTITYTESTER for Rational Stochastic Languages

Input: Known distribution Q, sample access to P, parameters $\varepsilon > 0$, $\delta \in (0, 1)$
Output: ACCEPT if $\|P - Q\|_1 < \varepsilon$; REJECT if $\|P - Q\|_1 > \varepsilon$ (w.p. $\geq 1 - \delta$)

Compute truncation length $\theta(Q, \varepsilon/3)$.
Let $k \leftarrow |\Sigma^{\leq\theta}| = \Theta(|\Sigma|^{\theta+1})$.
Draw $N = \Theta\left(\frac{\sqrt{k}}{\varepsilon^2} + \frac{k}{\log k} \cdot \log(\frac{1}{\delta})\right)$ i.i.d. samples from P.
Let η be the fraction of samples with $|x| > \theta$.
if $\eta > \varepsilon/3$ **then**
  return REJECT ; `// Empirical tail mass is too large`
end
Let $\widehat{P}_{\leq\theta}$ be the empirical distribution of the remaining samples over $\Sigma^{\leq\theta}$.
Let $Q_{\leq\theta}$ be the restriction of Q to $\Sigma^{\leq\theta}$.
Run a finite-domain *tolerant* identity tester on $\widehat{P}_{\leq\theta}$ and $Q_{\leq\theta}$ with distance thresholds $(\varepsilon/3, \varepsilon)$ and confidence $1 - \delta$.
return the output of the finite-domain tester.

Using the inequality $\log(1 - \rho) \leq -\rho$, we get

$$\left\lceil \frac{\log(\varepsilon/3)}{\log(1-\rho)} \right\rceil \geq \frac{\log(1/(\varepsilon/3))}{\rho} = \frac{\log(3/\varepsilon)}{\rho}.$$

Thus $\theta \geq \frac{n \log(3/\varepsilon)}{\rho}$, so $\rho^\theta \leq e^{-n\log(3/\varepsilon)} = (\varepsilon/3)^n$.

Hence $Q_{>\theta} \leq C \cdot (\varepsilon/3)^n \cdot \rho^{-n+1}$. For sufficiently small ε, this is less than $\varepsilon/3$ (adjusting constants if needed by the minimization over WFAs).

4.2 Correctness and Sample Complexity Analysis

We now establish the formal guarantees for Algorithm 2.

Theorem 3. *(Correctness of Identity Tester). Let $Q \in \mathcal{S}^{\mathrm{rat}}_{\mathbb{R}+}(\Sigma^*)$ be given as an SRE, and let P be an unknown distribution over Σ^*. For any $\varepsilon > 0$ and $\delta \in (0, 1)$, Algorithm 2 satisfies the following with probability at least $1 - \delta$:*

- ***(Completeness)** If $\|P - Q\|_1 < \varepsilon$, then output is* ACCEPT.
- ***(Soundness)** If $\|P - Q\|_1 > \varepsilon$, then output is* REJECT.

The sample complexity is:

$$N = \Theta\left(\frac{\sqrt{k}}{\varepsilon^2} + \frac{k}{\log k} \cdot \log\left(\frac{1}{\delta}\right)\right), \quad \text{where } k = |\Sigma^{\leq\theta}|.$$

Proof (Sketch). The proof hinges on the decomposition of the ℓ_1 error and the properties of the finite-domain tolerant tester.

1. **Truncation Guarantee:** By construction, $Q_{>\theta} < \varepsilon/3$.

2. **Tail Mass Check:** If $P_{>\theta} > \varepsilon/3$, then the empirical estimate η will exceed $\varepsilon/3$ with high probability given the sample size N, causing rejection. This handles soundness cases where P diverges from Q in the tail.
3. **Head Analysis:** If the algorithm proceeds to the finite-domain tester, we know $P_{>\theta} \leq \varepsilon/3 + o(1)$ with high probability. The total ℓ_1 distance can be bounded as:

$$\|P - Q\|_1 \leq \underbrace{\|P_{\leq\theta} - Q_{\leq\theta}\|_1}_{\text{Head}} + \underbrace{P_{>\theta} + Q_{>\theta}}_{\text{Tail}}.$$

4. **Completeness ($\|P - Q\|_1 < \varepsilon$):** The tail term is less than $\varepsilon/3 + \varepsilon/3 = 2\varepsilon/3$. Thus, $\|P_{\leq\theta} - Q_{\leq\theta}\|_1 < \varepsilon/3$. The tolerant tester, configured with a lower threshold of $\varepsilon/3$, will correctly accept.
5. **Soundness ($\|P - Q\|_1 > \varepsilon$):** Since the tail term is at most $2\varepsilon/3$, the head distance must satisfy $\|P_{\leq\theta} - Q_{\leq\theta}\|_1 > \varepsilon/3$. The tolerant tester, with an upper threshold of ε, will correctly reject.

The sample complexity is dominated by the finite-domain tolerant identity tester [6], which requires $O(\sqrt{k}/\varepsilon^2 + k/\log k)$ samples to distinguish between distances of $\varepsilon/3$ and ε on a domain of size k. The multiplicative $\log(1/\delta)$ factor comes from standard confidence amplification. The number of samples is sufficient to ensure the empirical tail mass check is also correct with probability $1 - \delta$.

Remarks. The algorithm provides a computationally efficient reduction from identity testing on infinite sequences to the finite domain. The sample complexity, while exponential in the truncation length θ, is polynomial in the effective support size $k = |\Sigma^{\leq\theta}|$. For rational stochastic languages with rapidly decaying tails (a common property), θ is manageable, leading to a practical verification procedure for models that are hypothesized to be close to such languages.

5 Conclusion and Future Work

We have established the first formal reduction from decoder-only transformers to weighted automata, creating a bridge between modern neural sequence models and classical automata theory. Our main technical contributions are: (1) a constructive proof that transformer self-attention can be computed by structured RNNs, (2) a spectral learning algorithm that converts such RNNs to weighted automata with provable approximation guarantees, and (3) an identity testing procedure for rational stochastic languages with sample complexity $O(\sqrt{k}/\varepsilon^2 + k \log k)$ where $k = |\Sigma^{\leq\theta}|$.

The Computational Barrier. Our analysis reveals a fundamental bottleneck: spectral learning requires Hankel matrices of size $O(|\Sigma|^{2\theta})$, leading to exponential complexity in the truncation parameter θ. This barrier underscores why automata-based verification of practical language models has remained elusive.

Importantly, this limitation is not merely an artifact of our specific construction. The exponential dependence on θ reflects a deeper tension between the expressivity required to approximate transformer behaviour and the computational tractability of automata-theoretic methods. Any approach that seeks to capture the distributional properties of transformers over realistic vocabularies must confront this fundamental trade-off.

Theoretical Implications. Our results locate transformers within the established hierarchy of computational models. The reduction provides the first formal characterization of transformer expressivity in terms of weighted automata. This connection enables transfer of results: closure properties, decidability results, and algorithmic techniques from automata theory now apply to transformer analysis. Furthermore, our identity testing algorithm provides a principled statistical framework for model comparison and verification.

Algorithmic Challenges and Directions. The exponential bottleneck suggests several concrete research directions:

1. Develop low-rank approximations or sketching techniques for learning that preserve essential spectral properties while reducing computational cost.
2. Design randomized algorithms that estimate automaton parameters without constructing full Hankel matrices, potentially achieving polynomial dependence on θ.
3. Exploit specific properties of transformer architectures (attention patterns, positional encodings, etc.) to reduce the effective dimension of the learning problem, and make it tractable.

We acknowledge that these challenges have not allowed us to implement and evaluate our approach on real-world transformers, and it remains a direction of future work. Beyond this, Several fundamental questions remain: Can the exponential dependence on θ be avoided while preserving approximation quality? What is the minimal class of weighted automata needed to approximate practical transformers? How do architectural choices (depth, attention patterns, normalization) affect the complexity of automata-based approximation?

In conclusion, our framework has provided new evaluation methodologies for language models. Rather than relying solely on empirical benchmarks, our identity testing approach provides statistical certificates of distributional similarity to reference models—a step toward more rigorous model validation. Through this work, we provide both a foundational connection between transformers and automata theory and a precise characterization of the computational challenges that must be overcome for practical verification. The path forward requires algorithmic innovation at the intersection of spectral methods, randomized algorithms, and formal language theory.

References

1. Angluin, D., Chiang, D., Yang, A.: Masked hard-attention transformers and Boolean rasp recognize exactly the star-free languages. arXiv preprint arXiv:2310.13897 (2023)

2. Balle, B., Mohri, M.: Spectral learning of general weighted automata via constrained matrix completion. In: Advances in Neural Information Processing Systems (NeurIPS), pp. 2168–2176 (2012)
3. Balle, B., Mohri, M.: Learning weighted automata. arXiv preprint arXiv:2007.08131 (2020)
4. Bollig, B., Zeitoun, M.: Weighted automata. Lecture Notes, ENS Cachan (2015), http://www.lsv.fr/~mz/wa.pdf, version of September 13 (2015)
5. Bowen, C., Sætre, R., Miyao, Y.: A comprehensive evaluation of inductive reasoning in LLMS. In: Findings of the Association for Computational Linguistics: EACL 2024 (2024). https://aclanthology.org/2024.findings-eacl.22
6. Canonne, C.L., Jain, A., Kamath, G., Li, J.: The price of tolerance in distribution testing. In: Loh, P.L., Raginsky, M. (eds.) Proceedings of the 35th Annual Conference on Learning Theory (COLT). Proceedings of Machine Learning Research, vol. 178, pp. 1–52. PMLR (2022). https://proceedings.mlr.press/v178/canonne22a.html
7. Cohen-Inger, N., Elisha, Y., Shapira, B., Rokach, L., Cohen, S.: Forget what you know about LLMS evaluations - LLMS are like a chameleon. arXiv preprint arXiv:2502.07445 (2025). https://arxiv.org/abs/2502.07445
8. Davis, C., Kahan, W.M.: The rotation of eigenvectors by a perturbation. iii. SIAM J. Numer. Anal. **7**(1), 1–46 (1970)
9. Delattre, B., Araujo, A., Barthélemy, Q., Allauzen, A.: The Lipschitz-variance-margin tradeoff for enhanced randomized smoothing (2023). https://arxiv.org/abs/2309.16883
10. Deng, C., Zhao, Y., Tang, X., Gerstein, M., Cohan, A.: Investigating data contamination in modern benchmarks for large language models. arXiv preprint arXiv:2311.09783 (2023). https://arxiv.org/abs/2311.09783
11. Ducotterd, S., et al.: Improving Lipschitz-constrained neural networks by learning activation functions. J. Mach. Learn. Res. **25**(83), 1–30 (2024). https://jmlr.org/papers/volume25/22-1347/22-1347.pdf
12. Hao, Y., Angluin, D., Frank, R.: Formal language recognition by hard attention transformers: perspectives from circuit complexity. Trans. Ass. Comput. Linguist. **10**, 800–810 (2022). https://doi.org/10.1162/tacl_a_00490
13. Hsu, D., Kakade, S.M., Zhang, T.: A spectral algorithm for learning hidden markov models. In: Proceedings of the 22nd Annual Conference on Learning Theory (COLT), pp. 403–414. Omnipress (2009). https://arxiv.org/abs/0811.4413
14. Hsu, D., Kakade, S.M., Zhang, T.: A spectral algorithm for learning hidden Markov models. J. Comput. Syst. Sci. **78**(5), 1460–1480 (2012)
15. Hua, W., et al.: Inductionbench: LLMS fail in the simplest complexity class. arXiv preprint arXiv:2502.15823 (2025). https://arxiv.org/abs/2502.15823
16. Huster, T., Chiang, C.-Y.J., Chadha, R.: Limitations of the Lipschitz constant as a defense against adversarial examples. In: Alzate, C., Monreale, A., Assem, H., Bifet, A., Buda, T.S., Caglayan, B., Drury, B., García-Martín, E., Gavaldà, R., Koprinska, I., Kramer, S., Lavesson, N., Madden, M., Molloy, I., Nicolae, M.-I., Sinn, M. (eds.) ECML PKDD 2018. LNCS (LNAI), vol. 11329, pp. 16–29. Springer, Cham (2019). https://doi.org/10.1007/978-3-030-13453-2_2
17. Khromov, G., Singh, S.P.: Some fundamental aspects about Lipschitz continuity of neural networks. In: International Conference on Learning Representations (ICLR) (2024)
18. Li, J., et al.: Mirage: evaluating and explaining inductive reasoning in LLMS. arXiv preprint arXiv:2410.09542 (2024). https://arxiv.org/abs/2410.09542

19. Merrill, W., eta al.: A formal hierarchy of RNN architectures. In: Proceedings of the 58th Annual Meeting of the Association for Computational Linguistics, pp. 443–459. Association for Computational Linguistics (2020)
20. Newhouse, L., et al.: Training transformers with enforced Lipschitz constants (2025). https://doi.org/10.48550/arXiv.2507.13338. https://arxiv.org/abs/2507.13338
21. Okudono, T., Waga, M., Sekiyama, T., Hasuo, I.: Weighted automata extraction from recurrent neural networks via regression on state spaces. ArXiv **abs/1904.02931** (2019). https://api.semanticscholar.org/CorpusID:102350402
22. Qi, X., Wang, J., Chen, Y., Shi, Y., Zhang, L.: Lipsformer: Introducing Lipschitz continuity to vision transformers (2023). https://arxiv.org/abs/2304.09856
23. Schützenberger, M.P.: On the definition of a family of automata. Inf. Control **4**(2–3), 245–270 (1961)
24. Shojaee, P., et al.: The illusion of thinking: understanding the strengths and limitations of reasoning models via the lens of problem complexity. arXiv preprint arXiv:2506.06941 (2025). https://arxiv.org/abs/2506.06941
25. Strobl, L., Merrill, W., Weiss, G., Chiang, D., Angluin, D.: What formal languages can transformers express? A survey. arXiv preprint arXiv:2311.00208 (2023)
26. Vaswani, A., et al.: Attention is all you need. In: Advances in Neural Information Processing Systems (NeurIPS), vol. 30. Curran Associates, Inc. (2017)
27. Verine, A., Negrevergne, B., Chevaleyre, Y., Rossi, F.: On the expressivity of bi-Lipschitz normalizing flows. In: Proceedings of The 14th Asian Conference on Machine Learning (ACML). Proceedings of Machine Learning Research, vol. 189 (2022). https://proceedings.mlr.press/v189/verine23a/verine23a.pdf
28. Xu, C., Guan, S., Greene, D., Kechadi, M.: Benchmark data contamination of large language models: A survey. arXiv preprint arXiv:2406.04244 (2024). https://arxiv.org/abs/2406.04244
29. Zhang, B., Jiang, D., He, D., Wang, L.: Rethinking Lipschitz neural networks and certified robustness: a boolean function perspective. In: Advances in Neural Information Processing Systems (NeurIPS) (2022)
30. Zhang, Y., Albarghouthi, A., D'Antoni, L.: A one-layer decoder-only transformer is a two-layer RNN: with an application to certified robustness (2024). https://arxiv.org/abs/2405.17361

Author Index

L. Lestingi et al. (Eds.): DataMod 2025, LNCS 16421, p. 163, 2026.
https://doi.org/10.1007/978-3-032-25552-5

The manufacturer's authorised representative in the EU is Springer Nature Customer Service Centre GmbH, Europaplatz 3, 69115 Heidelberg, Germany. If you have any concerns regarding our products, please contact ProductSafety@springernature.com

Printed and bound by CPI Group (UK) Ltd, Croydon, CR0 4YY
07/08/2026
02189605-0001